Secret Duties of a Signals Interceptor

Dedication

To my husband Jean–Marcel Nater, in gratitude for his constant patience, love and understanding

Secret Duties of a Signals Interceptor

Working with Bletchley Park, the SDS and the OSS

or A Long Time to Hope

Jenny Nater

Pen & Sword
AVIATION

First published in Great Britain in 2016 by
Pen & Sword Aviation
an imprint of
Pen & Sword Books Ltd
47 Church Street
Barnsley
South Yorkshire
S70 2AS

ISBN 978 1 47388 712 1

A CIP catalogue record for this book is available from the British
Library

Typeset in Ehrhardt by
Mac Style Ltd, Bridlington, East Yorkshire
Printed and bound in the UK by CPI Group (UK) Ltd,
Croydon, CRO 4YY

Pen & Sword Books Ltd incorporates the imprints of Pen & Sword
Archaeology, Atlas, Aviation, Battleground, Discovery, Family
History, History, Maritime, Military, Naval, Politics, Railways, Select,
Transport, True Crime, and Fiction, Frontline Books, Leo Cooper,
Praetorian Press, Seaforth Publishing and Wharncliffe.

For a complete list of Pen & Sword titles please contact
PEN & SWORD BOOKS LIMITED
47 Church Street, Barnsley, South Yorkshire, S70 2AS, England
E-mail: enquiries@pen-and-sword.co.uk
Website: www.pen-and-sword.co.uk

Contents

Author's Biography

Jenny Nater lives in East Devon but was born in the United States to American parents two years after the end of World War I. Her parents divorced and moved to England, placing her in boarding school when she was five. At seventeen, in 1937, she was sent to a progressive co-educational school in Switzerland run by German Jewish refugee teachers who had fled Nazi Germany. Here the young Jenny not only learned the German language, but also began to understand the political situation of the time and the approaching threat of National Socialism. Because of her knowledge of German, in 1941 she was accepted into the WRNS as a signals interceptor, and served on the Dover cliffs, monitoring German Naval radio traffic in the Channel. There she met her first great love Rick Cornish, 27, commanding officer of a Motor Torpedo Boat of the Coastal Forces. The letters between the two that make up much of this book are a personal record of the Second World War.

"… Ah love, let us be true
To one another! for …
… we are here as on a darkling plain
Swept with confused alarms of struggle and flight
Where ignorant armies clash by night."

from *Dover Beach* by Matthew Arnold

Prologue

While in hospital in 2008, without food but on a water and glucose drip for three weeks, I had what seemed at the time, an arresting experience. I would be awake most of the night sitting up in bed writing – scribbling in the semi-darkness. It seemed to me firstly that I had found the answer to all of mankind's problems and that I was also able to remember a great many incidents from my very early childhood. I decided to try and record these early memories, or rather sensations, for my children and grandchildren. These remembered 'sensations' are from the time before we left America – pre 1925. I will try and write what I actually remember – not reminiscences from family photographs or anecdotes.

I was born in the United States of American parents. My father's maternal side of the family had left England in 1645 during a time of religious persecution; they were Quakers, and like so many of these, they settled in Massachusetts, in their case Nantucket. Our first recorded ancestor, David O'Killia, both of whose parents became ill and died on the voyage over the Atlantic, had taken their son and a bag of money to the captain of the ship and asked him to see to the safety of the boy and his inheritance. By great good luck the captain was an honest man, and on reaching America took young O'Killia and his money to a bank. A generation or two later the local bank notes bore the portrait of his decendant Isaiah Crowell, my great great grandfather. His daughter Phoebe Kelly Crowell married Thomas Brown and their daughter Alice, my paternal grandmother, married Thomas Gill.

One of my earliest picture memories is of my great aunt Anna Maria Brown's house in Canaan, Connecticut. She had a Scots cook and I remember climbing onto a stool and from there onto the white counter to get at the cookie jar. They were oatmeal cookies and I loved them. Another vivid memory is of very, very yellow scrambled eggs on blue and white plates. The driveway was a mixture of pebbles and small blue-green stones (copper sulphate?)

with which I played for hours. Inside the house, under the bookcase, was a low white cupboard full of "magical" toys. I was only allowed to look at these when an adult was with me. There was a mechanical ladybird that crawled and flapped its wings, a jack-in-the-box, a little monkey on a stick who did somersaults, and a beautiful box of 'Jack Straws'. I was not allowed to touch these, but they are one of the things I have inherited from my father. Most of the exquisitely carved sticks are still intact. They were carved on long picnics in the Connecticut countryside. There is a bottle of Tokay, a book, *Diana of the Crossways*, the goose that laid the golden egg, and the egg itself; a heart dated 1899; a delicately carved pen with the initials AMB; a thin, fine, fretsaw; a furled umbrella and a quarter inch globe with the countries of the world quite recognisably depicted, among other things.

Anna Maria was a spinster, her younger sister Ella also. Of the three Brown sisters, only my Grandmother, Alice, married. Ella is a benign presence dimly remembered, except for the wonderful occasion once a year when she organised a Halloween party in the summer house for all the children. The building smelled of hot, sun baked cypress wood. The fall sunlight fell in beams on the wooden floor, in the middle of which stood an enormous pumpkin. It was hollowed out and many thin silk ribbons cascaded over its sides. Each child was given a ribbon, and the piano played the 'Pumpkin song'. We all danced around singing until the signal was given to pull our ribbons, and there on the end of each ribbon was a toy. The last game was to find as many walnuts as possible in their hiding places – and the ultimate prize was a golden walnut. (Years later my aunt Laura and I tried to find the words and tune of the 'Pumpkin song', but despite searching in Pheobe Kelly Brown's blue nail studded box under the piano, we never found them). Great aunt Ella died very young of tuberculosis. She was a talented painter, and had studied and painted in Paris at the same time as Mary Cassatt, a brave and unusual thing to do in that day and age. The Cassatt family were all in Paris together. They had gone there originally for the sake of their youngest daughter's health. My great aunt was alone. I wish that I had known her. She and great aunt Annie were taught painting by the family's companion, Miss Fidelia Bridges, whose water colours are very fine. I was told by my parents, both of whom loved and admired her, that she had a sad love affair with Lafkadio Hearn, who married a Japanese woman and never returned from

Japan, or recovered from his complete fascination with all things Japanese. An account of his life and experiences in Ireland, England, the Continent, the Caribbean and Japan can be found on the Internet.

The Gill's, like the Browns were also of English background and, at the time of the Monmouth Rebellion in the seventeenth century, at least one, or possibly two members of the family were arrested and condemned to be deported to Barbados to work on the sugar plantations. As far as I can make out the Gill's were non-Conformists and Protestants and could well have supported the Republican cause against the Monarchy. Fortunately for them, the family already had a small sugar plantation in Barbados so they did not suffer the fate of many Englishmen sent out to work as slaves in the extreme Caribbean climate. Many deported at this time died from exposure. They were subsequently replaced by black Africans at the time of the slave trade.

My grandfather Thomas Gill had been born in Barbados, later finishing his education in England. The family divided their time between London and Barbados until well into the twentieth Century. One of my very early memories is of being at my grandfather's farm in New Jersey. He, my uncle Hal and my father ran the farm, which Thomas had bought as a sort of *passe-temps* when he retired. My father took me there one winter. He made a wooden soap-box into a sled. There was lots of snow, bright colours and sun. I remember daddy pulling me.

Fresh water is also an early memory. Swimming in cool green woodland ponds, the goldfish pond in aunt Annie's garden; there are photographs of me, naked, running excitedly to the pond. Inevitably I fell in, my father pulled me out and comforted me. I was always conscious of his presence. He was the reason nothing frightened me.

The first record of my mother's family, the FitzGeralds, is when a Garrett FitzGerald left Ireland for Canada in the 1700s. He enlisted very young and was a drummer boy with the British Army in the entourage of the Duke of Richmond, who was, I believe, the first Governor General of Canada. By 1812, at the beginning of the war between the British-Canadians and the Americans, he was a Sergeant Major in the 100th Royal Canadian Regiment. He was also despatch rider to the General in Command of the battle of Niagara in 1830.

Although there are records of the family from the time Garrett FitzGerald left Ireland we have not been able to discover the name of his father. However, according to my mother, whose memoirs are very interesting, my grandfather Christopher FitzGerald would often say to his children 'We are Maynooth you know!' which seems to lead to a connection with the FitzGeralds of Kildare.

I have vivid early memories of my maternal grandmother FitzGerald's home in Riverside Connecticut. The garden was large and always seemed warm and balmy; there were long rows of tomato plants, between which I wandered at will. Sometimes Milo, my grandmother's chauffeur accompanied me. He would pick a warm ripe tomato, and give me a pinch of salt. I can still recall the taste. No tomatoes have ever tasted like that again. My grandmother loved her chickens. I spent a lot of time with her in the warm, hen-smelling chicken run. I remember seeing a headless chicken, obviously just killed, still running around the yard. My grandfather had a cider press in the stables, and I have another vivid sensory memory of the smell of apples as they were crushed. The other smells I connect with him are 'Bay Rum', cigars and sherry. I am not quite sure whether he died after I married in 1946 or shortly before. He had fallen on his way to the bathroom and broken his hip. Shockingly, the doctors did not discover it was broken for several months. The poor man must have been in quite considerable pain. A short time later he took to his bed, and was clearly close to death when one day I was called up to his room. I kissed him and he held my hand, and begged my forgiveness – saying that he was sorry he had been so hard on me. When I told my mother this she said 'Oh, he must have thought you were me' – He *was* hard on her, and that must have been the case. He was always a sort of twinkling, warm and loving grandfather to me.

My favourite FitzGerald aunt was my mother's youngest sister, Dodie. When I visited my grandparents she spent a lot of time with me. My Aunt Woodie, who had a great sense of humour, used to play the piano and sing Edward Lear's *The Yonghy Bonghy Bo* and *I am called Little Gutter Pup* to the tune of Gilbert and Sullivan's *Buttercup*. My mother's eldest sister, Margaret, played the piano for me to dance to in the cool, dim library among the mirrors and shelves of Dresden china and books. In the summer my grandmother used to sit almost all day, particularly during violent electric thunderstorms, on the front veranda in a rocking chair, and I often sat with her as she made and embroidered baby clothes for a charity called 'Little Child of Jesus'.

I remember a steep flight of back stairs that went down from the top floor of the house to the kitchen, where Jimmy the cook reigned. I often watched horrified, but fascinated, as he dropped live soft-shell crabs into pots of boiling oil, their claws scrapped the lid and there was a high-pitched wheezing sound. Of course I was convinced they were still alive.

My father, an architect at the time, had designed and built a house for my mother in Riverside. He had spent months touring around Connecticut and the East Coast with my mother, photographing doors, windows and architraves and all the American Georgian architectural details he loved and admired. He incorporated them into his house. It was very beautiful, and they called it White House. In the garden I remember there were pansies, velvety and hot, their scent delighted me. I picked them and took them into the dining room, where I climbed up onto the dining room table and tried to put them into the bowl of flowers. Apparently I left dusty foot prints all around the centre of the polished table top. I never wore shoes – the fashion of the time was for 'natural upbringing'. One day, crossing the open field to the neighbour's house, a snake was lying across the path, I screamed and my father came running out to me. He had an eggbeater in his hand and whirred it at the snake, which slid away. Like all other fears – bears in the corner of my bedroom, nightmares of foxes biting my head off, snakes, Daddy always shooed them away, and I knew they were gone and all was well. At this age I still had bad attacks of croup. Fighting for my breath was very frightening. My mother would sit with me on her lap under an umbrella with a steaming kettle beside us. I was given drops of ipecac and belladonna and after several hours the spasms would pass. While we lived in this house, there was another wonderful, much loved, presence in my life. Her name was Celestine. She was from British Guiana, her father was a Scot called McBride. She cooked wonderful meals of chicken and rice and Caribbean beans. When my parents went away they left me in her care. I took my first steps with her, and have never forgotten her.

I suppose it was when my father was diagnosed with tuberculosis and sent for a cure to Saranac in New York State, that I went to stay with my

FitzGerald grandparents; I don't know where my mother was. Years later she told me that while we were living in White House she had a baby aborted. This must have been very difficult for my father. She later told me that she had 'lost' the baby, and that it was a boy. Was this the beginning of the end of the marriage? Gigi (as my mother was called after she became Geraldine Gill) left us to visit her godmother in Spain, ostensibly to recover from losing the baby, but probably because of post-natal depression.

My father and I moved into a flat in Brooklyn. The lovely house he had built was put up for sale. My grandmother bought some of the furniture and gave it to my aunt Woodie who later left me the double bed my father had designed and a small footstool he had made for my mother. I do have some memories of the Brooklyn flat. We ate breakfast in front of the large window and watched the shipping on the Hudson River. One night there was a fire in a neighbouring warehouse, and I remember being in my father's arms watching the huge flames outside the window. Soon after this my mother returned and she and I must have left for England. My father told me, shortly before he died in 1983 that he had watched her walk away from him down the hill in Brooklyn. She was elegantly dressed in red, with matching shoes and hat, and he had said to himself 'There's a gal who thinks she's going places'.

Chapter 1

Early Days

In 1925, the first time I crossed the Atlantic, I was with my mother. It was memorable for several reasons. The first was the wonderful thrill of being asked by our dining room steward if I would like to meet the captain's 'tiger', to which I eagerly replied 'Yes please'. On most days, I was on deck running up to the bows and revelling in the weather when it was wild and windy. I often ate my hearty meals nearly alone in the dining room and never felt the slightest sea sickness. At last the day came when I was to meet the 'captain's tiger', and I was accompanied up to the captain's cabin by our dining room steward. There, on a mantelpiece that could have graced any formal sitting room, twined carefully around the vases and family photographs, was a magnificent Persian tabby cat. Somewhat disappointed I took him to be the 'tiger', but was soon disabused of this idea and told that the captain's personal steward was in fact called his 'tiger'.

Another of my pleasures on these Atlantic crossings was watching my beautiful and elegant mother dress for dinner. I particularly remember one dress of pale green silk appliquéd with pink flowers under a tulle overskirt. For the traditional fancy-dress farewell dinner she always wore a Nefertiti costume, and it is true that she did have a strong resemblance to the famous bust of Nefertiti in the Berlin Neues Museum. She was a sort of magical figure to me, an emerald and silver goddess to whom I wrote poems well into my teenage years.

She had a real talent for acting and for dress design, and an uncanny way of predicting what the latest fashion from Paris would be. She made her own clothes until well into her eighties, and made my wedding dress and trousseau when I married in 1946.

I loved these transatlantic crossings then, and on the consecutive summer trips from 1925 to 1928 to visit my maternal grandparents. It was the crew on these liners with whom I spent the most time. One, a very patient, kind and friendly deckhand who never seemed to mind my tagging along behind him as he went about his tasks, the deck stewards who let me 'help' them, and the members of the ship's orchestra who fiddled away for *thé dansants* – and late into the night after I was in my bunk. The only unfortunate encounter I had on one of the trips, when I was 6 years old, was with the man in charge of the gym and swimming-pool where I used to spend many hours swimming, climbing the bars and riding the mechanical horse. He was always very welcoming and helped me onto the horse, but one day he put his hand inside my panties and I fled. I told my mother, who did not know what action to take. However, on the last day when all the passengers were disembarking they had to walk down a long flight of stairs to the gangplank, and the ships crew would traditionally line the staircase on either side. One was expected to tip them all. My mother walked pointedly past the man in charge of the gym.

Story has it that on the first crossing in 1925 while my mother was having dinner, the stewardess came to turn down the sheets, and found me hanging head first out of the porthole, singing at the top of my voice. She apparently seized my ankles and pulled me into the cabin. I do have a sort of recollection of banging my hands on the side of the ship and seeing the water being cut apart below me. I suppose this is true – if not all of it, at least in part.

The summer before we left the States I stayed in my grandmother's house in Riverside, Connecticut. The beach at the yacht club was a paradise, as was my grandmother's garden. I, and my cousins Geoff and Hucko, played all day long together. At the beach they were both equipped with water wings, but my father wanted me to learn to swim and have no fear of the water as young as possible, so I never wore them. One day, when we were playing on the beach, the boys decided to go for a swim. We all ran onto the big flat rock which jutted out into the bay and from which the grown-ups would dive into the sea. Geoff and Hucko leapt in off the rock, and I followed. I sank like a stone, and came to the surface at least twice. The third time I saw my cousin Hucko, exactly my age, gazing at me in a puzzled way. I grasped him, and as we clung together a row-boat came round the corner of the rock. This incident unfortunately scared me off the ocean and swimming for several years. These summer trips to the US were only wonderful times – a light at the end of the tunnel during the long months of boarding school.

My first memory of London is of a flat, I have been told opposite the Victoria and Albert Museum, where I and my mother lived above a famous 'fine goods and grocery shop'. I slept upstairs in the duplex, and on waking early in the mornings would go down to the kitchen for a handful of raisins and cooking salt. This liking for salt had started at my grandmother's house in Connecticut, which was by the sea on the Sound. I would walk around the large clapboard building rubbing my wetted fingers along the top of the boards and licking off the salt. One morning in London, after my foray into the kitchen, I returned upstairs to my room and, to my delight, there was a large dragonfly sitting on my pillow. I rushed downstairs and found the help and told her in great excitement that there was a 'big bug' on my pillow. She gave a screech of horror and ran to inform my mother that there were bed bugs in the flat, and that one was on my pillow no less. So much for the different languages, American and English.

My other recollection of the flat is of being very ill with jaundice. I could not keep anything down, not even water, and the smell of mother's face powder or perfume made me sick immediately. My mother later caught it from me and was also very ill, with lasting effects on her liver. She later learned from a doctor to take the juice of a lemon every morning 'to give her liver a kick'. She did so until the end of her life at 106 years old.

As I convalesced, my father would come to visit. I can only assume that they were not living together at this time. I have a vivid memory of, what seemed to me, my first meal since my illness, fed to me by my father out of an antique American silver porringer as I sat at his feet in front of a gas fire. It was rice with chicken gravy – delicious. I can still see his face as I looked up at him and he fed me – I realise now, most tenderly.

Whether it was before or after this I do not know, but during the time of the General Strike in 1926, my parents were still, or once more, living together. They were in a flat in Lincoln's Inn lent to them by Johnnie Rothenstein (Sir John K M Rothenstein). They had met several members of the so-called Bloomsbury Group, and apparently after a day of driving buses or trains, such worthies as Evelyn Waugh, Ford Maddox-Ford, Douglas Goldring and others would turn up for copious drinks at 'the Americans' (all of whom were believed to be rich and hospitable). I have been told that Ford Maddox-

Ford described my mother in one of his books as a 'feather headed American beauty' - there is no-one more snobbish than an intellectual snob.

Two close American friends of my FitzGerald grandfather's, Mr Henry Selfridge, the founder of Selfridges department store, and R D Blumenfeld, Editor of the Daily Express from 1902-1932 took my mother under their wings. She wrote small articles for the female readers of RDB's newspaper for a while – and one rather different result of these friendships was that I had carte blanche at the American ice cream counter in Selfridges. It was in 1926 that the Blackbirds Revue, an American all black group of musicians came to London from New York. The cast were extremely popular and led a fairly hectic, racy life among the social set of the time. Since my father had a good voice, and quite a repertoire of Negro spirituals and songs, he too had a certain success.

At that time my future step-mother (Joyce Fagan) a friend of Evelyn Waugh's, met my father, fell in love with him and wrote a letter telling him of her love. As his marriage to my mother was breaking up, and my father had approached Walter de la Mare asking for his daughter Jeanne's hand in marriage, the situation must have been complicated to say the least. I suppose it was because of these facts that my parents decided to send me to a boarding school. I was only 5 years old and came from a very different environment. The experience was not a happy one. I attended various English boarding schools from then on until I was 17 years old. Sometime in the summer of 1925 we had gone to look at the school my parents had chosen for me. It was in Hampshire, called Wickham House, and was run by a medical doctor and his wife called Kinnear. The school was primarily for the children of British couples serving overseas, in the Middle East, China, India, Africa and Burma etc. Many of them spent all year at Wickham, even the holidays. The day we visited we had lunch around a big table and as we ate, I felt a very painful series of pinches on my bare legs and I started to cry. I was unable to tell anyone what ailed me. A small boy of about my age had crawled under the table and was tormenting me. The whole place, Doctor Kinnear and his wife, the other children, all terrified me. Here started what was to be my first experience of being away from home and family.

That autumn began my twelve-year stint in English boarding schools, but Wickham was only for three years. One of the few pleasant memories of the place was the yearly fair run by real gypsies. Swing boats, coconut shies, and best of all, the roundabout – gaily painted horses, polished twisted brass poles and the lovely hurdy-gurdy. I was allowed as many rides on this as I was years old – so being 8 years old was a great milestone.

However, most memories of Wickham House were not happy. The Kinnears had a 5 year old daughter called Evelyn, and we were supposed to play together. I was an ideal subject for teasing – my American accent, my easy tears, my fear of the dark and my enviable collection of fairy tales beautifully illustrated by Arthur Rackham, all led to meanness and envy. If we quarrelled I was always blamed, even when it was Evelyn's fault. Once when playing the 'fishing game' for instance – a cardboard pond and two fishing lines with magnets on the end to catch the magnetic fish – we both caught the same prize. She hit me with her fishing line, magnet first, and I was sent to bed on bread and water. My first experience of injustice. Being in the big brass bed in the daytime (with enough sunlight coming through the drawn curtains to light the two brass balls at the end of the bed) had me paralysed with fear. The big-eyed lion at the end of the bed, (as I conceived it to be) was going to eat me up.

We went on long, and sometimes lovely walks every day, but preparing for them was torture. We wore boots, and on top of them, leather gaiters, which were done up with a button hook, at least fifteen to twenty buttons on each leg. Quite beyond my inexperienced fingers. It always ended in tears, and my having to run on fat legs after the disappearing 'crocodile'. But I do remember the thick clumps of damp, sweet honey-smelling primroses I was allowed to pick in the spring, the marsh marigolds, or kingcups, down by the river, and the occasional sight of an otter. Once, climbing a bank, I disturbed an adder, and watched her glide away from the root I had grasped to help me up. I began to develop an intense interest in nature, and plants and flowers in particular, which has remained one of my major joys all through my life.

The school routine and rules were completely alien to me. I still suffered from croup, though much less intensely. The easy way to stop my struggling for breath, and my wheezing, was to allow me to suck a boiled sweet or fruit drop. This, the school decided was simply a ruse to get a sweet out of regimen. We were allowed only one boiled sweet after lunch, and so it was refused me. We sat for our meals at long tables on backless benches, packed close together so as to prevent us from sticking our elbows out, and we learnt to clip them firmly to our sides. Every day, breakfast was porridge with black treacle or molasses, except on Sundays when we were given a 'treat' of fresh rolls with the soft centres removed and a spoonful of golden syrup in the middle. The molasses made me gag, though I loved porridge with salt and milk. After several shaming breakfasts of gagging and being sick, my parents got permission for me to eat my porridge with salt and eschew the molasses.

At the age of 6 or 7, I decided I loved a small, curly haired boy of my age, who played the piano. Miraculous. I danced around behind him kissing the top of his head until he shooed me off in no uncertain manner. I then decided I must 'kill myself for love' and, having heard that celandines were poisonous, I picked some, put them in an empty bottle with a little water, and hid the bottle behind the school room bookcase. I checked the bottle every day, and when the liquid looked green and slimy, I decided that it was time to drink it. It had absolutely no effect whatsoever on my obviously cast iron digestion.

My young unhappiness and the strangeness of the surroundings must have affected me deeply, because I was *not* good at my lessons. My parents were informed, in all seriousness, that I was a little mentally deficient. I must have been about 7 when I contracted whooping cough and mastoiditis. I was very ill, and remember in my fevered state, only wanting my parents.

In 1928, my parent's divorce, which had taken three years in the English courts, became final. My years from 5 to 8 had been fraught with fears of abandonment and uncertainty. I well remember the day they came down to see me and we went off in my father's convertible AC car. They stopped in a country lane, and tried to explain that they were separating. I wept copiously and asked who I would be living with. I assume the more I wept and blew my nose into my father's handkerchief the harder it was for them. I finally leant forward, and for some unknown reason, wiped the face of the clock on the dashboard; of course I smeared it with snots and tears. My mother's control snapped and she upbraided me soundly, only making my weeping worse.

During the following years my mother and I lived in a series of rented flats and houses in England. In term time my mother lived (or rather PG'd as she would put it) with friends and acquaintances as a paying guest. One year she rented a cottage in Shere in Surrey. Before I was enrolled in my new school, I went for my lessons to a Miss Hulk who lived in a small, one room, wooden hut, little better than a shack it appeared to me. She was an excellent teacher, a very kind woman, and I had her exclusive attention. However, since she was unable to teach me French, I went once a week across the common, about three quarters of a mile, to a friend's house. Groups of older village boys would sometimes pursue me throwing dried cow-pats at my terrified fleeing back. This purgatory probably put me off French lessons for many years to come.

We can't have lived in Shere for more than eight or ten months. Our cottage was very pretty, old and thatched, with a nice garden. My favourite playmates were the younger village boys. We would go on long walks, play in the stream, catch tadpoles and go bird's-nesting. We once had a near disastrous encounter with a furious swan, from whom, I am ashamed to say, we had stolen an egg. Some days, when summer visitors were exploring the area, I would wait at the bottom of the lane by the ford, and 'guide' them across for a three-penny bit, or even sixpence. I never told my mother about these adventures.

Very often she went to London for the day, and I was footloose and fancy-free. I was 8 or 9 years old when I decided one afternoon to cook her supper, and have all the oil lamps and candles lit when she got home, (potentially pretty dangerous). Before lighting them, I made scrambled eggs. While they dried out on the stove, I waited, peering out of the bedroom window for my mother's return. We did have some good times together. Gigi could always make me laugh. She was a great story teller. We had picnics in the fields and woods which, in spring, were full of wild lilies-of-the-valley. My passion for wild flowers never left me and was a big part of my life. My mother had absolutely no sense of direction and I would take great pride in leading her home again.

At the end of the summer I was sent to my second boarding school in Bramley, Surrey. I do not remember much about it, except that I was lonely.

I made a graveyard for all the dead mice, insects and invertebrates I found. I planted a garden around them and spent my free time there every day.

It must have been in 1930 that I was sent to a school in North Foreland. At this age, and until 1933, I made more lasting friendships. One of my fellow students was Gogo Schiaparelli who seemed a very glamorous person to all of us. This had nothing to do with the fact that her mother was Schiaparelli of the fashion world, but rather, that she spoke with an Italian accent, her underclothes were different from ours, her hair was curly and cut in a fashionable way, and most of all she walked with a slight but very graceful limp, having had polio as a young child. On half-term weekends my mother and Signora Schiaparelli, would descend from the train together in a cloud of sartorial glory. By now Gigi had rented a flat in Chelsea, and although on a dollar allowance from her parents, she was also working for a dress shop in Sloane Square. In the holidays she limited her social life so that she could be with me. She had several admirers at this time, all of whom I regarded with deep suspicion. She later told me that some of them would telephone when term time had begun again and inquire if the 'ogre' was back in school.

In 1933 she married again. Her new husband, Geoffrey Marler, was a New Zealander. He was eight or ten years her junior, a very charming and sweet-natured man. I admit that I felt threatened by the marriage, in the sense that I did not know where I would be living or with whom. The wedding was in London in the Savoy Chapel. I was given two days off from school to attend the ceremony. They left for New Zealand shortly afterwards. It had been arranged that I should go and live with my father and step-mother until such time as they could send for me. It was a difficult period in my life and I am sure equally difficult for my father and Joyce, my step-mother. She made it clear to me that after supper in the evenings I should stay in my room as she and my father wanted 'to be alone together'. At this time I grew very fond of my two little half-brothers Mick and Jim, and played the role of big sister quite enthusiastically.

My mother's marriage turned out to be rather disastrous. She later told me how, en-route to New Zealand, Geoff, laughing wildly, suddenly seized her by the wrists and hung her over the ship's side. Luckily a doctor on board saw what was happening and came up to Geoff and said quietly 'Let's bring her in Geoff'. As soon as she was safely on the deck Geoff fell down in a fit. Apparently, when he was younger, he had done quite a lot of stunt flying. On one occasion he crashed the plane, and a piece of metal lodged in his skull pressing on his brain. His parents, who knew of his condition, did not tell my mother and it seems Geoff was unaware of his problem. In those days, an attempt to remove the fragment from his skull was considered very dangerous, and his parents did not give their permission for such an operation. Gigi also discovered that they had little or no money, and that they were to live with her in-laws, so there was little chance of sending for me to join them. I missed my mother terribly and still have some of the rather desperate letters I wrote to her at the time.

In 1936 she asked my grandmother to send her enough money for her to return to England from New Zealand to be with me. After she left an acquaintance told Geoff that she had gone because she was afraid of him and of his recurring fits. He too later returned to England to represent his father's company in London, but when Gigi tried to come back and live with him again, he told her he did not want anyone living with him 'out of pity' and so she was divorced for the second time and returned to her rather nomadic way of life, boarding with friends, until she went back to her parent's house in late 1938.

By 1937 I was finishing my twelve years of English education in Malvern. My last school, Lawnside, was particularly known for its Greek dancing and choral verse speaking and – as far as the Headmistress was concerned – perhaps even more importantly, for its rose garden. The only school prizes I ever won were for Deportment (I had inherited a good straight back) and 'Rose Names'. I knew all the roses by sight and each year I would win the Rose Prize – much to my Headmistress's displeasure as I was not her favourite girl.

Every second year the school would put on a classic, part Greek-dancing, part verse-speaking, play. A soundproof stage would be brought from London to the Malvern Theatre. The year I was acting and dancing, Bernard Shaw, the journalist and broadcaster S.P.B Mais, the composer Rutland Boughton and the poet Alfred Noyes were invited to attend. We performed Homer's *Odyssey*. I had the part of Calypso, but I also had to dance the 'Furies' and the 'Storm' when Odysseus is washed up on the shores of Calypso's island.

We were all measured for our costumes for the dances and had to wear rigid "liberty bodices". After the measurements were taken half an inch was deducted making them so tight that no sign of our burgeoning bosoms could be seen. I was flat as board at the time, but dancing very energetically in a restricting garment left one gasping for breath. Academically it was a very good school, and we learnt a lot. My favourite subjects were English, History and Geography, but the school ethics seemed to have remained enshrined in a sign over the front door 'A lady when entering a carriage does not show her ankle'.

Chapter 2

New Experiences

U p to now, my father had always allowed my mother to choose my schools. These were all paid for by my maternal grandmother, Margaret FitzGerald. When I was 17 and with a School Certificate under my belt, he decided that he would choose the next one. He had met a refugee German painter one night in a chinese restaurant in Soho, and they began talking about schools for their daughters. My fathers companion told him of a school run by a German couple in Switzerland, and said he was very impressed by the school system and the couple, and that he was sending his daughter there. After getting in touch with Max and Gertrud Bondy, the joint heads of the school, my father met them, approved of their method of education and he and my step-mother Joyce, took me to Switzerland in the Summer of 1937.

Late in the afternoon, we crossed the French border into Switzerland at Vallorbe. We had been travelling through France by train all day. The Jura mountains seemed to me very beautiful and mysterious. I had yet to become intimate and enchanted with mountains, climbing them, living under them and most of all learning to respect their moods and challenges.

It was nearly dark when we arrived in Gland, a small village about 4km from Lake Geneva. The station smelt of chocolate and cleanliness, there was a large and ornate music box against one wall, with crinolined ladies and elegant figures which danced when it was turned on. Our train was met by a blonde, good looking man who introduced himself in somewhat halting English as Harald Barushka. He drove us through dimly seen vineyards, past tile-roofed houses and over a small private air field, until we entered a gravel drive way.

We stopped in front of a very brightly lit modern building, with balconies running across the first and second floors. As we got out of the car I could hear male voices whispering, and laughter in the surrounding shrubbery. I had no experience what so ever of co-educational schooling, and the presence of boys – in all probability teasing boys – frightened me.

When we entered the house we were met by the heads of the school, Max and Gertrud Bondy. The couple came from Hamburg, where they had run a well known school called Marienau. Gertrud Bondy, who spoke excellent English – to calm my obvious nervousness, introduced me to the two girls who would be my room mates. I understood virtually nothing of what was being said – my German was completely non-existent, and my French strictly from English schooling. Seizing an opportunity to speak to my father, I begged him not to leave me in the place. Primed with lurid tales circulated in boarding school, I thought I was about to be abandoned in a white slave-trading centre and I could see myself being shipped off to South America or the Middle East to a 'fate worse than death'. What was the meaning of all the laughter and rustling in the bushes? Who was this incredibly handsome so-called teacher?

I calmed down somewhat when my two future room mates, Cecile Guigoz and Sigrid Bernstein, showed me around some of the grounds and other buildings.

Les Rayons, as the school was called, had been an English school for several years before the Bondy's bought it in late 1936. There were at least five separate houses in the fairly extensive grounds. There was a private lake front landing stage on Lac Leman. Back in our bedroom I learnt that Cecile was a Swiss girl from Gruyère with a serious but friendly manner, and Sigrid was a pert, snub-nosed, impish German from Hamburg.

There followed eighteen very interesting and formative months for me. My friendship with Cecile was a slow and steady enrichment of my everyday life in Gland, and she was later to become my oldest female friend. We remained close until her death in 2014. We spoke a mixture of French, English and German together – what Cecile called a '*melange de torchons a de serviettes*' – (a mixture of dishcloths and napkins). Neither of us had any formal language lessons and I, for one, learnt German more or less by a process of osmosis. She was, and remained, a very loyal friend, and despite quite different personalities we had a good understanding of one another. A quiet, undemonstrative, moral, and extremely practical young woman, she later developed into an efficient and caring head of the Guigoz clan and maintained the family home *Le Coteau* for any or all of the large family.

In our time at Les Rayons we were often in the kitchen trying to help Johnny, the bad tempered, and usually intoxicated cook. Since the school was struggling financially and run on a tight budget, I am sure he had a difficult time trying to come up with affordable menus. Breakfast consisted of a bowl of porridge, at ten o' clock we had a *Gabel Frühstuck* (fork breakfast) which was black bread and nut butter, and lunch was simple but tasty. For supper, again rolls with jam and butter.

In the first winter of my stay in Gland, Ceicile invited me to stay with her family in Vuadens in the Gruyere. I travelled by train from Gland to Romont where I had to change. There I had a wait of about forty minutes. I went into the waiting room where a large iron stove was thrumming with heat. The room was full of farmers and their wives, the smell of garlic was pretty overpowering, although I did not know it was garlic at the time – it was a new smell to me. Everyone was sitting quietly and patiently. Ruddy faced, and of varying ages, they did not greet me in anyway, in fact they did not seem to even talk to one another. This was not so surprising to me, as before the Second World War the English too were reticent and uncommunicative, particularly with strangers. The atmosphere in the little room was neither critical nor mistrustful. The faces seem to express a tolerance and acceptance of others and of their common lot in life.

These and other thoughts about the Swiss started in my time in Gland, and developed later in life on getting to know Switzerland and the Swiss very well. I grew to like, appreciate and greatly respect them. Apart from the happy time in Les Rayons itself, it was the overwhelmingly beautiful countryside that then, and today, lifted my spirits. I had never lived in the vicinity of mountains before. The school was right on the lakeside and Mont Blanc was to be seen on most days either shining in all its clarity or shrouded in clouds. We went on wonderful *Wanderungen* – I remember driving to the foot hills of the Rocher de Nez and being sensually, practically physically, submerged in field upon field of wild perfumed *poeticus narcissae*.

Although the beauty of the Swiss landscapes and flowers already impressed me, my appreciation of these things and love of the mountains has grown ever greater with age. The smell of Swiss alpine villages in winter – wood smoke and a certain spiciness in the air, or in summer after the fields have been cut and there is the sweet smell of drying hay in the barns, are not to be forgotten. I enjoy Swiss food and wine and appreciate Swiss private – as well as professional – hospitality. Sometimes in small, simple, high altitude restaurants; a good soup, bread and cheese will be brought to the table without any sort of servility or ingratiating manner. There is always a strong impression of personal dignity and individuality.

My husband and I spent several years working in Switzerland, and after we retired we started a small touring business. We met and became very friendly with a hotelier in the Graubünden. Sepp Waldegg was in many ways a typical *Wirt*, an excellent host in his working hours, but also a very thoughtful, spiritual and knowledgeable man. He and Jean would talk well into the small hours of the morning, and I would say that in their later years they were fast approaching the sort of relationship that had existed between Jean and his greatest friend Hans Imhof. Hans, was of course, an outgoing, warm and approachable Austrian, and Sepp a rather withdrawn and reticent Swiss at times.

To go back to 1938 and to Cecile's invitation to visit her family. Louly, Cecile's brother who was also at school in Les Rayons, met my train at the *halte* just below the Guigoz chalet where the train stopped en-route to Bulle. We walked up the hill, our feet crunching in the snow on the way, to the house. This was the first chalet-type building I had ever seen. On entering I was somewhat intimated by Monsieur and Madame Guigoz. She particularly, as she had a machine-gun like delivery of French in what I later learnt was a strong Marseille accent.

Later that evening Louly asked me if I would like to come with him to fetch the milk from the farm next door. We walked through deep snow to the back of the farmhouse, where I could see the carcass of an animal hanging from the eaves. When I rather hesitantly asked what it was, he said 'It's a dog, we eat dog in Switzerland!' Although I have since learnt that this was possibly true, I think it more likely that it was game shot for the table. It all added to my somewhat nervous incredulity!

In Gland, Cécile and I settled back in school, a *Schulgemeinde* (a student community school), it was run on the same lines as the Bondy's school in Hamburg, called Marienau (this school still exists and is run on the same principles). The students helped in various ways. The girls not only assisted in the kitchen, but darned the boys' socks, worked in the laundry and in the 'Mimi Haus', where the very young pupils lived. The boys made the sports field for football and athletics, and on Saturday mornings all of us were busy, singing and joking as we worked, cleaning the dining room floor with steel wool scrapers on our feet, waxing and polishing it later with so called *Blochers* (heavily weighted discs on handles). We also held a student's court, to deal with minor (or even fairly major) behavioural problems.

As I later learnt, the Bondys were part Jewish, and most of the children were refugees, for one reason or another, from Nazi Germany. None of these facts were known to me at the time and even if they had been, I was unaware of the connotations of Fascism and Anti-Semitism or of the gathering clouds in 1937.

In the early spring of 1938 the Bondys wanted to recruit more non-German students. The Germans could only bring ten Deutsch Mark a head out of Germany in those days – these controls were the so called '*Devisen*'. So non-German students were needed to pay the bills. The idea was to make a sweep through Northern Italy, Yugoslavia, Austria, Hungary and Czechoslovakia on a so-called *Propaganda Reise* (promotional trip). The Bondys realised that they could not take enough money for the journey on their German passports owing to the *Devisen*, without attracting attention. so, (I realise now somewhat cynically), they asked my father if he would like me to accompany them on this 'exciting tour, a wonderful opportunity to travel in the Balkans and Italy'. Of course, my father agreed and all the funds for the trip were declared on my American passport. We set off in a small convertible Fiat, which was Max's car, always with the roof down except in the pouring rain. I sat in the back seat making endless *Butter brote* (rolls and butter) for Max, as he suffered from stomach ulcers and had to eat lightly but often. It was early March and the beginning of *Fasching* – or carnival time. My next culture shock was when, on being left alone in the car in a Graubünden mountain village, I was suddenly surrounded by a yelling crowd of hideous masked figures clothed in ancient tattered *Fasching* costumes. These youngsters whooped and shrieked around me and I was very glad to see the Bondys returning with yet more rolls and butter. We set off to cross the Bernina Pass into Italy.

The Bondys were gifted pedagogues and very intelligent people. Gertrud was more practical than Max. Not only was she joint head of the school, but also a Doctor of Medicine and able to speak several languages. Max himself spoke only German and was, in many ways, the original 'absent-minded professor'. He certainly had little or no idea of what made a car run, and how it should be driven in extreme weather conditions. It was early spring and of course, deep snow everywhere. The surface at the entrances to the many rocky tunnels on the Pass was icy. At one such tunnel Max stalled the car and we began to slide towards the edge of the sheer drop. Widely spaced, upright stones marked the edge of the road, but there was no barrier. I leapt out of the open back of the slowly moving car and got some large rocks to put under the wheels. I succeeded in stopping the car and I and Gertrud managed to get Max moving again.

We continued over the Pass, but on the descent Max ploughed into a snow drift and we were stuck. It was getting on towards evening and Max and Gertrud asked me to walk back to a village we had just passed through to get help. I trudged into the snowy group of houses and had knocked on a couple of doors before I began to realise there was no sign of life anywhere. No footsteps of man nor beast in the snow, no smoke from the chimneys, no lights in the windows. It was completely deserted. I returned to the Bondys with my news and Max remarked that the village must have been abandoned as 'a sort of memorial to the First World War'. I have since learnt, that this was of course, a *Maiensäss*, a settlement empty in winter and only used by the herdsman for summer pasturage.

It was beginning to get dark, but luckily, and much to our relief, a horse-drawn sleigh came towards us. The driver and his horse managed to pull the Fiat out of the snowdrift and late that evening we arrived in Tirano to spend the night. Our next stop was Trieste, where we stayed in the villa until recently owned by Gabriel D'Annunzio, the Italian writer and proto-fascist. I met a lot of people, who today I would have found very interesting indeed – but I was entirely out of my depth. A few days later in Zagreb, I remember visiting a factory where they made linen goods; the Bondys obviously hoped that the factory owner would send his child to Les Rayons. I went to the market alone and bought an antique peasant blouse, with large embroidered sleeves, two pairs of red pointed slippers for my brothers and a terracotta drinking vessel in the form of a cockerel for Joyce and my father. Two days later we drove to Budapest, approaching Buda coming downhill with a fabulous view of Pest in the valley below.

My memories of Budapest are once again of endless meetings with grownups, and of details such as heavy felt and leather curtains inside the doors of cafés and restaurants to keep out the intense cold. I was nearly 18 years old, had a plait of thick hair hanging down my back and was tall for my age. I was also entirely innocent. Walking down a main street one day, an 'older man' (probably no more than 30 or so!) stopped dead in his tracks at the sight of us, and with an expression of extreme agony clutched at his heart. When I asked Gertrud what was the matter with the poor chap, she laughed and said, 'He thought you were beautiful'. What?

Our next stop was Vienna, where the Bondy's had many friends and family. Endless handshaking and *Knicksen* (curtseying). Rooms full of people all discussing, with worried faces, the current situation. The next day, after saying goodbye to family members, we picked up the Bondy's eldest daughter, Annemarie, from the University of Vienna where she was studying medicine, and proceeded on to Prague. It was 11 March 1938. Hitler invaded Austria two days later.

Prague, the Karlsbruecke and the Old City were impressively beautiful. I was to stay with a family called Lederer, whose daughter Anita later came to Gland and was my roommate. It must have been a relief for the Bondys to have a place for me to stay, at no cost, for a longer visit than anywhere else on our trip. On the first morning at the Lederer's, a knock on the door announced the arrival of an impeccably uniformed maid, who drew my bath, and then came in with a beautiful tray of breakfast, the finest china and silver, coffee, a boiled egg and delicious croissants. Mrs Lederer was an extremely elegant, rather intimidating figure to me; she took me with her on several mornings when she went out. As she left the flat, she was always handed a fresh pair of white kid gloves from a pile in the hall cupboard. One day she took me to a fashion show, where I sat in my school skirt and gym shoes and watched the models wearing Chanel, Déssés and Grés. I was entranced by many of them, particularly the beautiful tailored suits shown with little umbrellas topped with bunches of Parma violets.

I had my eighteenth birthday on 12 March; Mrs Lederer gave a dinner party for me. A great many young people were invited. The day before the party I had gone riding with the granddaughter of Jan Masaryk, the Czech diplomat, in the park (Masaryk was the Foreign Minister of Czechoslovakia from 1940–48, in that year his body was found on the ground outside his bathroom window. It is believed that he had been assassinated by 'defenestration' - the act of throwing a person out of a window, historically used in Bohemia and Austria). Another rider, when he passed us, lifted his hat and warmly greeted my companion, 'That was Dr Benes' (President of Czechoslovakia) she informed me. Duly impressed, I was further delighted to be offered the loan of a dress to wear to 'my' dinner party. I possessed the barest minimum of wardrobes, and even less than usual on this trip. The dress was of palest blue angora and silk. I was so terrified of sweating into it, that I lined the sleeves with layers and layers of lavatory paper.

We had an amazing meal. I have no idea what we ate, I was overcome by the array of cutlery and glasses at each place – water glass, Pilsen glass, red and white wine glasses, *digestif* glass, etc. Everyone was most friendly to me; after dinner we danced and I relaxed and enjoyed myself. A few days later I was invited by the Petschek girls, who had been guests at the party, to their 'Palais' to have dinner with one of them. The Petschek home in Prague was indeed a palace. A huge marble floored entrance hall with an imposing flight of marble stairs up to the second floor, where each of the three Petschek daughters had a private wing. Every girl had a staff of their own looking after them. We dined with Rita Petschek, and her staff were all in pastel green and white uniforms. After twelve solid years of British boarding school, and little or no social life until this time, I found the whole Prague experience pretty amazing. The Petscheks family managed to leave Czechoslovakia before the Nazi invasion and later settled in Canada I believe. The Petschek Palace, a city landmark, today serves as the residence of the US Ambassador in Prague.

The conversation among the adults in Prague in 1938 must, of course, have been tense and fearful. Hitler had invaded Austria; we had left just in time with Annemarie, and what would happen next? Germany was laying claim to the Sudetenland, and many of the people I met, including the Lederers and the Petscheks, I later realised, were German speaking and Jewish or part Jewish.

The only result, as far as I can remember, of all the hard work done by the Bondys to promote their school and raise funds for it, was that Anita Lederer came to Gland as a finishing school pupil, and the Petscheks and others came later that summer for their holidays. Making decisions for their children must have been incredibly difficult because of the political climate at the time.

Realising they could not return to Switzerland via Vienna, the Bondys and I drove southwest to Bratislava to cross over from there into Hungary, Slovenia, Italy and eventually home. At the Bratislava border crossing on the Austrian side, heading towards us we could see long lines of cars stretching as far as the distant horizon. All were waiting to cross into Czechoslovakia - all of them fleeing Austria and Vienna.

Max took our passports and went into the customs house. After half an hour Gertrud and Annemarie seemed to be getting anxious. After about an hour, Gertrud got out of the car and started walking about with Annemarie. Two hours later I could see that Gertrud was in tears. Annemarie returned to the car to fetch a handkerchief and I asked '*Was ist den Los*'? (What is the matter)? She replied in an irritated voice '*Ach Du, Du verstehst von garnichts!*' (Oh you, you don't understand anything), and I said '*Nein, ich verstehe wirklich nicht, also bitte sag'smir!*' (No I really don't understand please tell me!). She explained that the Bondy family were part Jewish, that they carried German passports, they might be delayed indefinitely and that Max might not even be allowed back out of the customs post.

Being 'Jewish' meant nothing to me. Nobody had told me that most of the pupils at Les Rayons were Jewish, and even if they had I would not have understood the perils that caused them to come to Switzerland. I grew up very fast in the next few hours.

Now I wonder why, or even how, this could have been the case. Once I had started living with my father and step-mother, I was exposed to, but I did not comprehend or analyse the fact that they and their close friends were very liberal – one could say left wing – in their political beliefs. In early 1936 we had Abyssinian refugees from the Italian invasion of Abyssinia staying in the house; later, in 1937–8, Spaniards fleeing from the Spanish Civil War were often living there, and in 1938 several Germans, particularly one German woman, who was a close friend of Joyce's. Nobody told me that these Germans were Jewish and in fact, nothing was directly said to me, or the subject even discussed with me. I simply accepted the presence of these guests in our home. I was already in my teens, and it would have helped me to grow up if these facts had been explained to me. The little that I did gather probably made me somewhat isolated in boarding school, as I began to have the first inklings of my political leanings.

Max finally emerged from the building and we continued on our way. I remember nothing at all about the return journey, and can only now speculate on what a traumatic time it must have been for the Bondys until we arrived safely back in Gland.

Earlier in the spring of that year, my mother had gone to the Tyrol with an old friend. She had bought me a thick Tyrolean knitted jacket, this was the warm jacket I wore in the back seat of the Fiat on our *Propaganda Reise*, and a pair of shoes known as *Goiserer*. These are still made today in Bad Goisern in Austria. They are traditional, heavy duty shoes, laced on the side, and I thought them rather smart. That same summer she went to Sicily for the second time. Her first visit had been with a friend the year before, and an Italian army officer, of Albanian descent, had fallen quite seriously in love with her, and wanted to marry her. She arranged for me to come to Palermo and stay with her in her Pension for the summer holidays.

I was very young for my age. I took the train from Geneva to Milan, where I had a five hour wait for my connection to Naples, from where the boat left for Palermo. I spoke no Italian, was very shy, and did not know what to do with my suitcase if, as was most unlikely, I had been brave enough to do some sightseeing. So I ordered coffee, sat in the main concourse of the railway station and watched the world go by. There seemed to be hundreds of people passing and re-passing in front of my eyes. Peasant women in local costume, elegantly dressed men and women, and fantastic *Besaglieri*, (Italian mountain troops), in black uniforms, with cascades of black and green shimmering cocks feathers, in their wide hats. I decided to write a letter to my father to tell him all that I was seeing. The letter ended up being twenty-five pages long. Unfortunately it was not kept by the family. I should have enjoyed reading it!

By the time I boarded my train for Naples it was evening, and the journey was to take most of the night. I found an empty third class compartment and settled myself in a window corner. Somewhat later and to my dismay, a middle aged man with peasant boots and many packs and baskets got into the same compartment. He smiled and nodded at me and I studiously ignored him. Shortly after we left the station, he removed his boots with groans of pleasure, and put his feet up on the seat next to me. I moved even closer to my corner. After dark he produced a large sausage, an onion and some bread from his basket – also a bottle of homemade wine. Oh God! I thought, he is going to get drunk and I am all alone with him. He smilingly offered me a piece of sausage on the end of his knife. I refused it. I probably looked scared out of my wits. So, after trying all he could to calm and placate me, he shrugged his shoulders, rose and put the lights out. I leapt up and put them on again. He obviously was planning to rape me. He sighed and put the lights out again, and I once more re-lit them. Finally, the poor man, probably the father of six with a farm somewhere, fell asleep and snored away the whole night. I remained alert and kept my frightened vigil.

By the time I reached Palermo the next day, I was exhausted. My mother met the boat with her admirer, Franco Ferrara, and we drove in a *Carrozza* to the Pension on Mondello beach outside Palermo. It was a charming simple place with no frills. What struck me most of all was that the owner's youngest child, a little boy, was allowed to wander around everywhere wearing only a shirt with his little penis exposed, because that way he could go pee-pee wherever and whenever he wanted, and there would not be constant laundry!

'Le Tout Palermo' used to come out in the evenings for supper. It was a very good and well known restaurant. This was the first time I saw, or even imagined *ménages a trois*; very often Barone, or Principe so and so, with their wives and mistresses all dining together. Franco kept us up on the local gossip and filled us in on every local personality. He ate in the most extraordinarily delicate way. He would cut all his fruit with a knife and fork. Delicately peeling and coring with his thin, dark, hairy fingers. He taught my mother which was the correct side to sit beside him in the *Carrozza*, I believe it was on his right for a fiancée and on his left for a mistress. The food was also something of an eye-opener to me. Several evenings there would be special orders of seafood, including large platters with an octopus, legs dangling over the edge, in place of honour.

At the age of 8, after years of pleading with my mother, I had finally been allowed to let my hair grow. By now, aged 18, it was very long and thick. My mother really disliked it, as she did not consider it smart or chic. She took me to a hairdressers in Palermo and asked them to cut my hair. The hairdresser looked at her without saying a word, but when he had shampooed my hair, he, with a dramatic gesture, smashed a small bottle of Coty Perfume on the edge of the basin and anointed my head with it. He then made two fat braids of my hair and twisted them around my head in a crown. He sent me outside to sit on a bench in the sun and said '*Eco*, when your mother sees you with your hair in all it shining glory she will change her mind'. I doubt if she did, but I was allowed to keep my hair. When it finally had to be cut, before enlisting in the Navy years later, my father was very sad to see it go.

I was invited to go riding with a young man, who had just come back from studying in the United States. His name was Salvatore Rossi, of the Martini Rossi family. We rode one day in the gardens of a ruined palazzo. He was always challenging me to further feats of equestrian skill. The final test was to take our horses, skittering and slithering, down a long flight of marble steps. He used his riding crop constantly and I angrily berated him. He told me he had learnt to use his whip on 'man and beast' in Abyssinia. One evening he gave me my first kiss, I broke away from him and ran upstairs to the bedroom I shared with my mother. I proceeded to brush my teeth furiously. She smiled and said 'What's the matter darling, did someone kiss you?' To which I replied, 'Yes and it's disgusting'.

Before we left Sicily, of course, I had lost my heart to a married Barone who enchanted my romantic soul by telling me he often slept on the ground in his orange groves, to guard the crop. He would loop his horse's halter around his booted ankle so the horse would alert him by lifting its head if anyone approached.

By the time I left Gland near the end of 1938, I was dreaming, thinking, and speaking in German. My written German was never as good as my spoken; I never learnt it formally and made many grammatical mistakes. I had also found new friends, chief among them of course was Cecile Guigoz and her 'brother' Louly. (Cecile had been more or less adopted by the Guigoz family, and later became Louly's wife).

Shortly after leaving Gland I returned to the United States. I entered the Arts Students League on 72nd street in New York and studied Anatomy under George Bridgeman. My mother and I lived in a flat in central New York, while she worked for a shop called British Tweeds, which was owned and run by an English couple. She was sent by them to Maine in the early summer of 1939. A short while later that year I told her that, as war was imminent in Europe, and all my friends and contemporaries would be involved on one side or the other, I felt my place was back there. When I returned to Europe in late July, I knew that if I wanted to see any of my friends from Gland I would have to go to the Continent right away.

At the beginning of 1939, Max and Gertrud Bondy and their three children closed Les Rayons and emigrated to the United States. They had been sponsored by several prominent Americans, including Dorothy Thompson. They opened a school in Lennox, Massachusetts, but it was not easy to inculcate their pedagogic methods into educating American children, and after a few accidents, and other troubles, the school was closed. Annemarie and her husband Georg Roeper however, later opened a very successful school in Detroit.

Staying in Switzerland with the Guigoz's for some time, I was reunited also with a young German, Heio (Heinz-Joachim) von Frankenberg-Lüttwitz, Louly's best friend, whom he had met when they were both pupils at the Bondy's school near Hamburg. I learned that Monsieur Guigoz had offered Heio a job in his powdered milk factory and strongly advised him not to return to Germany. His mother, who had lost family in WWI and who was already worried about her eldest son who had been recruited into the *Wehrmacht* also begged him to remain in Switzerland, but because of his devotion to his brother, he returned, was sent to the Russian front, and was killed at Stalingrad.

On leaving Switzerland, I went to Bavaria, where a young family of two boys and a girl, whom I had befriended in Gland, were holidaying on a farm near Munich. We were all recruited to bring in Hitler's harvest, and worked hard every day in the fields and barns. I had planned to continue to Hamburg to see Geeritt Joost, a former Bondy pupil who visited Gland occasionally, and who I suppose was my earliest admirer. I caught the train from Munich and spent the next few days getting to Hamburg. The train was constantly being shunted onto the sidings to let the troop trains go through. Passing through stations en route, one could often hear the sound of tramping feet and the marching song '*Und wir fahren, und wir fahren, und wir fahren gegen England*'. It did cause a certain frisson up the back of one's neck.

On arrival in Hamburg, Geeritt had somehow managed to meet the train despite the long delay. He greeted me by saying '*Du musst sofort weg!*' (You must leave immediately). I replied that I needed a wash, a meal and a night's sleep, and that the next day I would go to the US Consulate and see if my bank had managed to send the money I had asked for.

The next morning I went to the Consulate, where the Consul was one Charles Thayer. He looked at me wearily and said 'OK, I know, you're an American citizen and you want to get back to the US'. I replied 'No, actually, I was going to ask you to lend me £20, so that I can return to London. My bank has been unable to forward the money I had asked for.' He looked surprised and somewhat amused, and said he would certainly do so if I allowed him to collect the debt in London on his way through when returning to the US, for, as he explained, sooner or later America would have to enter the war. Thayer must have been in his late twenties, he was born ten years before I was. He was a charming and very amusing man, and I would have been only too glad to have met him again later in our diplomatic posts. I did meet him in London, just before I joined the WRNS in 1941 when he gave me an ice cream at Gunters and the debt was paid. Thayer, a specialist in Soviet affairs, was the trusted and skilled right-hand man of Ambassador George Kennan for much of his career. Alas, he was later hounded by McCarthyism, which in the end caused him to resign from the State Department. A great loss to the US Foreign Service. He ended his life living in Europe and died in Salzburg in the 1960's.

The train journey from Hamburg to Zeebrugge, where I was to catch one of the few ferries still leaving for England, was painfully slow. The lavatories were blocked and not maintained, and there was dirt and disorder everywhere. The stations were full of weeping women, and middle-aged and older men in ill-fitting World War One uniforms, for which they had grown either too fat or too thin. War had already been declared between England and Germany, and it was only twenty years since the end of the last war. All through Germany, as far as Aachen, the scenes were the same, and on into Belgium, where the fear and dread must have been even greater.

When the border guards came on board the train to check our passports, a good looking young man in a border guard uniform, came into my compartment and I handed him my passport. He looked at it for a short time and asked me in German 'Why are you leaving *Gnädiges Fraulein?*' I replied, also in German, that I did not like the way things were going in Germany. He looked sharply into my eyes and started to speak, but then stopped, collected himself, clicked his heels and said '*Schade!*' (what a pity), before leaving the compartment. The fear of 'Agents Provocateurs' must have been very great at the time.

On approaching the English coast at Dover, what should meet my unbelieving eyes, but beaches full of summer visitors, Punch and Judy shows, donkey rides, paddling in full swing, and an air of total insouciance!

Chapter 3

The War and an Important Decision

When I arrived at the family flat in London I let myself in and realised my father and step-mother were not there. I knew that they had gone to the South of France to visit friends, and thought they were probably already down at the farmhouse in Dorset where they had left my two young half-brothers, Mick and Jim, in the care of a Mrs Eaves. I telephoned, and Mick, aged 9, answered the 'phone. My Father and Joyce were not back from France. There were very few boats crossing the channel since war with Germany had already been declared. Mrs Eaves had fled in a panic with her young son. I asked who was looking after them and Mick replied 'No one'. Who was cooking for them? 'I am'. What were they eating? 'Mashed potatoes and apple sauce'. I told them not to worry 'Old Joan' would be with them as soon as possible.

On arrival in Dorset, I found the boys full of life and perfectly alright, but pretty dirty, with ragged shorts and broken sandals. Two days later the Rifle Brigade arrived in the area and a young Subaltern named Tony Rolt, came to Park Farm with his Corporal and announced they were going to billet a platoon of men on the farm. I told him I was alone in the house, and only 19 years old. He turned to his Corporal and said 'Make a note of that, Corporal, only 19' (he too was only 19 at the time). He then explained that the men were going to sleep in one of the barns and that they would have a Field Kitchen. The only thing they would need from the house was water. There was a tap near the back door into the 'baronial hall' as we called the large back kitchen. I explained there were a lot of chicken fleas in the barns. Tony once more turned to his Corporal and said 'Make a note of that, Corporal, fleas as big as chickens'. During the following days I grew to realise there was nothing to fear from the soldiers, they behaved with great propriety.

Later, Tony and I became good friends, and he was my first boyfriend. He was in the Regular Army, the son of a General but also a very keen and successful racing-car driver. One of the first Regiments to leave England for France, the Rifle Brigade were ultimately to hold off the Germans in Calais, thus helping to enable the Dunkirk evacuation. Those who were not killed, or managed to escape towards Calais, were taken prisoner. Tony ended up, after several attempted escapes, in Colditz, where he took part in the famous building of a glider in the attic of the castle. However, before he, Douglas Bader (of RAF fame) and several others attempted their escape, the castle was liberated and Tony returned home.

A week after the Rifle Brigade arrived I began to worry about money, since I had no more. I telephoned my father's bank in London and the manager told me he was sure there would be a few more boats from France, and that in the meantime, I should run up bills in the village shop. Next day with my last ten shillings, I took the boys to Dorchester on the bus and bought a new pair of shorts for Jim and sandals for Mick.

On our return the bus deposited us at Park Farm gate, and to my great relief the family car was in front of the garage. Joyce and my father greeted us, and Jim turned to the hedge and was sick. 'Oh darling what is the matter?', asked Joyce; Jim looked at me slyly and said 'Old Joan's cooking', for which, over the years I have pretended never to have forgiven him.

In the following weeks of what was called the 'phoney war', my father and Joyce, both of whom certainly had pacifist leanings, were making plans to drive ambulances in Poland. The war was 'certain to peter out soon'. However, as the weeks passed it was realised that the situation might well last for quite some time, and my parents could not leave their two young sons, so any such plans had to be abandoned. My father told me that I would have to find a job that 'Merits the food you eat off the British Government', or I would have to return to the United States. I started trying everywhere to get a useful wartime occupation. I was told that as an 'alien', i.e. an American, I could not serve in the British Armed Forces. The Censorship people, who I thought would be able to use my German and French languages, were also not allowed to hire aliens. I tried all sorts of different and sometimes very interesting possibilities, including the Canal Service. With petrol shortages, the canals were going to have increased barge traffic, particularly for things such as coal deliveries. They too turned me down.

In the meantime, I worked in the YMCA canteen in Euston Station. The railway stations were bombed regularly every night, especially on nights when the moonlight guided the raiders by lighting up the railway tracks. When the Dunkirk evacuation started, we began to get large numbers of exhausted, shocked, filthy troops on the way back to their units. It was fairly chaotic in the Euston canteen. I sketched a portrait of one very young soldier, which I later made into an oil painting. Despite the bombing, I used to walk most of the way home – anyway as far as Baker Street Underground station where I could catch the Metropolitan Line to Swiss Cottage.

I remember the Blitz with great clarity. At the age of 19, with adrenalin pumping and despite the bombs, the incendiary devices, and the huge mines dropped by parachute, I remember only the excitement of every day and particularly the nights. One actually leapt out of bed each morning, looking forward to the evening. I spent every afternoon and most evenings in the canteen at Euston. In the early days the porters and the RTO (Army Rail Transport Office) staff were more than welcome, and only later were our customers restricted to the active armed forces.

Sometimes groups of downed German pilots would be brought through on their way to a northern POW camp. I would go out to the army trucks with some cigarettes and chocolate and tell the scared, mostly very young men, that they had nothing to fear from their captors or their imprisonment.

I did not use the Underground very much, as the sights there filled me with horror. When people were first allowed to use the stations as shelters, these were not equipped for the crowds that went down there. There were no lavatories, the platforms ran with urine, and stepping out of the trains you would have to pick your way between the recumbent bodies.

One night, on arrival at Finchley Road, I was faced with quite a heavy stream of water coming down the stairs towards the platform. I waded my way up and as I reached the street I heard my father's voice calling 'Kid, are you OK kid?'. He was splashing down the street towards me. A bomb had dropped outside our flat, and the poor owner of the delicatessen shop downstairs was standing in the broken glass and contents of his window, wringing his hands and saying '*Alles kaputt, alles kaputt*'. A great many German Jewish refugees had settled in the Swiss Cottage, Finchley Road areas of London.

As the raids increased, and the stations became more and more vulnerable, the volunteers at the canteen were allocated an air raid shelter. The older staff would go down there when the bombing became very intense. One night, during a particularly heavy raid, I was left alone in the canteen. I decided I ought to take some food and drink to the elderly Scots Guards troops in the RTO. I made up a tray and carried it over to them. I was sitting on a high stool at the counter in their office, feeling extremely tired, when the RTO's commanding officer came in. It was 1.30 am. He had been wining and dining somewhere in London. He took one look at me on my stool and asked me to leave. The next day he reported me to the rather formidable lady in charge of the canteen as having been 'Hob-nobbing with the troops' and I was asked to leave the canteen. I suppose it had not helped their disapproval of me, that often, in the last weeks and months, letters had arrived addressed to 'Lofty' or 'Black Bess' etc. They would hold up the offending envelope between finger and thumb and say 'Miss Gill I presume this is for you?' These epistles were usually simple heartfelt thanks from soldiers or sailors that I had helped in some small way.

I was transferred to another YMCA canteen, 'Gattis' in the Strand, opposite Charing Cross station. The crowds of troops and sailors coming through did not lessen, but sometimes there would be an American voice. Several Quaker-organised groups of International Ambulance drivers had arrived in London. Lowell Thomas Junior (son of the well known broadcaster and writer) was one of the early ones. We would often leave the canteen together when my duties were over. I suppose this only added to my bad reputation. One evening I went to the cinema with a young sailor. When we came out of the theatre at Oxford Circus, there was a deep red glow in the sky. He took me back home to Swiss Cottage on a bus. When we climbed to the top deck we could see that the whole of the sky over the East End was red. The Docks and the entire area around them were burning fiercely. It was possibly the worst raid on London during the war.

A girl I was working with asked me to spend the night with her, as the flat next to her had been bombed and she was afraid to be alone. She told me an aunt of hers had lent her a Mews flat and we could go there and sleep in the 'horse shelter'. These so called horse shelters were no more than the garages attached to the flats. That night we carried our mattresses down and lay on the concrete floor of the garage. There was an incendiary raid, and one of the fire bombs landed in the courtyard of the Mews. Grabbing and dragging my mattress, I went out and threw it on the small burning bomb. I knew that the purpose of these fire raids was to light up the area for the heavy bombers. I jumped up and down and stamped on the mattress, yelling insults in German at the top of my voice. The fire out, we returned to our shelter and tried to sleep. At about four o'clock the next morning I heard voices and on looking out, I saw members of the AFS (Auxiliary Fire Service) preparing to take away the bomb. I called out 'Oi, that's my bomb' (I had hoped to have it as a souvenir), but they refused to leave it for me.

Finally my father, through his connections, managed to get me a job in the US Embassy. He knew John Ehrhardt the Consul General – (later American Delegate to the Allied Control Council in Vienna when we served there in 1947). I became 'Miss Gill in Immigration Information'. My office was in the back of the old Embassy in Grosvenor Square. Outside the back entrance was a courtyard, which became more and more busy as the year went on. Towards the end there were as many as 500 people waiting in all weathers, to find out when they could, *if* they could, get to the United States. Almost all the people I interviewed were European Jews, terrified the Germans would invade sooner rather than later, and that their persecution would continue.

Towards the end of that year, shortly before my twentieth birthday, I was seeing as many as 400 to 500 desperate people a day. I developed a test for myself, I would write down the nationality of each person as they walked in the door. A few times, Dutch diamond merchants would, with a look of piteous appeal, empty handkerchiefs full of uncut diamonds onto my desk, and reacted in disbelief when I begged them to take them away immediately, and never to try that with any consular or customs officials. I explained to them that, as Dutch citizens, they were not on any immigration 'quota' and therefore – providing they could get a passage – there were no long delays involved in getting to the US.

On the quota system, the German would-be immigrants, most of whom were Jewish, had to wait five years for a Visa, and provide a viable Affidavit guaranteeing support from family members, friends, or institutions before they would be eligible. After several months of witnessing such fear and distress, I made what might be called a fatal mistake, and spoke German to one poor frightened woman. Before I knew it, the word had spread like wildfire '*Sie spricht Deutsch!*' The following weeks and months were very hard for me at my age. Every desperate would-be immigrant wanted to tell me their stories, hopes and fears.

One day a young, blond German boy by the name of Hans Boxer, came in and asked me if I could find out what had happened to his Visa. His family were already in the US, he had waited the requisite five years, and the Affidavits had been sent to the Embassy long ago. I promised I would look into the matter. That evening I marshalled my friends the doormen and porters, and persuaded them to let me into the filing archives in the basement. The racks of files reached up about 10 ft almost to the ceiling, I climbed up with a foot on each side of the aisle and lay on my stomach on the As to Bs. At the back of the file racks on the floor, were three files which had fallen down. The porters got them out for me the next day and, sure enough, one of them was Hans Boxer. I immediately went to one of my friendly consuls and he saw to it that the Boxer file was expedited. Next time Hans Boxer came in, I was able to give him his Visa. I thought no more about it, but to my amazement, two weeks later, Hans once more waited two hours in the courtyard, and presented me with a gift of a wine glass he had painted with a Tyrolean design, as a thank you.

Years later, in the 1950s when my husband and I had been posted to Zurich, one of his contacts was an American called Oswald Boxer who was representing Pan paperback books. He and his German wife were living in Thomas Mann's villa on the lake, and he invited us to come for a glass of wine and dessert one evening. We were all sitting around the tiled stove, when Oswald mentioned that his younger brother, John, would be joining us later. A young man came in and sat down at the far end of the bench around the stove. I could feel him staring at me for some time, and finally decided to put a stop to this 'unseemly admiration'. I turned my head sharply, and as I met his eyes I said 'Hans Boxer', and at the same time he cried 'Miss Gill'. He turned to his brother and said 'Here she is, here she is Oswald, Miss Gill!' Apparently the fact that I was American but had an English voice, had first alerted him to the fact that he knew me.

Another day an elderly French woman, (Mademoiselle L) and her niece, came into my office. She wore three hats one on top of the other on her head, and at least two overcoats. The niece, a woman of a certain age, and very nervous manner, stood in the background. Mademoiselle L explained she wanted to go to New York, where her brothers 'Had a bank'. She proceeded to excavate her passport and papers from the lining of one of her overcoats, and behaved in a very frightened and furtive manner. I assured her, that providing she could get a reservation on a transatlantic crossing, there was nothing to delay her entry into the United States. There was no French quota. I begged her, however, not to have her documents secreted about her person when she applied to the consul for her Visa, or was interviewed by customs. By this time there were very few berths available for transatlantic crossings. In 1940 the war at sea was well under way. I went to my father, who was Secretary of the American Chamber of Commerce in London, and asked him to pull some strings with his contacts in the 'American Lines' to try and get a cabin for the two women.

My father did manage to get them a passage, and I prayed that Mademoiselle L would freely produce all her documents for the customs officials. A week or so later, my father phoned me to say that the two women, on being interviewed by the Customs in Liverpool before getting on board, had run into trouble. Mademoiselle still had her papers and passport hidden about her person, and further more, when the customs officer approached the two women, the niece had screamed 'Heil Hitler!' and tried to kick the customs officer in the stomach! They were arrested and kept overnight in prison, but did eventually reach the United States.

My habit of guessing a person's nationality as they came into the room, almost got me into real trouble. I would get very tired, particularly emotionally, by the end of the day, and on one such late afternoon a woman in English tweeds and a felt hat came in. She put her British passport down on the desk, and said she wanted to visit her daughter in America – 'How long would it take to get a Visa?' Without thinking, I said 'I am afraid it will take five years,' I had put her down as German when she walked in, clothes and passport notwithstanding. She was horrified, but on looking at her passport, I found that in fact she was a born German, who had married an Englishman before the Treaty of Versailles, and therefore, had she wanted an Immigration Visa, she would have indeed been on the German quota, unfair as this seemed. In fact she only wanted a Visitors Visa, and had no problem in securing one. It was a stressful job for me at this time, particularly as I had so many German and Jewish friends and colleagues.

I continued to try and find useful war work, and although I do not really remember how it happened, my efforts paid off and I was given an interview with the Royal Navy, who I had heard were looking for German speakers. I was asked to attend an appointment with a Lieutenant de Lazlo (son of the well known portrait painter). I went to the Admiralty dressed in my best, a tailor made green tweed suit, red felt hat with a green veil and shoes with green bows. After all I was still greatly influenced, by my elegant, clothes-conscious mother.

When Philip De Lazlo saw me, he must have been aghast; however he put me through my paces and my German vocabulary. He bombarded me with questions, in technical wireless and naval terms and, when I told him I had learnt 'the language' and not the technicalities of wireless and Naval Operations, he said 'Well go away and swot up for a month, and then come back and we will see'. I gave up my job at the US Embassy without telling my father, and spent all day in the library doing just what the Lieutenant had ordered. When I returned, he asked me how many times I had been out to dinner and dancing. When I huffily told him 'None at all' he looked at me and said 'OK you're in'.

Chapter 4

Dover

Just after my twenty-first birthday I joined the WRNS as a Petty Officer. We were a small group of girls, all pretty fluent in German. The official title of our service was 'Special Duties' or 'Y'. We were to be trained to intercept and listen on VHF (Very High Frequency) radios, to the German surface craft operating primarily in the English Channel. Most of the 'traffic' was from German E-Boats or *Schnellboote*, which were preying on the convoys still using the Channel. They communicated in an R/T (voice), three-letter code, which had been broken – I assume at Bletchley Park – early in the war. This code was in no way as complex or as difficult to break as the so-called 'Enigma' code, used by the U Boats.

In her book *I Only Joined for the Hat* Christian Lamb, as well as describing her time in the Navy, has gathered recollections from former Wrens in a variety of branches in the Second World War. She writes of the 'Y' Service as:

> *Another deadly secret, never described or advertised because of its work for Naval Intelligence, which consisted of listening to intercepts and passing the, usually coded, messages to Bletchley Park* [Which we in Special Duties called 'Station X']. *Until the 1970s, this veil of secrecy remained intact, and like many of the jobs we did, no-one who had worked in that department ever discussed it.*

The Special Duties (Linguist) WRNS were known as, 'Freddies Fairies'. We were trained at Greenwich Naval College by a Lieutenant Freddy Marshall. I had always thought he was a born German and that German was his mother tongue, but according to Christian Lamb he had lived in Denmark, and German 'was a language he spoke'. He certainly sounded entirely German when he read – at breakneck speed – the dispatches from the *Oberkommando der Wehrmacht* – the German High Command's daily radio reports. According to Christian Lamb he had joined the Royal Navy in 1939 and had been ordered to Dover early in the war to intercept German Naval traffic. WRNS Linguists were sent to assist him and he subsequently started the training courses at Greenwich, *'Where he taught the WRNS Nautical German,'* (and Nautical English in many cases!), *'wireless proceedures used by the German Navy, and manipulation of the knobs and controls on the radio sets'*. We were trained to search slowly and painstakingly over a small area of frequencies listening for, sometimes very faint, 'carrier waves'. We then had to switch off the 'BFO' (Beat Frequency Oscillator), when the speech or signal of some sort became clear or clearer.

While at Greenwich, because of the bombing raids, we slept in the cellars of a beautiful old Christopher Wren building. We were issued hammocks but, alas, no stretcher boards, so most of us opted for sleeping on the stone floor, except for 'Cookie'. She was terrified of the mice. We had to heave her considerable bulk up into a hammock every night. As we were often kept at our training overtime, we were sometimes late for meals in the Mess. I was always delegated to knock on the galley hatch, and explain that we were 'Special Duties', and apologise for being late. They would reluctantly give us our food, until one fateful day when the response was 'You may be Special Duties – but you ain't God Almighty!' and so saying the hatch was slammed closed. So no lunch that day.

After finishing training I was posted to Dover. We worked and lived in St Margaret's Bay, South Foreland. We were billeted in a lighthouse and a windmill, which are still plainly to be seen on entering Dover Harbour. Our Watch Room was in the windmill and some of us slept there. I had a wonderful bedroom in the light of the lighthouse. Behind us, the Royal Marines had their cross Channel guns. There were frequent barrage exchanges between them and German batteries on Cap Gris Nez. On clear days, with binoculars, we could see the German gunners walking around on the cliffs of France. Eventually the shelling from both sides of the Channel was causing quite considerable damage, mostly in the form of large cracks in the masonry of both our buildings. At about this time Admiral 'Bertie' Ramsay, the Commander in Chief at Dover Castle, came to inspect us, and according to Christian Lamb, who was told this story by my former Third Officer Daphne Humphrys, he told her that we would have to be moved.

When Daphne said we were all very happy and would rather not be moved, he apparently replied 'But what I am going to say to your fathers?' Daphne was a very charming and extremely pretty young woman. Alas, when we were moved from St Margaret's Bay, she did not come with us, but stayed in Dover working in the Intelligence Centre in the Castle. One comical memory I have of her is that she would frequently say 'oh balls!' When things went a little wrong. When I explained the real meaning of the expletive she was profoundly shocked.

A newspaper report in 1944 near the end of the war described Dover thus:

Never has a British town suffered so long and so much. For four weary years this 'lock and key of the kingdom' as Matthew Paris called it, has continuously been under fire. Dive bombers, 'doodle bugs', an infinity of shells – Dover has had them all. ... The difference between London and Dover was that since the first days of the Luftwaffe's onslaught in 1940, Dover has known no surcease. It could not forget how close together the front lines ran in the Straits.

In late June of 1941 I had been invited by a young MTB (Motor Torpedo Boat) Officer to the mess of HMS Wasp. All MTB bases were named after stinging insects. 'Wasp' was in the Lord Warden Hotel, which is still functioning as a hotel in Dover today. While we were in the bar, talking to several other officers, I sat next to a tall Lieutenant with very blue eyes and a quiet manner. I noticed his remarkably beautiful long hands and cheekily said 'You have beautiful hands, what do you do with them'. He smiled wryly and said, 'I'm a butcher'. Although I doubted this was true, I later learnt his father was in fact an inspector at Smithfield Market.

Shortly after this meeting with Eric Cornish, or Rick as I later called him, he was sent to Portsmouth to pick up his first command, MTB 220. He wrote to me from there, and so began an extremely profound and important relationship in my life. His first letter from HMS *Hornet* was formal but humorous:

H.M.S Hornet
c/o G.P.O London
17.7.41

Dear Jenny
I thought I had better type this letter to you because it looks more formal and I am making an official apology. ... I am terribly sorry I have not got in touch with you before this (and if that sounds ambiguous I am still very sorry), but – and this, to use a foreign, i.e. American expression, is where I shoot a line – No, you are much too intelligent to require excuses, and my line shooting needs improving too. (By the way, does a girl like to be told she is intelligent or is that a faux pas (French)? – amongst other things I suppose. There is one thing, I thought "Wasp" was well enough represented anyway.

Well, how are you? If it isn't an official secret, I should like to know that you are quite well and happy and not too much troubled by this war. In the note you sent me you suggested we might renew our rather maudlin phone conversation – I would like to take you up on that, either over the non-Naval line you suggest, or the couple of drinks. In the former case I should require a number and in the latter a spot of leave. Of course, I used my hands before the war, but not to any particular purpose. I still use them but only for the same tasks. But I have known for some time now that I should have been trained to use them in some way, instead of having to rely on my brain. I must confess I was very embarrassed to have it pointed out to me so directly.
Cheerio and best wishes
Yours,
Eric A E Cornish Lt. RNVR

Rick and I exchanged a few more letters while he was in Portsmouth. Shortly after he left Dover, we, the Special Duty WRNS were, as had been threatened, moved from South Foreland to Capel-le-Ferne, west of Dover. The large house requisitioned for us was called Abbotscliff. It had been condemned before the war as being likely to slide into the sea from the top of the crumbling chalk cliffs. (In the late 1980s, my husband and I went to look at Abbotscliff. The house and grounds were surrounded by a security fence, with guard dogs prowling around the perimeter. As far as I could see the building was still perched on the edge of the cliff).

A short time later I received another letter from Rick in Portsmouth:

…. Forgive me for having put you in a quandary. It would however, be nice to see you in one, as I have only seen you in Wren's uniform … It is rather interesting to hear you say you never feel yourself in Dover, because it leads to the obvious question 'Where do you feel yourself?'. … I don't know whether that question even makes sense, since there cannot be an unqualified answer to it, particularly in this complicated twentieth century way of living. I knew you were going to move. … You didn't sound very thrilled at the prospect. I have always felt that the Dover area was a bad place to stay for any length of time – there aren't any trees for one thing. You say you haven't been in the Service long enough to acquire a 'cotton wool' mind, an attitude of indifference, and living for the moment. Just how long have you been a Wren and what were you doing before, so as not to attain that state of mind?. … It is 2.30am so I think I ought to turn in. … An explanation for the rambling nature of this letter. I can lay no claim to an 'ingrained unorthodox manner' to explain it.

Good night, Eric

And again, shortly after this letter he wrote:

…. I should like to pursue the subject of being oneself with you. To know oneself is difficult, for it involves being completely honest about it, not accepting the picture in the mirror of ones own self-esteem. Am I that dumb, embarrassed fool in a room full of people, is that me, surly and morose, poring over the morning paper at breakfast, the lazy one lying in the sun dreaming the afternoon away, that barmy irresponsible person, when the sun first shines after an English winter? When am I being 'Myself'?. … The psychologists tell us that every individual is a single personality – but not necessarily integrated – or do they!. … I had not written to you as soon as I intended because I have been very busy – a facile excuse but sometimes not unreasonable. I have just taken over a new boat – the technical expression is 'Command', but a literal interpretation is not as yet very near the truth. All

sorts of people keep coming up to me, asking my opinion of this, shall they do that, what leave can they have etc., perpetually driving me into a corner so I have to make decisions. I live constantly in fear of KR and AI and my diet consists almost entirely of AFO's, CAFO's and conversation seems to consist of initial letters like that – a code language for which I haven't the key. But in fact, all one needs to do is to hang on to one's sense of humour. Are you as remote from the 'gay life' of Dover as you were formally, or are you compensated by the proximity of Folkstone? How I envy the good fortune of those 'going foreign' [being posted abroad]. *The chance to see something new and possibly interesting, the possibility of constant sunshine, the opportunity to exercise one's foreign languages or acquire new ones…I should very much like to hear from you again if you have time and inclination. I still have the prospect of those 'couple of drinks' before me.*

Cheerio and good luck
Eric

When he writes, it is obvious that he doesn't realise how young I am and that I have little or no history of an earlier occupation. I wrote to him from Dorset when I was on home leave, describing the countryside and telling him a little about Park Farm, he replied:

Dear Jenny

How are you? That's rather important because I hope you are not feeling down. … I feel inclined to admit that I did rather mock before. I thought I might sting you into replying, since I could think of no other reason why you should. It is perhaps not fair to take you up on everything you say. … I suppose there is some other way of getting beyond the subject of weather. … to say that your leave sounded delightful is only to recall the past – to peep through the hedge of present, grown too thick to get to the other side through the lapse of time. To live on a farm within reach of the sea seems ideal to me, not only for a holiday, but for normal living. I must confess, I think I am an escapist, and to judge by your rejection of the 'twentieth century way of living' you are too. … I am really interested to know whether you are actively concerned with the farm when you are on leave, and to what extent you were in peacetime. For some time before the war, I had been of the opinion that I should try and work out a way of living so that I spent part of the week in town and part in the country. ... That for the development of a balanced personality one needed the intellectual life of the town sifted through the sieve of the more natural countryside. I am not certain now that I wouldn't give you the town and just aim at simplicity. We have done little else but make life more complicated in the last two hundred and fifty years. ... Do you know it was very nice of you to ask me over to see the Farm, (but you make a lot of excuses for my not coming – 'even though it is awfully far, a bit uncivilized and you don't know me'). I should have loved to have been able to come over whilst you were there. ... Your description of the surrounding countryside – the hills, the woods, the deer, the river and the sea – make it all appear even more charming and intriguing. Tell me, have you much experience of sailing? I ask because that is one of the things I was intensely keen on. I liked it for the animal reasons – the sun on my body in fine weather, or the wind and spray on my face in bad. And for other reasons too – the isolation and the fact of being self-contained, the practical jobs of painting the boat, the cooking of one's own meals, the hundred and one odd jobs that required one's common sense and hands. It is one of the things I look forward to most after the war – when I look forward – I hope you will write to me again if you have time and tell me how you like the new place and whether it is as dreary as you made it sound.

Cheerio and best wishes

Eric

Having been spared almost all the usual childhood illnesses in my youth, I had contracted chicken pox at the beginning of the war while I was still working in London, and came down with measles in August while serving in Dover. Rick, who had returned to HMS *Wasp*, came to visit me in Sick Bay, and wrote me a letter in the form of a fairy tale. From his letters I had begun to know this young man, and to like him. He had tried to come and see me twice in Sick Bay, but was too shy to do so whilst other people were present. Finally he came up, and we had a long talk, after which he left me the following letter:

There was once a youth who lived in a small country, he was a shy serious fellow who did not laugh much though he often wore a smile. He lived a lot inside himself. Even then he had little ambition except in one thing, though he liked to do things well.

He dreamt a lot too when he was alone. Sometimes his dreams were fierce and frenzied things to set the world aright. But often they were quieter – for he was a sentimental and romantic chap – and they took him into the hills and sunshine across the grassy downs, through the wooded lanes or across sparkling blue seas – dancing. He was never alone for there was always someone with him to whom he talked or with whom he rested. She was a spirit for he never quite saw her face.

He never really grew up, for the world never got at him. When things were dull and grey he would often go to the land of sunshine. But there were times when the real world was beautiful and then he was alone and it was then that this beauty hurt him. He lived like this for ten years – a whimsical, earnest, empty fellow, and one day when he was in his hovel, he heard a voice and saw it was a princess. He had seen fine ladies before, but never a princess, and, poor fellow, it was a little too much for him. She spoke to him and he stammered and blushed, so she left and it wasn't until after she had left that he found his tongue.

It was some years later before he went back to the place. The princess was rather famous and everyone sang her praises. He went to the house where she lived, but ran away. He was, however, a little desperate poor fool and went back again. He saw the princess and she smiled at him and he became a slave.

Now he never believed in miracles so he hadn't understood when she spoke to him. But the greatest miracle was yet to come, for she turned out to be the person who used to go with him over the hills and across the blue waters. So there was music in his heart and the sunlight entered his soul.

When I recovered from measles and was back at work, Rick and I started to see more and more of each other. We grew close as time went by, I learnt he had an Honours Degree in Economics from the London School of Economics, where he had studied under Professor Laski. He told me that he dreamed of working for the League of Nations after the war. His other plan was to buy a Lunenburg Schooner and to sail it across the Atlantic or even around the world. These schooners were made in Lunenburg in Nova Scotia, Canada '*For centuries this port was renowned for the fleets of Grand Banks fishing schooners – the most awe-inspiring fore and aft working sailing vessels ever to put to sea*'. Nowadays they are being built again and are reputed to be '*simple, elegant cruising craft, modelled to be extremely seaworthy. Vessels built in the tried and true, time tested way, with stout wooden planks on double sawn frames*'.

We were seeing each other sometimes only for an hour or two every three days. We would usually meet in Dover in the evening and often go to 'The Crypt', a bar-cum-restaurant very popular with the Armed Forces, and one of the few such places still functioning. I had told Rick about Tony Rolt, and how I felt about his being a prisoner of war. I also said, somewhat immaturely that I 'loved' Tony, as well as a new and mutual friend of ours Geoffrey Elton, who was also a Coastal Forces Officer.

Rick and I wrote to one another frequently, despite the many times we saw each other. As our relationship became ever more serious in one of his letters of 29 September, which had been partly destroyed by the censors scissors, he wrote:

Midnight September 29th/ 30th 0700 hrs.

As usual I am spending about the last hour of the day talking to you before going to sleep. In this case the conditions are a little different for I am on board my boat in the lower bunk, in the tiny cabin one is pleased to call a "Ward room". .... -turned in fully clothed and with watches set. Usually I just let my thoughts drift and talk to you one sidedly and inconsequently. I'll do the same now, but I'll try to put it down, even for the sole purpose of trying to clear my mind. I have almost come to the conclusion that I shouldn't talk to you on the phone, because I cannot express adequately in words all I want to say, nor tell, merely by the inflections in your voice, whether I am making sense. (yet I must talk to you or the world for me will end......)

30/9-0700

Since you. ... know all about. ... being 'in love' with and 'loving' someone and since I am merely trying to clarify my own ideas, may I try and put down what I think I mean by either expression.

When I was very young, i.e. eighteen or so, I believed one could only fall in love once in a lifetime and that only if you met the one suitable person. ... I didn't believe that Troilus and Cressida, Romeo and Juliet, were accidental happenings, mere figments of the imaginations of word twisters. They might happen to anyone and this sort of relationship was the only one worth having. But it required a lot of patience and self-control, not to accept anything less.

I believed this sort of thing for years and though I was quite frequently attracted by this or that pretty face, or charming figure, I rejected these attractions much more quickly than was normal. ... I don't know how it grew up, but then you would realise that it wasn't anything more than a temporary attraction. You didn't want to hurt the other person, and you made the unforgivable mistake of continuing – half-heartedly. I used to think then that I had done something wrong – had sullied the ideal.

These ideas were, of course, gradually broken down, because they didn't seem to square with common, every-day experience. ... but the whole wasn't quite blotted out. ... And now I have met you and you have uncovered everything that was blotted out, and I am living on something more real than hope. Do you understand then, that I am always wanting to be near you – to see your face and hair and throat and ears, to hear you – move and breath and speak. ... but there is so much more than that – something not quite intangible but difficult to express – a sympathy and understanding, an identity of aspirations, a spiritual harmony, and so – I have written this at very odd times – late at night and early in the morning. I have not read it through, I never do. I don't know whether it makes sense, but it seemed to whilst I was writing. It is inadequate particularly in the last part, but I have only just got to there and I want to send this off.

Adieu Darling

One evening after supper we walked down to the front – Rick took me in his arms and kissed me, but then shocked me by saying 'This is only physical' at which I pulled myself out of his arms and ran dramatically towards the sea. The beach was cut off from the front by large rolls of barbed wire to stop people from straying onto the mined area. Rick ran after me and told me in no uncertain manner to pull myself together. His next letter explained his feelings about kissing before meeting me:

October 41

…. Except for a brief glimpse yesterday, in 'The Crypt', I don't think I have yet been really happy with you – not happy the way children are when they play together. I think it is because I am too conscious of you near me. I think too, that is why I turn away from you, when I am trying to think out something I want to say to you. And I have to work it out first because I want to be completely honest both to you and to myself. It frightens me a little when you ask me 'why I went away then'. It frightens me too to think that you find Abbotscliff so lonely – why are you so much alone there?. … I am never alone now, before I go to sleep and as soon as I awake I am talking to you. Paul [Paul Berthon his roommate] *must be getting tired of one subject only. It is just as though you are always there, except that when you are actually present, you do the talking and at other times I get a word in! I have never been able to kiss anyone without realising it. I seem to stand apart with my mind – analysing, sneering slightly. It was like that when I said that I didn't like kissing you. And now that's not true anymore, everything just stops and there isn't any world outside. … I love you with all my heart – it tears me apart when you are unhappy or knotted up inside and I am in heaven when you are light and joyful – and with all my soul – for your greatness of heart, courage, your fierceness and tenderness, that you find beauty where I find it. But you bring me so much more than I bring to you. …*

See you later darling,
Rick

Later that month, when we were once more in 'The Crypt', Rick told me he wanted to marry me. He didn't expect me to answer right away, but to think about it. I confess I was really astonished, and almost frightened by his seriousness. We were standing in front of the mirrored over-mantle in the bar, and I vividly remember my shocked expression. Shortly after Rick's proposal, he wrote to me:

I am writing this, because I can think better when I am away from you. And because I wanted to get down some of what had been simmering for most of the night. ... I believed in my innocence that two people that were in love got married – by married I don't mean either the physical or legal thing – these followed but waited upon circumstance. That was why, though I had nothing to offer you, I had enough nerve to ask you to marry me. It seemed quite natural, but when I look back I sometimes feel aghast and a little awed with myself. I can understand why you feel you want to play safe with marriage, faulty ones, ones that just didn't work out right – have touched you very closely – have in fact hit you harder than they would ninety nine people out of a hundred. I have watched marriage from the outside (a difficult place to do it from and liable to lead to many misconceptions), and the effect it had on me was to make me careful about falling in love. Unfortunately, I am not certain that marriage is a thing you can play safe about – I am inclined to think it isn't – except when you reject it all together. I suppose everybody wants a real 'made in heaven' marriage, and probably think they have got it at the time. But there isn't anything to be done to ensure it. I do not understand about Tony. I know you tried to tell me and make me understand. I know that I am being dense about it, masculinely dense, I believe. ... I understand that a letter from the POW camp after such a long time, and in the circumstances of war, would knock you over. I thought you got them regularly. I know he is the main ghost you once mentioned. I am extremely conscious of the fact you carry his picture with you. I am puzzled by these things (I think about them a lot). ... I am putting two and two together to make four, and perhaps afraid of the four, none of which is conducive to straight thinking. And there is the other side – you see – I try to make out how much of me, to you, is a result of the war - ABC (Abbotscliff House), bloody Dover and all the rest. You see I am with you constantly – Tony isn't (and for that matter Geoff isn't). ... If you are not going to marry me and I have rather assumed you would (perhaps unreasonably) after, or rather when, it is possible – I would like to know, for though it wouldn't make any difference to the fact that I love you and hope to marry you some day –

I would stop building silly pictures and hopes, that would probably never be realised anyway. ... In growing up, I have had before me constantly, the ideal of balance – not only was I trying to develop a balanced mind and body, but the spiritual and physical, thought and emotion and so on. For various reasons the ideal is maybe erroneous, certainly I haven't been successful. What I am trying to say is the whole thing predicates self-control, which itself may be carried too far and so may destroy the balance in favour of something much too cold. ... Good God don't I take myself seriously.

Shortly after we moved to Capel, a group of sailors under the command of a young officer moved into the village. It was in the early days of RDF (Radio Direction Finding). One of their jobs was to build an RDF tower about a quarter of a mile from Abbotscliff House on the edge of the cliff. The WRNS would be out there listening for signals day or night, on which they could take bearings. On winter nights, clad in duffle coats and sea boots, (if we were lucky enough to own them), we would walk out to the tower in all weathers. On arriving we would unlock the door, close it before putting on the light, and then, torch in hand, climb the ladder into the loft where the aerial was housed. We had to lift the trap door and shine the torch around 'to make sure no one was up there'. Anyone crouching under the aerial would have had ample opportunity to hit us on the head! There was no lavatory in the tower, and one of my nightmares was having to go out in the dark, and often stormy, night to squat on the grass. I was not only afraid of cliff-climbing Nazi invaders, but of any other 'persons of evil intent' – I have never felt so vulnerable in my life.

My only 'coup' during this time was one night in the tower, when I intercepted a regular speech signal, which was repeated at frequent intervals. After the first message '*Ich lege ein Spiegelei*' (I'm laying a fried egg), I took a bearing of every following repeated signal. It occurred to me that a mine dropping into the water at night would look dark in the centre with the froth of white surrounding it. Rather like a fried egg in fact. I rang the Intelligence Centre in Dover Castle and told them what I suspected. In the very early hours of the next morning the minesweepers went out and, allowing for drift, found most of the mines. The only other unusual signal was on watch one day, when I received, as I thought, a three letter W/T (Morse code) message all be it on the wrong frequency, which read 'MUS SPI SSE NGE HEN', "must go for a pee" when I started to re-read the message to the Intelligence Centre I understood the meaning and said 'Forget it'. One of the Coastal Battery operators caught short!

Sometime later four of us were moved to the Lodge at the bottom of Abbotscliff drive. There was running water in the cottage, but no bathroom or lavatory. We had to bathe in the main house and had an 'Elsan' privy in the garden. Oddly enough all our names were of the same origin. We were McGill, Gilliat, Gillies and Gill. Margaret Gillies was the daughter of Sir Harold Gillies the famous plastic surgeon who was working with service men, mostly from the Tank Corps and the RAF, who had suffered severe burns. Rosemary Gilliat became, and remained, one of my nearest and dearest friends.

Rick wrote to me on 18 and 27 of October respectively:

18/10/41

That I love you, you know. How much I think you know too but refuse to believe it or credit me with it. But I don't know whether you understand that much of you is incomprehensible to me as yet ... not only are you a woman, you are also a fairly complex person. So it will take time. I think it is easier for you for the opposite reasons – I am a man and fairly simple...you say you 'love' Tony and you 'love' Geoff and you love me. And although it knocks all my ideas cockeyed. I have to believe that. ... in a pessimistic mood I feel I cannot compete with either of the others. You see I'm here, and they are away. Particularly do I think that I don't stand a chance with Tony, because he is a prisoner of war, and because of your greatness of heart. I am prone to moods of self pity – do you think I am being self indulgent now?. ... I really believe I've reached a stage where it is more important to me that you should be happy than I should ... I wanted to dance with you the whole time last night. Maybe I don't do it very well but I would like to. But whenever I am with you and there are other people present I turn away and just stop and watch. ... for fear of monopolising you or hurting you – maybe one day I shall be able to put into words how much I love you – that there is nothing beautiful unless I share it with you, no sun to warm me like your presence. ... I love you,
                                                            Rick.

27/10/41

It's been hell not seeing you these last two days, but almost refreshing. Hell because on Saturday night, after I left, I felt you had been trying to throw me out – out of your heart; Hell because you were shrivelling yourself up on Sunday and taking it out on me and I couldn't help you; Hell because I'm always thinking about you, wanting to be with you. Refreshing because I've been able to look after my boat more, to write letters, to read, and in reading, to rest. Refreshing too in that I have been able to look around and think what I must do to catch up with you, to feel even that I have started on that road.

I have, I suppose like most people, always wanted to learn to be fluent in several languages, to find the inspiration of music (even to play something myself), to paint, to travel and get nearer to other peoples. None of those things have I done by myself –. ... knowing you, I could do these things – that's what I meant when I said I always had to have a goad (the wrong word) and that I needed you. You are the future for me, and also I'm in love with you – I think that's necessary too. I could go away to enrich my mind, but it would be much more fun to do it with you – though perhaps more dangerous for us. ...I get to this point and ask myself 'what can I bring on the other side'. Nothing! (That's when I'm pessimistic). Sometimes I've thought that, though physically very courageous, you have not yet learnt moral courage. Also that in your thinking and your emotions there is very little control – direction. That I hope to bring you these things sounds conceited and I don't believe it either. I've thought too that I might show you patience. But what worries me is that none of these things are exciting – they are dull and difficult things, smug perhaps, and conventional.

If I were a poet I could have told you these things in a much better way. I could have said less logically and less coldly how you are my eyes, and ears, and hands. I could say too how your profile makes me catch my breath at times, how the line of your lips as you begin to smile haunts me, how the feel of your hair soothes me, the touch of your hand strengthens me, your ears delight me. ... Ah hell!...

One day I shall have the courage to swear at you and really chastise you (what an archaic word), when you start telling me what an awful mess you

are. Though it hurts and enrages me I am too much afraid I shall say the
wrong thing, or pick the wrong time. But I don't know any other way of
curing such a mood – such self-pity?

I don't know how true these things I write to you are, for there is nothing
to measure them by. What is truth but that I love you

Rick

I suppose the building of the RDF tower attracted the attention of the
Germans, because one night we were attacked by 'screaming Stuka' aircraft,
I ran out of the house and shook my fist and howled at the plane before I
realised that one of the guards at the entrance to the property had been hit.
His left arm was pumping out blood at an alarming rate. I got the other
guards to carry him into the basement kitchen of the house and put him on
the kitchen table. I knew enough, from reading, to realise that the heavy flow
of blood meant that an artery had been severed and that we must stop the
bleeding urgently. Again, from books that I had read I realised that I must
get some sort of tourniquet on him. I took a dishcloth from the stove and a
wooden spoon and, by twisting it, managed to stop the bleeding. Although
It took forty-five minutes for an ambulance to reach us from a nearby RAF
base, his life was saved.

The next morning I found that my nightgown was stuck to my leg, and I
thought that it must be from the guard's blood until I saw a hole in the back
of my lower leg. Shrapnel from the diving Stuka had hit me. I was taken to
Dover hospital and put to bed. There was an older civilian woman in the bed
next to me – I don't know what she was suffering from, but her distraught
husband was seated beside her, begging her not to leave him. I had been
given a morphine injection, presumably to calm me down and put me to
sleep, however it only served to make me extremely wakeful. I have never
forgotten the sad build-up to her death that night. Rick's letters to me in
hospital and later on sick leave were a great comfort to me:

(14/11/41)

.... I phoned Joyce (is that taking a liberty? It's much simpler) yesterday at half past four. ... Joyce said that they were sorry to hear that you were in hospital again that you seemed to be unlucky with your legs (I had to agree though I think they are alright), that we could go down any time but not to leave it too late or the boys would be home from school. I said 'Eh?' several times and 'Thank you very much' after every sentence but otherwise I wasn't as stupid as usual. ...

You have asked me several times about the first time we met. I find it difficult to remember my reactions though the various pictures are there complete. First of all the grouping of people around the bar, you in a chair, Geoff sitting on the fender, David on the table, me also on the fender after a peremptory order to sit down – from you. Another – very strong picture – of you abruptly jumping up and leaving; but particularly of you pushing the door open. What else? – an attractive mouth, a manner and voice I liked (not American after all!) – the remark about my hands – a pose?; I was of course knocked off my feet but you were obviously much out of my reach. That you should subsequently remember me I couldn't believe – I thought it somebody else's idea of fun. I don't think I really believed it until this last week. I wonder whether that tells you at all why I thought your remark that I was so sure and calm – almost complacent – about you, one of the grossest misstatements I've ever heard. I believe and feel now that you love me but it's incredulous and I don't see why. It's the most precious thing I've ever known but that's not saying anything. ...

...Generally speaking – I'm still hopelessly in love with you. One day I shall just be in love with you and there will be no other world but you and me (the 'hopeless' and 'incredulous' are the same). Get well and I'll be as patient as I can until I see you again.

I have nothing left to give you. Rick

In another letter to the hospital he says:

.... I suppose you feel it's a bloody nuisance being in bed again, (even though honourably wounded!), but please take it easy and let me know if there is

anything at all you want. And if you find you have nothing much to do you
might even write to me. … (at the moment I am a little uncertain whether
the Gods are for us or against us. If they are on our side they certainly have
a torturous way of showing it!) …I shall certainly dislike not being able to
see you in the next day or two, I can't even phone you, but you may be sure
that I shall hear of you indirectly – the Doc at least takes a friendly interest.
I don't know that I can trust him however to tell you how much I want to
be with you, how much I love you, and would like to be beside you now. (Do
you think anybody would mind?)

Rick

And then on 16 November he writes:

Darling,
Doc has just been telling me that you are to go on sick leave from Sunday
next for as long as it takes for your leg to heal…it looks then very much as
though you will already be at home by the time I get my leave, and I suggest
I join you there after having been home to collect my gear etc.
. … Goodnight Darling

I did go home on sick leave, and later Rick joined me there. Every time I
went home I always brought my ration book with me, even on my rare forty-
eight hour leaves. These were very few and far between. However, as more
people were recruited, and more 'Y' stations were opened on the East coast
things became a little easier. I used to feel guilty when I arrived home for
these short visits and saw how little of everything the civilians were having
to make do with. They were allowed 4oz of butter, 8oz of margarine, 8oz
of sugar and 2-4oz of tea every week. Coffee was off the ration but hard to
come by. Our family stretched the tea ration by adding Maté to the teapot
which actually tasted very good. Fish and offal were also off the ration if one
could get them. My ration card augmented the 1s 2d or 1lb 3oz family meat
ration and afforded a treat. Babies, like my young half-brother Dominic,
were issued bottles of concentrated rose-hip syrup which, when diluted
with water, provided them with vitamin C. There were no lemons, oranges
or bananas to be had. In the Forces we had ample food, although no luxuries.

When Rick came down to Park Farm we had four days together. He met the family, and helped my father dig in the garden. We baby-sat Dom for an evening when Joyce and Don (my father) went out, and we grew ever closer. On his return to Dover Rick wrote:

25/11/41

Darling, it is always that way. I passed, spent, stayed, lived (I don't know the word) four days with you and 20 minutes in the car waiting for the train wasn't long enough. I know that it was four days because I can count them on my fingers. … I know that 20 minutes wasn't long enough because it went so quickly and there suddenly seemed to be so much that one wanted to say.

I suppose it has happened before, is happening now, to other people but for the last three months I seem to have done little else but say goodbye to you. And each time seems to get more difficult – there is such an empty burst-bubble feeling afterwards, but it was certainly much worse on Tuesday than anything before. I know now how a prisoner must feel as he returns to his cell after his twenty minutes exercise in the open air and sunshine. Everything seemed set to emphasise that feeling. It was a beautiful evening and just had to be a that time between day and night when the light is so soft that the countryside looks eternal and the very smoke from the cottage chimneys pulls at your insides – you feel so much a stranger – alone and desolate. Those first twenty minutes on the train were – not awful or terrible – rather sad.

I liked being at the farm. I liked being inside the house. The place itself and the people inside were so nice and friendly to me. Can I say any more than that I was quite happy.

I was rather – shocked – when you asked me if I still wanted to marry you, for I told you once before, originally, when you had so much against it – that I wanted to marry you but that it was up to you and I would not mention it again…that I must keep to the present and let the various new 'pictures' be sufficient.

The other obstruction, the war, I can understand for I think there is a big risk in wartime of things going wrong and unfortunately it is you that the risk falls upon. …

How poor a thing is memory compared with reality. I am remembering that I kissed you that I couldn't hold you any tighter. ... oh Lord for the reality.

Rick
PS. By the way did I mention that I loved you.

My leg healed very slowly, and I was away from Dover for about three weeks. It was wonderful to have Rick meet my train on my return. The next day I received another letter from him:

2/12/41

. ... As usual it was very difficult to say goodbye to you – I find that that difficulty lies in my mind – perhaps subconsciously for the most part – from about an hour after I arrive. The time seems so short anyway.

I have always distrusted being happy – that is why I'm such a gloomy person I suppose. I used to think that happiness and sadness were portioned more of less equally in a person's life – that if I had been particularly unhappy or depressed then the pendulum would swing to the other side with just as wide an arc. I suppose I thought that way because I seemed to live in those kinds of moods. It all seems to me to be utter nonsense now whether there is any external direction to our lives or not, but it does mean that there are left occasional moments of apprehension almost – during such times as say this last weekend. And there is also always the question 'Why should I be so lucky, what have I ever done to deserve this?'

That Joyce thinks you are too young to get married I'm not surprised, but I don't think it (her opinion on that point) too important. One might as well say you are too young to be in love. But I think she is too clever to say a thing like that and not realise it as more than a hypothetical discussion. I understand vaguely why you want to see your mother first.

I want to marry you – urgently. And I know that it is not only a wartime neurosis that makes it so. But being married to you wouldn't make me able to see you more often. I don't honestly think that it is reasonable to have any children in wartime – there are many pessimistic reasons for that – and they are to me a 'sine qua non' of marriage. I don't see any point in a marriage in which the girl either returns to live with her parents, as some do, or flits from flat to furnished house to flat following her husband around. Is there anything more in the alternative of taking a house somewhere for the wife to make a home of to which the husband returns for five days every two months or so? The only alternative arguments I can think of are that things done unreasonably often turn out better, and marriage is essentially founded best on difficulties. But the most powerful feeling is that it is so bloody difficult to wait, and to think all the time of 'some-day'.

… When I came away from the Farm and sort of returned to the outside world I had the curious feeling of being much more self assured and confident. I say it was a curious feeling because it seemed to be founded on a greater harmony inside me. The Farm, the rest and change may have had something to with it but I think it was much more that I had been living with you for a few days. …

…. Apropos of nothing in particular I have come to loathe the telephone with an almost inhuman hatred. They invade every sanctuary with their imperative call, scatter the wits, trap the unwary, enrage even the most patient of men, and finally condemn whoever touches them to the nethermost hell for the blasphemous. They're obviously an invention of the devil.

I've heard of people writing to each other daily. I used to think that they suffered from some sort of strange affliction. It seems more reasonable now. I practically live around the letter rack here these days. It's a curious paradox that on the one hand the whole world seems to be narrowed down to you, and yet on the other hand, because of you, there is so much to be done and seen and learnt…

Stay with me darling, Good night,
Rick.

Our letters were more and more frequent, and there were some revealing excerpts from them from 4–7 December:

4/12/41

'I wish I were there to comfort you' – you said. That sounded so lovely to know you mean that.

I hate to sound depressed to you on the phone for fear that it might worry you. I know that in similar circumstances when I have thought you have sounded 'flat' that it is just as though the sun has gone out and my whole being seems numb with helplessness. I was only tired and stifled by the hot lifeless air in these blacked out rooms. I have been driving about the harbour and the surroundings getting on 'fish' (Torpedos) and fuel and doing engine trials from about eight o'clock this morning until just after five without lunch etc. – and the whole program went wrong. And I missed being inspected by the King and Queen.

PM. 6/12/41

Oh Lord,... it was lovely seeing you today after such a long time and all I wanted to do was to put my arms around you.... it is rather difficult to determine now just why the hell I didn't simply do that. But, though I make such a show of not caring what people think, I believe it does influence me. I am wondering half the time what their nasty minds are trying to construe and what effect it will have on you – how it will affect you. Maybe it's only that I'm nasty minded. I don't know whether it would make any difference if we were married or engaged – I think it probably would.

7/12/41

I have just read and re-read your letter. You say a lot that I have been wanting to express for a long time. I think I fell in love with you a long while before you fell in love with me – I believe I fell in love with you the first time I saw you, but I was suspicious of it and it was for such a short confused period that afterwards I wasn't certain how much you attracted me physically – whether you were as beautiful to me as I thought you were. I didn't have that confirmed until I saw you in hospital the first time. I don't know whether you ever understood the state of mind I was in when I came to see you and why I couldn't come and see you when somebody else was there; or how tense a period it was to wait for a couple of hours or so until I came back again.

You write of 'some mysterious tie' which two people are born with and 'fate wills them to meet'. I have, I know said something of the same thing to you when I said that I used to think that there was for an individual only one other person to fall really in love with. And the first time I told you I *loved you I said at the same time that I had never said that to anyone else before. ... whether or not you love me or are willing to marry me – didn't affect that, for if it were 'not' it is conceivable that I could have married somebody else but it wouldn't be the same sort of thing.*

You mentioned this 'stimulus of spirit' – that too I meant when I told you that you had taken off the lid that I had clamped down on my feelings and thoughts – and dreaming-when the war started. I could have kept it there but there was no seal sufficiently strong to retain it once you had started the things boiling underneath. The world and life were mine again to enjoy with you...to say goodbye to you is like going from a warm room out into a cold night down a long desolate road. How much one wants to return indoors again!

On 7 December the Japanese attacked Pearl Harbour and the United States came into the war. Rick wrote to me immediately:

I wanted to ring you up as soon as I heard the news about the commencement of hostilities against Japan. I wanted to know how you thought it might affect you that the States were involved directly. My first reaction as always was that I wanted to talk about it with you.

It was rather depressing to realise that Switzerland and some South American states are the only countries not at war. It would have helped to be with you because there is this strange feeling of not facing the world except with you – sort of you and I in a mad world in which there is nothing real except our love for each other. And in a world of death, life has come to mean so much now. It isn't altogether peculiar that I should ask myself the question 'how does this affect Jenny and me'. I feel that the prospect of a real marriage to you is put off even further by these new imbecilities so that I want to act as though you were my wife and not bother about the formalities. I don't mean that in any vulgar sense – that I want to rush off and go to bed with you (though I would like to do that) but that I need your spiritual companionship in the sense that we are together always. I have a curious mental picture of you and I walking up a deserted street with shattered houses on either side – trying to figure out what we can make of the mess. We go off independently into the side streets, to see what is there

but come back to each other to continue up the main road together I suppose
I am being foolish and romantic – I know that I'm not expressing my mood
very well – this Adam and Eve idea. I am rather letting my imagination
run away with me and I know that tomorrow the people I meet and see will
be just the same and that there will be no signs of the catastrophe that seems
to be happening in the world now.

Good night and God bless you,
Rick

About ten days later I do not remember why or what conversation triggered
the following reaction, Rick wrote a letter which makes me feel guilty and
sad now when I read it:

19/12/41

You once told me that it is our lives that we have to live, and that I believed
because it is the answer to the world. But if I or my previous environment
are not good enough for your people – if I am not cultured enough or well
enough known or whatever it is – and that matters enough, then I won't
marry you. I don't know what that would do to me, to lose such hope now,
but that doesn't matter for all I want is that you should be happy, you before
everything – you are everything anyway.

The irony of it is that if you don't marry me because of that reason you
would never be quite so happy as you might. And worse still, I might become
'well known' – for what I need is something to harden me – I have the
patience and possibly the brain (I think).

I have I think been afraid of this thing for some time. I believe this fear
was behind my remark when I asked if your father meant what he said about
me, or was merely trying to be easy with you. The future would be a gamble
for you with me. I have no worldly ambition – yet. Often I feel as I look
ahead, that one has only one life, and there are so many places to see, so
many things to know, so much to learn that one hasn't time to be 'successful'.
That's all wrong because it doesn't fit in with a wife and family and a home
– all things I crave for.

Wartime is a bad time for many things, but is a particularly hard time to fall in love. It jumbles up the social classes in a most peculiar way and there is no future but what one's dreams provide. Personally I just do not see what I shall do after this war – and you would probably like to know that now – what sort of work I shall do, how much money I shall have, where I shall go. It doesn't worry me in the slightest now but it might if I were married to you.

I cannot advise you in this matter of getting married to me because quite obviously I am not an unbiased or disinterested person, and therefore I cannot be sufficiently honest however hard I try. That's why I said I wished I knew somebody who could help you...

But as I said yesterday, and I think I was right, let us postpone the answer – I don't know how long – for you have to see your mother (maybe she has to see me too), and you have to meet my people on their ground. It won't matter if we do because you are young in years, and I can wait (since there is nothing else to do).

This is an awful letter – I wrote only because I had to. I don't know whether I shall give it to you. In any case as I won't see you for a few days, I'll try to write a better one. I ought to have enough time to think it out properly – what a bloody awful Christmas to look forward to.

Sweetheart – my heart goes out to you. It's awful to be the cause of worry to you and not be able to do anything to help you. I want you always to be as happy as you have been at times recently. I wish I knew if there were any means of ensuring that. R

Towards the end of December I was sent to Greenwich for a week's course to qualify as a W/T (Morse code) as well as R/T operator. I was to go on leave when the course was finished and would be away from Dover for the New Year. The course in Greenwich did, I suppose, improve my W/T skills but I was never going to be able to read rapid traffic. During the training we had to march in squads from our quarters to the college in Greenwich, and had to take it in turns to be in charge of the squad – a group of almost entirely untrained participants. When my turn came we were marching along fairly smartly until we almost walked smack into the back of a parked lorry – the only thing I could think of to say was 'Oh God, left wheel or something!'.

Rick's following letters were written immediately after I left Dover:

28/12/41
Sweetheart (R), Darling (R).

Jenny,

I have been working like a slave the whole of the afternoon on flotilla wine and tobacco accounts. Now that's a serious business and my long training as an economist has fitted me admirably for carrying out such a job. It's difficult to concentrate and none of the bloody things add up right. And as soon as I stop it's there again – that dull sort of lost feeling. It's still Sunday the 28th. If there was any meaning to time at all it would at least be next week by now…

I feel the need urgently for some place to be with you alone – remote for a time from the world and the people in it. I don't think that in wanting that I am running away from reality, for you and the need of you are the only things that are real to me now. That need, to be alone with you, has been very strong at least ever since I was at the farm with you. Even there, and lovely as that was, I wasn't quite alone with you…Oh God! Just for a while now. Maybe, if we lived alone, after a few thousand years we might want to have a look at the postman or the milkman and even eventually the rest of the world (or some of it).

Please write and tell me you love me.
Rick
PS may I get my hair cut?

And again on the same day:

I think I'm constantly needing an English dictionary these days when I write to you. I try very hard to put into words what I am feeling and I want to tell you about it exactly. I would like to look up the word 'paradox' now. Is it not a paradox that because we love each other so completely our lives at present are so incomplete. I want to be with you always – to talk to you, laugh with you, see the beautiful things with you…I am not the same person I was three months ago, for I am you.

My life is incomplete too. I ought to be able to speak to you just whenever I want and not have these one sided conversations inside my own head, but when I do see you we are alone for such a short time. ...

I have for some time been living very much like an ostrich (one does I suppose in wartime), and it must be something of a habit. It wasn't until yesterday afternoon that I was conscious that you were going away for such a long time. The sudden realisation was like a shock – a dull blow somewhere between the stomach and the throat. And I said last night that I was just beginning to feel it – to know every second as a minute, every minute as an hour, a day as a year – a fortnight just incomprehensible.

I want to say that I hope you will enjoy your course and that you will have a nice leave. But it sounds rather like a mockery; you know that I shall be thinking of you the whole time that you are away, that I wait only for the day when you come back again. If the sun shines at all while you are away it will just about end me. But there is no sun, or light, or colour, no cloud or sparkling sea, there is nothing while you are away...

Rick.

29/12/41

Sweetheart how are you? Or mustn't I ask that. And how is Greenwich – not I'll warrant as dismal as you prophesied. I certainly don't envy you getting up at 6AM just for the fun of it...

It is curious that I have only known you for about six months and this is almost the first time I haven't seen you for more than three days (or spoken to you). It's curious in that I might have known you for years and years or only for a few moments. Certainly I haven't seen you for years. Why should time do such queer things. Why if I'm with you for a few hours or away from you for a few hours shouldn't the two things be the same.

I have been very busy today. I have done nothing. I invent lots of small jobs to do which keep me occupied. They are not particularly interesting but they pass the time away. I know I ought to be frantically learning German so that I don't look so dumb beside you. But the brain won't function. Maybe I am exhausted, though the other day when I said that I was merely silly or depressed ...

So – I was 'ready to fall in love with anyone' – just ready for it. And 'it might as well have been you or any other person' (provided it was a she I suppose) I wish you would explain all that. I'm sorry – I'm being a little unfair and possibly vindictive. (Why do I mention these things I remember instead of those others you say which are so much more pleasant and thrilling) ...

I wish I had that dictionary because I want to look up the word 'jealous' I am so jealous where you are concerned that I am frightened. I am afraid that it might do some damage. And I am sick because it is so small and mean and petty. I would like you to help me to get rid of it but I don't think you can because you don't know what it means. Oh Hell what a bloody thing to talk about ...

> *Rick*

30/12/41

My heart,
I have been writing to you all day today though I haven't put pen to paper. I suppose that is much the same as saying that I am always talking to you. I imagine that people here think I'm daft – certainly unsteady – since I have also been looking in the letter rack at approximately 10 minute intervals. I liked your letter a lot but I must have you.

I am unhappy to hear that Greenwich is such a dismal place. How much more do I wish that I could be with you when I know that you are not happy. I feel rather foolish and inadequate when I can only tell myself that there is little I can do about it. What good does it do to tell you how I long to be with you when I can't come to you.

I know I want to marry you, but I know too that it wouldn't make any difference. It wouldn't make it any easier to be parted from you, it wouldn't make it any more delightful, exhilarating, thrilling to be with you than at present. ... I am however not certain that we can go on for years without being complete lovers, in spite of the 'pre-meditation' you speak of, without at the same time doing some damage to ourselves and to our love. I am not certain because I don't know – nobody has ever told me what is and what isn't possible. It's hard enough anyway to leave you when the whole of my mind and body is crying out to be with you. ...

How I wish I could get off next Friday to come and see you – but there isn't a hope and I wanted so much to be with you for New Year's Eve.

Rick

1/1/42

Darling I don't think I wished you a happy New Year when I phoned you yesterday although that was the chief excuse for doing so. In other respects it wasn't very successful either, your voice sounded very strange and artificial ... so I cursed the telephone again.

I hope your cold and throat are better I've never known before how miserable one can be made to feel if the person one loves isn't well and happy.

Lord how I wish I was coming down to the Farm with you this weekend. Shut Up! (That's to myself – mustn't let myself dwell on that or I shall go crazy).

I have to go and get my hair cut – though I have been waiting for you permission, or else buy some ribbon to tie it up in, but I haven't any coupons.

I quite agree that the most foolish thing I ever said to you was that this fortnight wouldn't be a long time. Maybe sometime in the future it won't have seemed a long time but now it's an eternity. I think you'd better wear some kind of protective padding like American footballers wear the next time I see you ...

2/1/42

How are you? ... I really am annoyed with the postman by now, it's Friday PM and I've received one letter from you since you've been away. Much better men than I have been driven to drink and for much less reason. It's bad enough you are away, but not to get your letters either is very discouraging ...

Loving you has given me a greater understanding of other people, made me perhaps a little more tolerant towards them, but it has also made me less self-sufficient ... Surely I ought to be a better person than before even though you are away, and not a great sulking, ill-tempered brute who nothing can please or even cheer.

I had a letter from Paul Berthon today telling me that he was gradually making headway with his physical malady. He ends with a rather cryptic PS "do you still intend to wait until the war is finished? 1944, perhaps more probably 45-46. Madness! Utter folly!" I think is it optimistic? ...

... I would like to be cutting the hedge with you now, or even sawing wood or perhaps giving Mrs Parsons (The Village shop) *a thrill! ... Please remember me to all at home and wish them a Happy New Year.*

For yourself what would you have of me – take it - but just give me your hands or just one sight of you. Hell!

Rick

3/1/42

I am several degrees more light-hearted today than I have been all the week because I have found three of your letters in the rack this morning. ... I would much rather have them on separate days and in any case it is better for the letters belonging to the other people, for if they don't remove them as soon as they are put there they get worn out from my searching through them practically continuously.

Queen Anne's block from your letters sounds particularly bloody – as antiquated as it's name ... Greenwich, I know, even at the best of times is depressing enough, though the flowers at some times of the year in the park, and the view across the river have a certain attraction. Though to me those things only emphasis how unnatural is the civilization we know in England and particularly in London. The London suburbs never failed to give me an utter desolation of spirit – to induce a sort of chronic melancholy which only the sunshine and sailing could dispel. Maybe I am an escapist if I want to run away from that, but I don't know any other answer that is entirely satisfactory to this problem of millions of people living in a confined area. It's all a vicious circle kind of argument in applied economics. Greenwood [Arthur Greenwood – Politician], *and his team are trying to solve it, but from what I know of them they are much too academically minded and will only produce a beautiful report to pigeonhole.*

Is the new Walt Disney worth seeing? Did it give you this 'belly laugh' that I "wot" of? I've never been able to understand why one 'splits one's sides with laughter'. It isn't there at all. I suppose it's alright to laugh until it hurts in a 'nice' place. ...

... It just isn't fair that I have to think every time I look at my watch or a clock what we would be doing at the Farm ... I try hard to console myself with one day!

Rick

Actually I was at Park Farm on leave with the flu for nearly two weeks. Though feeling pretty low, Rick's letters and the reality of our love for one another were a constant source of happiness and wonder to me. His letters were virtually every day:

9/1/42

Here I go again how are you ... I think I shot a bit of a line to your Father the other day on the telephone – at least in a mild sort of way. He said 'I suppose it's cold in the Channel'. I merely agreed – but so heartily that I must have given the impression that I spend all night and every night at sea – half frozen, miserable but sticking it. Doing my bit for the old country – proper Empire builder's spirit and all that. How could I tell him the facts over the phone?

Nevertheless it is perishing cold playing about outside especially if one's all wet. It's worth it if only for the hot bath afterwards ... if we only went to sea and got wet often enough I should never get high.

... I have now spent about 26 winters in this country. As far as I know I'm a fairly honest sort of fellow; not particularly a snake in the grass and so on. I cannot discover what I have done therefore to deserve such treatment. There just isn't any justice.

After I returned to Dover Rick went on his home leave, I was to join him on about the twenty-first of the month for forty-eight hours. Just before I came up I received some letters from him. The last one I had describes an abortive day's shopping in London and again shows something of his personality:

19/01/42

It was sweet of you to take me to the station today – but of course you always are incredibly sweet to me even when I am late, or more than usually stupid etc. … I am looking forward so much to seeing you on Friday but I am a little nervous – especially as you said you would probably be embarrassed. Oh well.

All I know is that I'm in love with you so much that it is a dull ache to be away from you that it is practically impossible to say goodbye to you when I am with you. That I'm not worth one of your little fingers and I'm afraid you will find it out some day. …

21/1/42

Sweetheart it did me a lot of good to speak to you on the telephone last night. I had been careening around London all the afternoon in the filthy slush and managed to achieve practically nothing. An abortive afternoon was capped by a train journey home in a very crowded carriage. As usual and in spite of the phone you took me from the nadir to the zenith. I went to bed feeling like a million dollars – I haven't the remotest idea what that means …

I had to go up to town again this morning to change our tickets, and I spent the rest of the time trying to get people to sell me some perfume. But in spite of the uniform, and the most charming smile, nobody would be persuaded to do so. I went to DH Evans, Pounds, John Lewis, Peter Robinsons, Waring and Gillow, C&A, Bourne & Hollingsworth, Liberty's, Dickens & Jones, Galleries Lafayettes, Swan & Edgar etc. I would never do it again, certainly not for anybody else. People have earned medals for less. I did it all without any help from alcohol. God how I needed it though. It's alright to go in through the swing doors but then the thing starts. I would stand nervously just inside the doors looking at the carpet until some kind person would come up and ask if they could help. Since none of them looked the type that would carry a flask I was reduced to asking the way to the perfumery department. I think that was the worst moment. Having finally got there and pronounced the name of the bloody stuff in about 9 different ways without any success, the next problem was how to get out – always this seemed to involve going through the most embarrassing departments. You have no idea of the feeling of relief I experienced when I managed to catch a glimpse of daylight at the end of an avenue, and so made good my escape. One thing – it certainly kept me warm.

But on each occasion I have come back with the same feeling, it is a feeling of utter despondency which is due to the lack of faith in my dreams and imaginings which London and particularly this shopping part of it induces. I see so many beautiful things I want to give you and why shouldn't you have them…there is a lot more to it like that but it's all rather tawdry.

Since you are not now coming up until Saturday this will seem the longest leave I have ever had, until then be good and careful,

Rick

When I arrived at his home on the twenty-first I was little apprehensive about meeting his family. He had told me when we were going into Folkestone on the bus, quite early on in our relationship, that his family lived in a house like the ones we were passing and about which I had made some thoughtless disparaging remark. I knew his background was different from mine, but by this time such considerations had no relevance at all. I immediately felt drawn to his mother and felt that the feeling was reciprocated. She was a sweet faced, gentle woman and very welcoming. Bill, Rick's father was a little reserved and perhaps less immediately reassured at Rick's choice of girl.

I heard many stories of his youth, and of the part that he had played, soon after he joined the Navy, in the evacuation of Dunkirk in 1940. I grew very fond of Lil, Rick's mother, and sometime later she became, for me, 'Mother C', she remained a part of my life for many years after the war until she died.

At the end of our leave we returned to Dover together on the train, and continued to write and see each other very frequently.

In early February 1942 it was decided that four of us from different Special Duty stations were to be sent to Falmouth in Cornwall. I spent the night in a fellow Wren's London flat before taking the train to Falmouth the next day. We were to try and intercept traffic from the German battleships *Sharnhorst*, *Gneisenau* and *Prinz Eugen*, which were some of Germany's biggest warships. They were reportedly trying to return to a German port from Brest. Ours was an attempt to intercept some 'traffic' which would give an idea of their intended movements. The wireless sets were sent up in barrage balloons to increase the range of our reception. The theory was that we would be able to use an automatic searcher to monitor the frequencies used by the Germans. However, the automated searcher was too fast and certainly not able to hesitate and retrace when passing a possible signal. The carrier wave was gone over far too rapidly and only one possible signal was received on one of my watches.

An excerpt from the book *Very Special Intelligence* by Patrick Beesly tells of the subsequent events in full. Apparently the German Admiral Räder wanted to keep the battleships in Brest after their repairs were completed, despite the danger they faced from fairly frequent raids by RAF Bomber Command. Hitler was said to have realised that they were bound to be put out of action sooner or later and so commanded them to return to the area of North Sea operations. He also intuited 'that a sudden dash up the Channel' would be so unexpected that it stood a chance of success.

Beesly writes:

An almost incredible sequence of failures and misjudgements followed. The Germans left Brest on February 11 and succeeded in getting as far as the straights of Dover. Admiral Ramsay was informed of their presence on the morning of February 12. ... But by this time it was far too late for effective and coordinated action to be taken. ... one after another the MTBs, Swordfish, Beauforts and Destroyers made gallant attacks, but were all driven off or shot down by the powerful sea and air escort which the German's had organised.

Alas, probably partly because of lack of inter-service cooperation between the Bomber Command and the Navy, the German battleships succeeded in getting through to the safety of a German port.

In his letters written to me while I was in Falmouth, Rick spoke – albeit very securely – about the Dover Coastal Forces encounter with the German Ships:

I did mention the excitement that went on in this place for a few days – with press reporters and Paramount cameramen, and heaven knows what. But underlying all this exhilaration of being still alive was a certain despondency at the thought that such a thing as three large warships going through the Straits in daytime could happen. The excitement has gone, and only the gloom remains. Amongst some, even the urgent fervour they had for 'Pongo bashing' (ridiculing Army officers and personnel) *seems to have cooled. And it is a shocking state of affairs, though quite foreseeable I think. It may have the effect, however, of shaking this nation up, a thing it requires in wartime far too frequently. It is rather a costly business when every time a certain amount of stimulus is required it is necessary to have a Dunkirk or Crete etc. That is where the newspapers do such a poor service in not 'blowing cold' often enough. They are too fond of lugging out the Battle of Britain. I cannot write anymore while my head nods over the paper as I form the letters. ...*

Earlier Rick had written to me:

Exactly – I can say I love you but it's not enough. It's true but it conveys little of what I think or feel – of the mental or physical state I'm in through this longing to be with you – 'with you' – as if it were as calm as that! I don't long to be with you – to walk by your side, to sit with you over a cup of tea, to talk to you. It is not a peaceful tranquil feeling – though I know I can find that too with you...but sometimes I dream with you too – of the sunshine that we will feel together; of the colours in the sea and sky and trees that we will see, of the 'warm' house that we will live in, of the days brilliant and blue when we go sailing together, of the hills and houses, the people and their ways. Of other countries we shall see together. Of the many things that fleet away the future. I suppose they are nonsense but they are nice. No! They are not nonsense – they are strong – one has to be strong too that's all...God keep you sweetheart.

Rick

13/2/42

I said in my last letter to you that I would write to you presently. It was my intention to write to you immediately, after I had changed, for we were as usual at short notice …

As you know there has been a great 'to-do' here in the last two days, and for the people who took part it was a thrilling experience and sight – something which they will always remember. They have now been very busy recounting the story both for the official reports and for the press. (Not to mention the several celebrations of their safe return, which was truly remarkable). It wasn't a particularly exhilarating thing as far as I was concerned, to watch them go out and then wait in the operations room for their return – particularly as there was nothing wrong with my boat – I was merely lending someone else one of my petrol tanks, but having just put myself into the dock I couldn't get out until the evening. It is particularly tough on my crew, who have the routine tasks of keeping the boat fit day after day and then miss the excitements for which they do it. The worst part for them is to have to listen to the talk of the other crews, and to have to stand their jibes and leg pulling. This must all sound rather like a big moan to you, and, I am inclined to agree with you that perhaps I am not the type of person you were meant for, since 'settled domesticity' of one kind or another is bound to be my lot. That's rather horrid I'm afraid but I won't scrub it out for it is right that you should know how mean I am on occasions – even though that is written with my tongue in my cheek.

… Though it is the one thing I want all the time – to be with you – never to be away from you, it isn't the greatest of fun to have to do it continually in the environment of restaurants and tea shops, buses and uniform, for snatched half-hours or at most a short evening. As you once said – you didn't want to fall in love at the present time or perhaps in the present conditions, and it must be rather annoying to have done so with someone in MTBs and the peculiar restrictions they 'work' under.

… I often feel that I am being weak willed or something – certainly inadequate – in not being able to influence the circumstances in which we are able to meet, and forever come up with the same conclusion that it's difficult to see what else can be done about it. I often look round for 'inspiration' to

see what other people do about it. The ones who see their wives only when they are on leave, the others whose wives follow them around – and so on. But I cannot see that they have come to any improvement and in any case you are not my wife.

I am scared too that one day you will wake up to discover that I am not the person I appear to be, that I am a sham. I suppose any man who wasn't completely conceited would feel the same if he were loved by a person as lovely, intelligent, sweet as you are. (The disheartening thing is that you will probably say 'pah!' to that – those last few words).

And not least, I suppose we are both doing something when we are on duty, that isn't particularly good for the nervous system. Certainly you are and without the excitement that some of us get. By which I think I mean that psychologically we require a certain amount of seclusion to find the utmost comfort and internal quiet in each other which the environment of say dinner at the Esplanade doesn't provide. That is why those few days at the Farm and the weekend in town stand out as monuments whereas in truth they are the normal and all else isn't (that's very awkwardly put).

… I'm practically dropping off to sleep as I write. …

Rick

On 16 February he writes:

… I know how great your annoyance must have been (still is) at being in Cornwall and not at the ABC [Abbotscliff house]. I didn't appreciate it on Thursday when I talked to you because selfishly I was too full of my own bad luck. I suppose I wanted somebody to feel sorry for me – no I don't know what I wanted, and all I said to myself was 'Shut up, that was yesterday, the past, irrevocable, so get on!' in any case I should have been very frightened if I had been working.

'The best years of your life the early 20s' is that a fact, are they supposed to be the best years of one's life? If so that frightens me because mine will be gone by the end of the war, but I know I shall look back and say 'the best years of my life?' yes I can remember when they began … I didn't believe before then that there could be anyone like you. I just hoped there might be even though I knew she wouldn't look at me. But would you believe it – even

now I can't – I did see her and meet her and this is the unbelievable part, she fell in love with me too. And now if I still look a little startled ... that is the reason because as anyone will tell you these things don't happen in real life ...

... Until next time,
Rick

I had been thinking quite seriously of trying to go away somewhere with Rick, possibly to Cornwall. I had plenty of time to think. Except when we were on watch, our lives were pretty boring in Falmouth, our quarters cold and uncomfortable, and I don't even remember where we ate. Obviously I mentioned some of these thoughts to Rick when I wrote because on the seventeenth. He answered:

.... I think the scheme by which we might be able to take a cottage for a week is the most wonderful idea. I have told you that the River Crouch looks a bit of a wash out as far as sailing is concerned, and as far as I have been able to gather the lakes are full of hobble-de-hoys (is that how it is written?) If you can fix it it's almost too much to think about – dangerous too, for I am sure I shall go crazy if I do. I am almost tempted to suggest a further corollary, that if it works out alright i.e. it is possible to make leaves coincide and all that sort of business, that it would be very nice to look around for a more permanent place that we could, at least for the war, call our own. Or is all that too ambitious? I am afraid I am leaping along in strides that are much too big but it is rather thrilling. I suppose I shall think it silly if I consider it, so I won't. I can get my car taxed and insured before my next leave, but the difficulty will be to scrounge enough petrol, for it's about 500 miles there and back from London. We wouldn't be able to use it much there so I suppose that wouldn't matter; and too it's such an old thing that I don't know if it would stand the journey. I wish it could all be managed by your birthday but I'm afraid it doesn't look possible. Whoopee! I'm sorry I must calm down.

*   I don't quite know what to say about your remark that it is possibly better to be apart like this and meet for longer periods as when we are on leave. I am inclined to think that it is better. It's not that I don't miss you – for I do*

badly ... but I think that the knowledge when we meet, that one of us has to be back at a certain time, that the consequences of the failure of unreliable transport arrangements, are important, and finally in my case, the prospect of a recall – all colour to some extent the atmosphere when we are together and affect us subconsciously. The constant goodbyes have similar effects ... I just don't know the answer, perhaps you can see straighter than me. ...

You know Mark Arnold-Forster I think? I was writing to you in front of the fire and I suppose I must have had that daft kind of look on my face for he said 'Are you writing to Falmouth'? apparently his people have a house at St Ives ... if you got bored or nattered at by the Chief Wren would you like to go and stay there for a weekend?... it sounded rather interesting to me. Background: Mark was at school in Germany near Lake Konstanz (Bondy at Salem) *for about two years when he was 12 or 13 – went to the same school in Scotland when the Headmaster was kicked out of Germany and started up over here* (Gordonstown). *Also something about being at school in French Switzerland. He was in the merchant service before the war. Now CO. of MTB 219.*

... There were not any MTBs lost last week, nor any casualties, nor any damage, sounds a bit tall, but perfectly true.

I passed over the idea of kissing your 'Snotty' [Midshipman] *for you and I was rather embarrassed at trying to kiss the Lieutenant you spoke about. Of course, there wasn't much of a description so I had a bit of bad luck with the first one or two, but I finally found one who knew something about it. I know him quite well and I know how he likes you to kiss him. But since he knows it wouldn't stop there either it was even more difficult... Good night,*

Rick

18/2/42

... Please tell me as soon as you know at the end of the week whether you are going to be kept where you are, I have already said something about this in my letter yesterday. For the most part I think you will like it there and in a most unselfish manner and for that reason, I hope you will stay there...that attitude results only from the fact that it hasn't yet penetrated into my full comprehension that this will be a long war ...

... I borrowed your phrase 'settled domesticity' because I thought when you used it that you wanted to convey the idea of a life which was merely a placid, complacent, even existence, narrow and suburban. And since I always seem to be at some other spot when things are happening, both before and during this war, I used the expression to convey that impression of the way I'm fated. It was, I suppose, an ill chosen expression for I don't believe that 'domesticity' in the sense of 'being married' is necessarily any more dull than action, events, are glamorous except in retrospective conversation or the newspapers. And in the above sense of a conventional life many men are 'doomed' to domesticity. The doom part comes either from the spiritual inadequacy of western civilization (that's a phrase that makes you laugh nowadays), or from a wrong sense of values. They are probably one and the same thing. I know the very great appeal of wanting to travel – to see the strange out of the way places of the world; to see the natural beauties of the earth, to meet and try and understand other people and their ways of life, to have a crack at a variety of jobs, to sail about the world as I would with no master and no ties. I told you once I wanted to learn several languages – the purpose being to understand better, to get more out of such an existence. But none of this squares with the satisfaction of the natural instincts of man, or at least the strongest one, marriage and reproduction – the perpetuation of the species. In my more philosophical moods (what a grand way of saying it), it is the failure to square these two ambitions – that's not the right word – which I find the most perplexing of problems. And I think much of this is behind my contention that one ought to organise one's life so that it is fairly close to the rudimentary and natural things – the earth, the seasons, the wind, the sea, the sun. That it is wisdom rather than knowledge which counts, and that there is more to be learnt from twenty-four hours sailing in a yacht when you are dependent upon yourself than a six month world tour in a luxury liner – from growing one field of wheat than making a million on the stock exchange. But there are so many questions – is the world an oyster to be eaten with the utmost enjoyment, is life merely a span of years to be lived entirely for one's own enjoyment – or is there some continuity and purpose to it, is there a meaning to such a phrase as 'service to humanity', have I any responsibilities to other men, and particularly those who come after me? There are lots of these sort of questions which seem to me fundamental and

also I think need to be answered in some way during this war. If they are not then it is even more of a pointless waste of time than it appears now, and there will be no progress in the peace which follows it. And the conclusion of all this is 'what's the bloody use of talking so much'.

I too want badly – always have wanted – a place of my – now our own, where we could keep our things, furnish, decorate, arrange as we wanted. Where I could do 101 things with my hands during the day, and find peace with you in the evenings ... I think that was why I expanded on this cottage idea yesterday with rather an overdose of enthusiasm ... I am trying to put down things and leaving you to sort them out, analyse them, draw your own conclusions. But Oh Lord! How I wish I could be with you while you do it ...

Rick

In another of his many letters to me in Falmouth, Rick talks of a conversation with Nigel Pumphrey, his much admired Senior Officer:

19/2/42

... It's rather a coincidence that you should mention education and economics for I had quite a long discussion with Nigel last night on these very points. I have spoken with him before about the mess we call civilization and consistently insisted on education being the only solution. Everything we spoke about I brought back to that. So yesterday he turned up with a fairly radical educational system.

Primarily it is the same for everyone – they go to school to learn the fundamental things until they are about 12 and then they spend the next 5 or 6 – even more – years learning to do things with their hands particularly, and also perhaps getting fitted for an occupation. And then they do more or less a University course – this to some extent being mainly their cultural education as apart perhaps from their social education.

But since education is so poor nowadays any improvement will require first of all the production of teachers, and at the same time a change in the social order which regulates it to a comparatively unimportant and to some extent traditional role. And this involves, first, a change in the economic system which has for its driving force now the acquisitive spirit and fear. Yes, I'm back to it again.

I'm not a very good person to teach you economics I don't know the subject well enough to be anything other than sketchy. But I ought to be in a position to help you learn about it if you really want to. Actually it is mainly common sense, camouflaged with high-sounding terms – that is pure or theoretical economics. Applied economics as found in the business and administrative worlds are mainly expediency, though it is probably more of a science in a place like Russia or Germany. ...

Rick

21/2/42

My darling Jenny, I didn't get to bed before a quarter to five this morning, though I was 'in' some time before that, all of which means I wasn't able to fulfil my promise to write to you before this morning's post ... I do know so well the despondent feeling if anything delays a letter from you. (I always feel that I am taking a lot for granted if I admit that you may have similar feelings).

It is snowing quite hard again today; it has been off and on for the past week. I hope you will never ask me to spend a winter unnecessarily in England – what is the good of being half-dead half the year? And snow, while we are out, is the very devil, because you can't see very far. It wasn't cold last night because we could keep dry – and with the gear I had on it's not surprising – woollen underwear, Pusser's (Navy Issue) thick stuff, serge trousers, shirt, white submarine sweater, monkey jacket, two pairs of stockings, thick scarf, fleece lined gloves, a thick bulky suit overall made of kapok, and over everything an oilskin thing like combinations, not to mention a tin hat or my cap – it all depends on the weather. It's difficult to be very agile dressed up like that, but thank heaven agility isn't required – except of the mind, and there is nothing I can do about that...

I must say I hope you are not setting out on a campaign of depreciating the moral standards – should I say the high moral standards of the Women's Royal Naval Service. I'm sure the Officers, particularly those of more senior rank and years are, quite unnecessarily of course, already sufficiently burdened by the responsibility for the welfare of some of these high-spirited young women. I know that if I had a daughter of their age I should be very worried to think of the multiplicity of temptations to which they are exposed! It is always a source of amazement to me to see how well they resist them. ...

Rick

I returned to Dover in March and Rick wrote to me from his parents while on home leave. This letter is primarily from memory as a few of Rick's letters were stolen:

... your letter – another precious one ... it scares me that you should seem so insistent about losing me...and you didn't <u>look</u> morbid – it seems to be the natural fear lovers always have, carefully nurtured until it is something bigger – I keep wondering if you are not giving me veiled marching orders, and keep reminding myself that when I get them they won't be 'veiled'. (It is veiled or vieled or veighled? It's such ages since I wore one) ... I keep on getting back to the consideration, let's not make our lives any more full of complications than the fates already have up their sleeves for us – it isn't often given to two people to love one another as we do and I think we should be grateful for that and not worry - for it will make us sick. I always say Jenny is somewhere in the world and she is thinking of me now as though we were together – time and distance in themselves are only material things – the essence of our love is spiritual. I can live on that for some time and then too I can talk to you – ask you if you see the colours in the sky and trees and earth, or at other times the grey and sombre tones like today, ask you as I walk along what are we to do about these people who look weary and depressed, these others who look poor and. ... or smug and .... ? discontented. ...

Rick

In April of that year Rick and I rented a cottage in Itchenor in Hampshire for five days leave. We were 'going away together'. Some time before we had decided we were going to get married. Rick had taken an unset, pale topaz stone that I had been given by Moishes Oved of Cameo Corner for, what Oved, called my *Schlüpfwinkel*, (hiding place) and had it made into a ring for me. I had given him a large silver cigarette case, inscribed 'To the Captain, from the Crew', for he was determined to sail across the Atlantic in his converted Lunenburg Schooner after the war, with me serving as crew! We had a few days of playing at married life; I cooked, we went on long walks and learnt more about one another. Without actually becoming lovers, we became ever closer, and on returning in the train to Dover, we sat in a bemused state of amorous bliss. In one of the last letters he wrote to me, he said:

Sweetheart, oh! I don't know what to call you – I have amidst this waste of time and futility of war been looking at the stars, and in their immense and breathless beauty I see that you have, these days, become an obsession with me – I don't mean these days, for you have always been that, but that in this sense I need you more and more each day. I am constantly thinking of you, and walk within the orbit of the mantle of your spirit – I cannot work when I am away from you. … even at the cottage I could not bear to be in another room from you and when I was, I listened for your movements and watched for you to come in. …

I am writing this lying on my bunk in the wardroom of my boat, and I think of some other boat, nodding sleek and sturdy in some other distant harbour. Instead of the shuffling of the 'pongos' there are strange indeterminate sounds and rustlings and laughter of people for most of whom the days work is done … Is it all foolish dreaming? No it is not foolish and if it is dreaming, it is for us to make it true. Oh Jenny my sweet … you see I am back at the beginning again.

Rick

On 24 April Rick telephoned me and I said I could not see him that evening, unfortunately I did not explain why I was not going to see him. I was feeling rather sick and had just washed my hair. The terrible result was that Rick wrote a rather unhappy letter, which I confess I have always avoided reading properly, as it makes me feel ashamed. His letter shows his recurring lack of faith in my acceptance of his background and family. It seems to me now that by the end of the letter he is uncharacteristically showing signs of stress caused by the constant dangerous nightly sorties:

April 25

Your insistence that I love you less, has occasioned on my part a certain amount of heart-searching. Though I disagree with your conclusions – because – though I am as much in love with you as I ever was (and that couldn't be more) – I do find that there is now somebody inside me standing aside with a large question mark.

The reason for this is very much past history, and ought to be forgotten, but whilst the facts are probably untrue, the psychological results are as far as I know them true. Though I forget the date, I remember it was a Tuesday (probably the 19th of December). *I spent the afternoon and evening with you and because I was with you, I was as happy as it is possible for a human being to be. I felt that we were spiritually, completely together, though on a plane much above common, mundane, daily experience. I imagined that we both felt the same, and for this reason there was such a quality of beauty as to approach absolute truth. I didn't in the circumstances, believe that to be a temporary experience, and so, although I had to leave you, when the only real thing would have been to stay with you, I was still in the midst of that feeling when I rang you up next day and you said you couldn't see me. Does this explain why I was surprised tonight when I found you didn't want to see me ... It isn't a question of whether I am in love with you or not for I am ... but rather that I am a little shy of the heights, because I haven't the same faith in them. And lacking that they aren't so easy to achieve. I know that I have only to be with you sufficiently to exorcise the little man with the question mark and his restraining influence. He went yesterday – for a time!*

The schooner was an antidote – and so the remark I made about it yesterday shouldn't be taken out of context. Sometimes it is possible to say things that have one meaning taken along with a train of thought, and a different meaning when taken alone – or even no meaning at all. The schooner represents something I wanted to do before I met you. There is all the difference in the world between that dream and one of it now. But I imagine that I thought that if the one thing wasn't the truth, then the schooner wouldn't be either. So the introduction of the word 'Anyway', meant that I had given myself something to think about. ...

.... Because I haven't been with you for a day or two, the next few days will seem even more empty than before. However – to stop being selfish – I

hope you will rest and find that quiet which you need more than anything else.

The following weekend we went to Canterbury and spent a wonderful day. We visited the cathedral, the antique shops – and bought an inlaid walking stick for Rick. On 12 May Rick telephoned me and told me he was not on duty that night, so when I heard the MTB engines, I thought there was nothing to worry about, at least until tomorrow. It fills me with sad guilt, that perhaps doubts had been on his mind, and I had not come to see him before he went to sea that night.

On 13 May 1942 there was a larger German convoy than usual escorted by E boats and minesweepers off Cap Gris Nez. Rick, SO of the Sixth Flotilla MTBs, went out to engage the Germans. His boat, number 220, did not return. I was not on duty that night, and of course, I remain convinced that I would have been able to get more out of the intercepted traffic than those who were on watch. One message was in normal speech, probably from one of the minesweepers, and it read '*Wir haben an Bord Der Kapitän ein …* *Bootes*' (We have the captain of a ..boat on board).

Could the rescued captain have been Rick? Or was it the German captain of one of the larger boats sunk that night? A German news report was picked up, stating that one of the MTB's was 'sunk by ramming and another English MTB was sunk'. The body of Tony Lovell (Rick's young Sub-Lieutenant) was found clinging to a buoy in mid-channel, apparently with the body of a German sailor nearby.

A fuller German account of the battle tells of the *Handelsschutzkreutzer* (Trade Protection Cruiser) *Stier*, which had been formally commissioned into the German Navy in November 1941, leaving Kiel on 9 May 1942 and proceeding to Rotterdam on 10 May:

On May 12th as she headed through the Ärmelkanal [English Channel] she was preceded by sixteen Motor Mine Sweepers, in three large V formations. She was surrounded by four torpedo boats of the 5th Torpedo Boat Flotilla – the 933 ton Wolf class 'Iltis', and three Möwe class boats – the 'Kondor', 'Falke' and 'Seeadler', each armed with six 53.3cm torpedo tubes, three

100mm guns and four 20mm Flak guns, deployed in a diamond shaped box formation around her.

The large escort convinced the British that she was important, and in the early hours of May 13th she was attacked, first by the fourteen inch batteries from Dover, which could not reach her, and later by Motor Torpedo Boats, which surrounded the convoy from both sides under cover of fog off Cap Gris Nez. In the ensuing chaos, with all the ships involved firing indiscriminately in all directions Stier *and her escorts fired star shells, in the light of which two of the MTBs were hit and set on fire, with one, the MTB 220 later going down. As the British pressed home their attacks, the* Iltis, *which had had to slow to keep station, was hit by a torpedo fired by MTB 221, she sank within three minutes taking all 115 members of her crew with her. The* Seeadler, *having successfully put one of the attacking MTB's out of action, was resuming her position in front of the* Stier, *when she too was torpedoed – this time by MTB 219, and also split in half. As the raider ploughed past the drifting forward part of the boat, her gunners, who had been ordered to fire at every suspicious shadow, raked the wreckage and the desperate men clinging to it killing their own. In all 85 members of the* Seeadler's *crew lost their lives. After escorting the undamaged raider into Boulogne, the surviving torpedo boats* Kondor *and* Falke, *went back out to look for survivors, rescuing 88 Germans and 3 men from MTB 220.*

It was very difficult for me to telephone Bill and Lil and tell them that Rick was missing. But I felt that hearing it from me, with the real possibility that he had been picked up, would give them more hope than an official notification.

Chapter 5

A Long Time To Hope

I was determined to stay in Dover. I stayed on for more than a year after Rick was lost and wrote him a letter every day. Writing these letters convinced me that he would be found to be a prisoner, and I would be able to send them to him. I saw a lot of his parents and became close to them. My roommate, Diana Davis, had a Jack Russell-mix terrier also called Jenny. When she left Dover, and ultimately the WRNS, she gave 'Little Jenny' to me, and the dog was my constant companion and comfort. At the end of my time in the Navy, I gave her to Rick's parents, where she had a wonderful life and a special entente with Bill until she died.

I have not copied verbatim all of my letters, which I kept, along with Rick's, from 1942 until today. There will be only a few lines in many cases, but they show how I felt each day, for weeks, months and years. They are in most cases, cries of loving despair, and perhaps cannot interest anyone, other than those involved. However, some of them may act as a sort of diary of the events of the next three years of war. Because of censorship, names of towns such as Dover or Folkstone and of Naval establishments such as HMS *Wasp* are written only as initials. One was constantly aware that nothing should be construed as 'insecure' by the British censors, or conversely helpful to the Germans.

In my first letter written on 13 May I tried to set the tone of what were to be daily letters:

If I start writing these letters now, maybe it will help to pass away the time until I know that you are safe. ... Oh God if only we had been married before!. ... I wish words were not so empty. I told your family tonight, because I could give them a much better chance to see hope. We were, 'working very hard' and close to you, and I have such hopes that are founded upon it. I am staying here so that you will be able to picture me more clearly and know what I am doing from day to day. I am going home on Saturday, but really I will be going to Itchenor with you – it is not a dream Rick darling – it is the truth and it simply means we will have to wait apart for the war to end … We will still marry when the war is over. … and the Lunenburg Schooner will grow much faster without money being spent on dinners and cinemas for an 'unsatisfiable girl'. … I know too that you are with me now stopping my tears in your compassionate love … I don't know how to contemplate that you are not alright. … when I 'look over' [the Channel] I feel that you are looking too and I can hear you telling me how near we are … I know that the reason I can hold so much sorrow, is because you gave me so great a capacity for joy. … I will 'stay with you' just as I did when we had to say goodnight on the phone. It is all too vast to write about. How can I give an inkling of my love.

My love, Jenny

14/05/42

My dearest heart,
How can I write to you and tell you anything at all of this thing I am carrying around in my heart, and the thousands of things I have said to you all last night and today. It is still very hard for me to believe that you are gone away. I suppose the reason for that is that you really never will be gone, and I shall always be with you. I wish most desperately that I was married to you, and, even as I am now, I wish I had your child to help me stay close to you. Rose [Rose Knight] *is coming to N.F* [North Foreland] *and so we will be quite near to each other, which I hope will help a little to lift the weight in me. Nothing seems to do that except, temporarily, weeping. Please take good care of yourself and look after everything I love – which means all of you. … How can I express this ineffable love I have and how can I tell you that outside of you there is nothing that matters – I love you Rick and wait for the first word from you – but do not feel sad if you send it to your people – I shall understand always. I wear both rings now. ….. You will be able to grow a beard in peace and polish up your German and Spanish. I will also study Spanish and seriously try to study navigation – so that I can be of some use to you on the schooner. The sun will shine again when I can*

Chapter 1: Early Days

Clan gathering: My great-great-grandfather, Isiah Crowell, front row, second from left, and his daughter Phoebe Kelly Crowell Brown, front row right, and back row, 2nd left, Thomas Brown, my great-grandparents. The Crowells, of English emigrant stock, traced their own ancestors in Nantucket back to the mid-17th century.

Phoebe Kelly Crowell Brown, my great grandmother, who married Thomas Brown.

Phoebe's daughter Alice Brown, who married Thomas Gill, and was my father's mother.

Miss Fidelia Bridges, a famous American watercolourist, who taught my great aunts to paint and was their companion.

My mother's father Christopher FitzGerald, with Geoff and Hucko Wood, my cousins.

With Celestine McBride, Connecticut, U.S.A., 1921.

In my first boarding school, Wickham House, England, 1926.

My first home, White House, designed and built by my father Donald Gill, Riverside, Connecticut, 1920.

With a deckhand, 1926, on my first crossing back to the States from school in England.

Second marriage: My mother Geraldine Gill, née FitzGerald, weds New Zealander Geoffrey Marter, 1933.

Pigtailed and 16, with great aunt Anna Maria-Brown ('Aunt Annie'), in her garden, Canaan, Connecticut, 1936.

I and my mother Geraldine, single again and now returned from New Zealand, Connecticut, 1936.

Chapter 2: New Experiences

Max Bondy, Gland, Switzerland, 1937.

Gertrud Bondy, Gland, 1937.

Morgenmusik, Gland, 1937.

Our Fiat on Bernina Pass, 1938, Switzerland.

Taken when I was 18, in Gland, 1938.

My best friend, Cecile Guigoz,
Gland, 1937.

Chapter 3: The War and and Important Decision

My father Donald Gill with (from left) me and
my half-brothers Jim and Mick, Park Farm,
Dorset, England, 1939.

My unfinished painting of returning Dunkirk
soldier, Euston Station, 1939.

Tony Rolt Missing

LIEUTENANT A. P. R. Rolt, of
the Rifle Brigade, one of the
missing defenders of Calais, will
probably soon be
recognised by the
Germans, assum-
ing he is a pri-
s o n e r, if he
should mention
the word "Don-
ington." It would
be taken to refer,
not to the prison
camp for Ger-
man officers in
the last war, but
to the m o t o r
racecourse on the
same spot.
It is the only
British course on
which the Ger-
man teams of
Auto-Union and Mercedes have
raced. And this Lieutenant Rolt is
that Tony Rolt who began racing
when he was still at Eton and leapt
into fame one afternoon at Doning-
ton just over a year ago.

A Faultless Race

THAT afternoon he drove a faultless race to win the British Empire Trophy from the best opposi-
tion we had.
His performance put him into the
E.R.A. racing team, the crack team
in the country, but that meant sadly
little, partly because the new E.R.A.
cars had so much trouble that they
were persistent non-starters, and
partly because Lieutenant Rolt was
kept busier and busier on military
duties.

Lieut. Rolt.

News of Tony Rolt's capture by the Germans at
Calais, 1939. Tony, my first flame, spent the entire
war in German captivity.

Nineteen year-old racing driver and
professional soldier Lt. Rolt, who billeted his
platoon at Park Farm, 1939.

21.9.43. My Dear Jenny, just had yours of 22.8.43, and I'm afraid I must again act as a bearer of bad news. I have re-questioned Mickey W., and to avoid any possible error have got him to write out what he knows & how he knew it. I give you his message word for word, and can only leave it to you to interpret it as you think fit. "I was at Mödag (Naval camp) when the survivors of Eric's boat came in, and talked to them. I asked about Eric who I knew was the C.O. of that boat, and was told that he was hit in the face, (at the same time as the boat received several heavy hits) and was given up as dead; and that as far as they knew he went down with the boat almost immediately." I'm extremely sorry I did not send you the details in my last letter, but Mickey was so emphatic, and the facts reported facts apparently so conclusive, that I thought the bare statement sufficient, without the further — statement of the details. You won't be in the mood for comparative trivialities when you read this, but I'd better fill up the rest of the space somehow so please forgive me. Although I can't say I quite understand your feelings about Dover, I'm afraid I'm another who is v. pleased to hear you've moved — it must be better for you in the long run. Yes, I'm glad we agree about the Huxley's — do read (or rather re-read) "The Uniqueness of Man" — particularly the essays on religion and his own philosophy at the end; I find his "scientific humanism" more convincing than anything else to date, and also a great help to one's morale in times like these. Cures that "what's the point in living" feeling.

all my love, Tony.

Kriegsgefangenenpost

An Miss J.R. Gill

Highlawns

Trimingham

Nr Mundesley

Norfolk.

Empfangsort:

Straße:

Kreis:

Land: ENGLAND

Landesteil (Provinz usw.)

PASSED

P.W. 6104

07.10.43 - 17

Gebührenfrei!

Deutschland (Allemagne)

Lager-Bezeichnung: Kriegsgef.-Offizierlager IV C

Gefangenennummer: 6 78

Vor- und Zuname: Lt. A. Rolt

Absender:

POW, letter (verso) from Tony Rolt, 1943.

Chapters 4 & 5: Dover

Lighthouse, St Margarets Bay, England.

Windmill, St Margarets Bay.

Beach fortifications, Dover Front, 1940s.

P.O. Jenny Gill, WRNS, 1941.

Lt. Eric Cornish, RNVR, 1941.

Mortor torpedo boat (MTB) on manoeuvres.

MTB in Dover submarine basin.

Crew of MTB 220, the boat that was lost with Rick Cornish on 13 May, 1942.

WHAT A CHANNEL BATTLE LOOKS LIKE : FROM THE BRIDGE OF A GERMAN ESCORT VESSEL
Our light naval forces make a night attack on a German convoy. The German escort throws up a protective barrage. A British M.T.B. is lying behind the curtain of tracers (top left). The barrage is coming from the German boat—outlined top centre—and another vessel at the end of the tracer bursts (top right).

WHAT IT WOULD LOOK LIKE FROM THE BRIDGE OF ONE OF OUR LIGHT NAVAL CRAFT
...man ships answer our fire. The illumination in the sky is caused by star shells thrown up by both sides. The smudge ...e (centre) is a German escort vessel. The spotty pattern is made by the barrage of tracer bullets from the same ship.

Coastal Forces action in Channel (clipping from Picture Post Magazine, early 1940's).

Dogfight over Dover cliffs, as seen from Abbotscliff House.

Dover coast as seen by Germans across Channel.

Lt. Geoffrey Elton RNVR, died of wounds in 1942 on the MTB he commanded.

Cmd. Nigel Pumphrey RN, commanding officer of Coastal Forces, Dover.

Lt. Mark Arnold Forster RNVR, true naval hero, survivor, a close friend of Rick's. CO of MTB 219.

My friend in the Wrens, CPO Rosemary Gilliat WRNS, fellow German-speaker.

Coastal Forces crew members retelling the narrow escape of the German battleships *Scharnhorst* and *Gneisenau*.

A brief holiday with Rick in Itchenor, Hampshire, spring of 1942, just before he was lost.

Rick's mother, Lily Cornish.

Rick's father, Bill Cornish.

MRS. ROOSEVELT AT DOVER

TRIBUTE TO SPIRIT OF THE W.R.N.S.

FROM OUR CORRESPONDENT

DOVER, Oct. 30

Mrs. Roosevelt, accompanied by Mrs. Churchill, visited Dover this afternoon. The Mayor of Dover, Alderman J. R. Cairns, received her, and with him were the Regional Commissioner, Lord Monsell; the Vice-Admiral, Dover; and the Brigadier Commanding the Garrison.

Large numbers of women gave Mrs. Roosevelt a great welcome as she passed through the streets. After an inspection of the control centre she viewed some of Dover's war damage. Going into one of the town's deep shelters she spent more than an hour with the W.R.N.S. Speaking to the W.R.N.S. on parade Mrs. ROOSEVELT said that they in the United States were only just beginning to organize the women of their country, and what she had seen here was extremely valuable to her. She concluded: "The thing which has impressed me most is the spirit which all of you show, the willingness to take whatever comes without complaint, and I hope we will do as well."

Earlier in the day Mrs. Roosevelt visited Canterbury and Barham.

From *The Times*, Oct. 30, 1941.

Mrs Roosevelt and Mrs Churchill, inspecting WRNS on parade, Dover Castle, 1941.

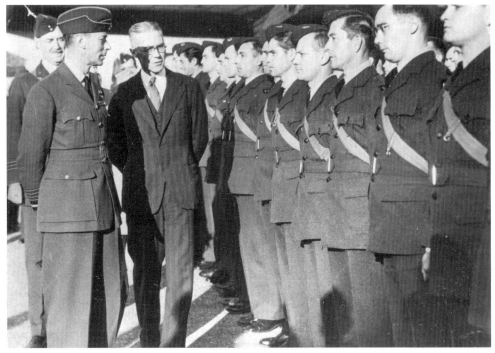

King George reviews the Civilian Technical Corps (CTC) with my father, Donald Gill.

A distant cousin and chance encounter on a train, Patrick FitzGerald, 1942, killed in the Fleet Air Arm.

At a US bomber base near Norwich, England, 1943.

Chapter 7: Post-War Germany

Henkel Trocken Sekt factory, Wiesbaden, Germany, OSS headquarters, 1945.

Jean Nater, 1945, Wiesbaden.

Jenny Gill, 1945, Wiesbaden.

Jean's friend Carl Muecke, 1945, Wiesbaden.

My first horse, the gelding Prima.

Now in U.S. Army uniform, with Julia "Bimba" Cuniberti, Wiesbaden.

My *Reitergruppe*, Wiesbaden, 1945.

World War II

JOAN B. GILL

Honorably Served
The United States of America
As A Member of
The Office of Strategic Services

WILLIAM J. DONOVAN
MAJOR GENERAL, U.S.A.
DIRECTOR

THE 1 DAY OF OCTOBER 1945

My discharge certificate from the OSS.

Chapter 8: Jean

Kastellorizo, Greece, 1944.

Jean Nater, Greek
islands, 1944.

Kastellorizo, 1944.

Kastellorizo, 1944.

Crew of Mosquito and Jean Nater (right), England, 1945.

Jean's crashed Mosquito, England, 1945.

I marry Jean Nater, Stratford, Connecticut, U.S.A., 1946.

*once more walk over the hill hand in hand with you, and can watch your
face when you look at the shifting colours in the landscape. All I can feel now
is my fear, love and need. But also I dread to think that you are worrying
about how I have taken the news. Don't sweetheart.*

15/05/42

*I have found out I can write two pages to you at once, but I must get all the
details from the Red X. It's a pity I can't write to you all the time, for I
think of you without cease and wonder how I could possibly tell you all my
thoughts even in a thousand letters.*

*I shall not 'live' until you return, you are my breathing, my living and
without you I do not exist. ... You once said you were afraid this place, this
town, had some effect on my loving you and gave me reason to – but you
were wrong Rick – I loved you before I was born.*

Jenny

16/05/42

*I am home now ... on the train ride the countryside looked beautiful, and
I was conscious that everything I saw, I must be seeing for you too and
tell you of it. There were two small foals in the New Forest, and the banks
everywhere were a riot of flowers. Summer is on her way – a Summer that
rightly belonged to us, and which I swear later we shall claim, and many
after it. Daddy met me and it was good to see Dominic. He 'helped' Joyce
and me weed the flowerbed, crawling between us all the way down, cramming
his mouth full of good Dorset soil every two minutes. His eyes are very dark
brown now, and of a peculiar dreamy and yet alive expression. I love blue
eyes – large blue eyes that look into my soul. ... The Lilies of the Valley
are out in garden, and the scent would penetrate even your nose. The apple
blossom is lovely. It is the first time I have seen the Farm at this time of year
and it is perfectly beautiful. I am afraid my atrocious handwriting will irk
the censors, so I will try and write a little larger and more clearly, although
I am jealous of every minute space. Still, I can write you everyday, and it is
you who must economise on space. Why I wonder, should I find it so difficult*

to say anything to you – I suppose because what is in my head and heart is just repetition and also no help to you and so better not said. I have decided to spend the last day of my leave or my next forty-eight hours with your Mother... If I once relax this attitude of hope and steadfastness I am lost. It must not happen. ... I sometimes feel that it is an impossibility to be away from you; by impossibility I mean a positive <u>seizure</u> of my heart in dread and a frantic denial of it being possible. ... I have a large tin on top of my dressing table into which go all my contributions to the bank (which means of course the Lunenburg Schooner). ... Tony Law and Mark [two of the Officers serving in Rick's flotilla] *came and gave me all the details and what hope there was .... Everyone seems to think you are the cat's whiskers – can't think why! But then if they didn't I would soon tell them. ... I can't find my feet yet. I send you my heart and know that it has flown straight and swiftly to its resting place.*

Jenny

17/05/42

Daddy's been out in the workshop all day. I have been helping him a little. If I do things furiously I can feel that the fear and pain is dulled and it is better. Watching Dominic I begin to doubt if our 'baby' is going to enjoy being tied down on the deck of the Lunenburg Schooner, and wont set up the most unholy screeching. ... Even the weather is weeping today, and all the apple blossoms are filled to the brim. The starlings have nested in the holes of the granary walls, and are slowly, year by year, tearing the poor granary to bits. ... Do you remember the train journey back from Itchenor? I shall never forget it. How you sat in the sun and suddenly began to talk, with your eyes wide open in happiness – and I was so happy I could only laugh for joy. I have only one thing against the Lunenburg now, and that is that I will have to let you out of my sight sometimes, if there are only two of us on board to sail her. We will have to go somewhere we can moor for the first year ... I do not understand how I am lucky enough to have you loving me. What can I say? I can only pray that it is not too long for me to bear, although I feel an hour is that right now. I always discover to my surprise that I have got through another day ... I am remembering now how you stood outside W

[HMS Wasp] *and talked to me one night, with your sea boots on and your white sweater, and how your eyes shone out of the dark. I am remembering the sunlight through the curtains in Itchenor, and the blue-bell woods behind Houghham, the sheets of violets and primroses which I shall never see the same way without you. ... God knows it is a good thing you cannot see how many ladies wept for you – it might make your head burst with so much inflation! God! Sometimes I am so afraid I can't think. These letters are written to give me some reassurance, and so they are only self-reassuring. I know if I don't believe in their purpose utterly, believe that you will receive them, or that I shall send them, I shall go crazy. ... But you are my strength, my comfort, my joy, my wisdom, my patience, my life itself. ...*

I am your Jenny

18/05/42

We've just put Dom to bed. He is the best antidote for sorrow I have seen. I wish your mother could have him for a while. I discussed the idea of a proxy marriage with Daddy and Joyce last night, and they seemed to think you might not be so keen on it, and would be just as happy if you knew from my letters I considered myself married to you. ... I am going to spend the last two days of my leave at 26 [his parents home] *and hope I can help your mother, from whom I had the sweetest letter this morning – which made me weep again. Silly! Because I* <u>know</u> *you are safe. My thoughts just go a merry-go-round of past and future with you, and never dare dwell on the actual present for long. ... I love to look at the picture of me lying in the grass with your jacket under my head, and to remember so poignantly the feel and smell of it, and have again the still joy and peace that moment actually had.*

These letters gradually began to show an increased desperation, which was soon almost derangement.

19/05/42

Not without you – I can't bear the beauty of this place. The blossom is lovelier than I have ever seen it – the lawns are a sheet of daisies, (of course *they shouldn't be)! The sun is out today, but there is still a pretty strong 'blow'. You can see for miles, as far as Poole Harbour. There is a light mist over everything, the colours are made very soft by it, the browns and greens, the black – green woods are more muted and made more tender. Joyce and I have been mowing the lawn like mad beasts. It is a sweaty job but a good one, and requires no thought whatsoever, only a blank mind, which is what I am trying to acquire. ... Come back to me, I can't <u>be</u> without you. It is a week now since I heard your voice, and week and a day since I saw you – that Canterbury day!. ... I shall be here for you when you need me.*

Jenny

20/05/42

It really seems that everything is trying to rub it in that you have left me. The morning sun doesn't seem to come out until about nine o'clock and then it burns through the valley mists and shines through the blossom where I lie collapsed on the lawn...Diana (my roommate) rang up today to say that Tony Law had been talking to her and given her great confidence. If ever I lose that I am lost. ... I hope you find the camps bearable...I wish I could come to you as I do in my dreams – they are so vivid – I welcome them but dread going to sleep. ... This is a three day letter – if I wrote as often as I thought of you, it would be a never ending book.

I am your Jenny

21/05/42

My dearest love, I have today planted a lot of onion seeds, caught the baby's cold, and of course, non-stop thought about you. I almost wish at times I could stop – but the idea of living completely without you, even in my thoughts, is too terrible to contemplate. I wish I hadn't slept through all your ordeal. I did not get up till 7.30 on Wednesday morning and you needed me at least four hours before that. Everyone is being so very kind. I have so many consoling letters – but none help to ease this fear, and I must bear that alone. It must be even worse for your Mother, she loved you longer, and you are her son. ...

J

22/05/42

Tony's body [Sub-Lieutenant Tony Lovell, Rick's young 'number one'] *was picked up on Sunday and I had some flowers sent to his mother. I am in an agony of suspense until I hear from you. Poor little kid –* (he was only 20 years old) ... *I am too afraid and upset to write any more until later ... I hope the news of Tony will not upset you too much, I am afraid you may have some foolish notion that you could have done something for him. ... I am taking a big bunch of flowers from the garden to your mother – and hope to stop her collecting honey for my brother Jim! She is the sort of person who gives and gives and saves nothing for herself...I seem enwrapped in your presence tonight, I walk in the radius of your spirit and feel you must be thinking of me to make it seem so close.*

Jenny

23/05/42

I arrived for a late lunch at 26. It's been a hard day. I think I have cheered them up, but succeeded in getting myself into a fearful state of despair. A commander Cunliffe, (presumably an Administrative Officer from Dover Castle), *wrote a terrible letter to your Father which terrified me. Oh God!. ... I have seen photographs of you from eight years old to twenty-five, and heard all the most intimate details of your childhood! How you would have raged if you had seen the regular orgy your mother and I had! Both your parents are sweet to me, but whenever I mention marriage to your Father he seems to close up – maybe he is not quite sure of the girl you have chosen, and he sees that I am not half good enough for you. ... There is an inconsolable ache in my heart which could only be cured by you walking in the door now.*

J

Next day: coming back here to Abbotscliff was the hardest thing I have done in years, you were not there to meet me ... I can't say anything – I see you at every turn. ... I am sleeping with Diana for a while, she has been incredibly good to me ...

25/05/42

I went into D today and saw Geoff [Elton]. He was still the inimitable poker face, but was very kind to me. Do say in your letters sometime if you would prefer me to move from here, as everyone keeps telling me I should. I only stay because I seem nearer to you that way. ... You never leave me for a moment here, and it is very bitter sweet to have you constantly by my side. Last night and today have been rather terrible – I never knew before that one could visualise so exactly – remember each detail of, a person's face – I keep seeing you coming out of the Officers Mess, standing outside Sick Bay tossing a coin, while you held your hat in your hand and spoke to Doc. Walking beside me, and the disgraceful way the Navy went around hand-in-hand or rather hands-in-glove! But I do hope I do not have to move – I seem near to you every time I am hurt by a street corner, the trees on the drive, the grass hill, the road to Mrs Sinclair, W, and of course, every inch of the town and F [Folkestone] too – enough of this. Gamble [Hillary Gamble a more senior RN Officer in W], has been giving me an evening's entertainment and surreptitiously sounding the depths. He has an uncanny way of looking at one at the wrong moment. He will leave here within two weeks – about time – he has had long enough in this job. I am 'au fond' tonight and so in no fit state to write as I should. It is so awful to consciously (almost out loud) love someone who is away, and for all one knows even worse, when in the company of others.

Jenny

26/05/42 0200 hours

As you know this the longest time we have ever been apart, two weeks have now elapsed and I am not sure I can sanely live without you. If I knew you were alive I could plan the future – but I don't even know that. You come between me and the written page of any book I try to read, the words on the sheet of paper I try to write, and you are constantly, vividly, in my head. I could almost beg you to leave me – yet I know that I would hold you back if I felt you going. ...

J

27/05/42

Without you I can never come to anything much. I could perhaps be someone – we could be someone – get from life the truth we believe to exist, live our lives as we believe they should be lived, try to establish even the merest base for a better world after this mess. But I need you – I cannot have a single aspiration, inspiration, without you and your spiritual oneness with me. ... I know now you are not only my hope, but also a necessary hope for the future of the world which we are destroying. ... I have only one faith – in you – and in what you believed and told me of. It is the profoundest agony to be so uncertain of the future. ... The fields by the house were heavy with the scent of cowslips as I came over to 'Solitary' [the RDF tower]. *The French Coast was so clear, I had a feeling that you could look over too and see where I was. ... Do you remember the letter you wrote to me after Japan declared War on the USA? You said that your idea of you and me 'Facing a mad world was romantic and Adam and Eveish'? It is not. We stand together and are lost apart. ... so please take good care of yourself.*

Jenny

29/05/42

My darling, Hillary succeeded yesterday in filling me with such confidence, and is so very sure of your safety, that I feel infinitely better today. ... I had a charming letter from Paul Berthon, it is amazing how much people like you! It makes me terribly happy to have people tell me how much they admire you. I feel that we belong to one another in the eyes of the world and it is a wonderful feeling. Daddy has got to work with the Red Cross by cable to find out your whereabouts. It ought to be quicker that way. ... I do hope your cold did not suffer from your 'immersion', and have been worrying about it a lot... Your Mother and Aunt insist we are very much alike, and in fact, every thing I did and said was greeted with 'just like Eric'. ...

Your Jenny

30/05/42 5am

'Toothie' [the dental surgeon], *took me to a very formal dance last night … I wish I could tell you how much I love having these people label me as yours. Do you remember how I used to kick about that! It just shows you how perverse I am. There are so many places I could be now, but Itchenor would be quite good enough! We should have gone yesterday or this morning. Perhaps it's better this way – because I know I shouldn't have been able to leave you again for this place. I feel sure you had to get rid of your sea boots when you were in the water, and keep wondering if you will manage to get some other foot gear. … By the way I look lovely in the pale blue shirt your mother gave me and will show you when you come home. I was so pleased to see you still have your* Lederhosen! *Darling I feel this may be becoming maudlin (like our first telephone conversation) but look at the hour! I wish I knew for certain that you saw the same skies I see.*

I love you Rick
Jenny

31/05/42

…. The magnitude of the chaos today is terrifying me. I want to take you away somewhere utterly safe, and keep you free from all possible harm. You represent to me not only all that I love – but all that I hold good in the world. … Shall Our Children Live or Die, *(a book by Victor Golanz) I find very satisfying, and not too abstract for my 'feminine intelligence'. Our life together is just beginning now; the fact that we should actually have been together on leave in Itchenor, and the contrast of the present situation doesn't make any difference to that fact. I am unbearably uncertain about you now, but that must pass. You are my future. … I suppose knowing me as you do, you will see that in talking to you this way, I am reassuring myself.*

Goodnight Jenny

On 1 June I went to Canterbury to meet Rose Knight from North Foreland. I took the same journey Rick and I had made three weeks earlier. Canterbury had been badly bombed the night before. There was a lot of damage. As the bus approached the city I could see clouds of grey smoke, and when we were forced to stop, I realised the road was blocked and we could go no further. After climbing over rubble, still warm from the raid, Rose and I managed to meet. She too had been forced to leave her bus and walk to our meeting. On the journey I noticed the things Rick and I had seen together, and I could feel him beside me. But once I arrived at the town centre there was no resemblance to that other day. Canterbury had been ravaged.

1/06/42

It just so happened that today was the only day I could see Rose, so I went on the same journey we took three weeks ago. The boys from my last school [i.e. German planes], *had been there last night and had left a lot of mess behind. Rose (coming from NF) and I managed to make contact with one another. The trip there on the bus was incredible Rick. Every time I saw the things we had noticed together,* The Bell Inn, *the church spire in the beech woods, the Georgian farmhouse, the red colour of the ploughed field, I would turn to you beside me, leaning over me to look out of the window, wincing at the little row of red brick houses – and I would almost say out loud 'Look darling, there they are again'. But once I arrived there was no resemblance to that other day – I can't really say anything tonight…the town depressed and saddened me. … The next time I look at you someone will have to lead me around, because I will never take my eyes off yours.*
Take care of yourself, J

2/06/42

There was nothing new to tell you yesterday. One day simply follows the last in a long suspense of waiting. The weather has become wonderful, fields just yellow with buttercups, and the sun is out until late in the evening. This time last year I first met you and you left D almost immediately. … I must try and see Hilary again before he goes. It is awful not knowing in the morning what has happened to those in CF [Coastal Forces]. *… I know now how blessed I am to have met you – for there will not be enough people like you to go around after this is over, and God knows they will be needed. … I find now that I am unable to think outside of you and what is happening to you.*
My love J

04/06/42

.... Here in 'Solitary' again, I can sit on the stonewall outside the window and gaze through the sunset at the sea and the opposite coast, and try to will these enigmatic waves to tell me what has happened to you. I can read and re-read your letters, wear your scarves, look at your photographs, and make, for a short time, an illusion of your nearness. I can go off into long day dreams of days together, in the sun, the snow, the rain and on the boat. ... Our first sight of new lands together, our first impressions – I feel when I do dream that such certainty and sureness of their coming true, couldn't possibly be unless you were safe. ... But I cannot all the time fight off this black and sudden fear.

Goodnight Jenny

Next day

It's hot today, too hot for me in my thick blue serge. ... Let me know soon how you are, whether there are others in the same place as you and what you need. ... I have written to John [Rick's brother] and hope to God I have not done wrong.

I have been washing down the woodwork in the Watch Room and re-painting it. The weather is sweltering and not a breath of air in the room. ... Your mother and I write to each other continuously, she has been wonderful. ... I wish you and I could have had the first swim of this year together – you never told me you were a good swimmer or a good shot – in fact, you carry your modesty and lack of conceit almost too far. ... Do you remember the night after we returned from Itchenor? By April 25th the weather was really warm and early summer had arrived, you came out to Capel and we met in the little inn The Royal Oak at the top of the hill. Thinking about that evening I tried to write a poem – for your eyes-only. ... How long will it take me to believe I cannot run down the drive to you, go to W and find you standing on the steps, get off the bus and find you waiting?. ... My darling I know that any steadiness and sane balance I have now in my mind, is acquired from you – any clarity of vision, knowledge of what I consider right, all yours.

Goodnight, just below your chin lies my head.

7/06/42

It's very late, or rather early and there is a moon in the sunrise. A star shines quite serene over the Barrage Balloons, untroubled by their ungainly reminder that it is not the time to shine on peace and quietude. ... I shall never forget as long as I live the train journey from Itchenor. It was somehow a sort of hilarious, yet perfect finish to those five days. The train full of khaki, and no room. But I was beside you, and could literally feel your mind working inside my head, my heart beating in your breast. Nothing could touch us that day. I have at last heard from Mummy, she wonders if I shall go to her, but I know that even if it had been possible I should stay here, even if they had assured me you were gone I should have stayed – until I could breathe no more and therefore hope no more.

Jenny

Three months after Rick was lost, our best friend Geoffrey Elton, was wounded in action off Boulogne. It was only a thigh wound, but since he suffered from thrombophlebitis, he died before they could get him back to HMS *Hornet* in Portsmouth. On the morning of 7 June I woke early, despite having been on watch until midnight, and asked Diana to go and fetch the newspaper, which was always delivered to Abbotscliff House. I said 'I think something has happened to Geoff'. When she returned I opened the paper and discovered, for the first time since the war began, that a Coastal Forces action had been reported. The article stated that Lieutenant Geoffrey Elton had died of his wounds after an encounter with German E boats off Boulogne. I had experienced a strange premonition about Geoff before, when I dreamt he and I were alone in the big house, and that a group of Japanese were slowly approaching up the hill. Geoff had turned to me in the dream and said 'Don't worry I have a pistol with three bullets in it. I will save one of them for you'. Two days after this I had a letter from him saying he had dreamt we were in Abbotscliff House together and that the Japanese were attacking it!

8/06/42

*My Darling – Geoff was killed in the early hours of yesterday morning. ...
He was, as you know, back at his old base – not here. No-one else was
killed. ... He loved life. I guess I haven't much to say. I need you an awful
lot. Oh this confounded war. ... But thank God I still have no revengeful
reactions. Because I lose a lover and a best friend, I do not want to take
someone else's away from them. ... Will write again tomorrow.*
Goodnight Rick, Jenny

9/06/42

*I hope I never have to go through days like these again without you beside
me. I have written to Geoff's mother, but what can one say?. ... That it is a
cruel waste of someone young and sane and good. Just 'So sorry'. I wish so
much I could hear you were alright now, it would help. I feel so deeply sad,
it is beyond anything I have imagined. So many people of all countries are
going through just such times. I wish I could be with you to help you when
you hear the news. God! Let me hear from you soon! I wish I could believe
in Him. But where is the 'gentle, just Lord', now?*
My love Jenny.

10/06/42

*.... Your enlarged photos arrived today, they are lovely. I hoped that I
should have heard from you when they came, or of your safety. I do not
believe I can wait much longer for that news. But what a futile thing to say
that is, for what can I do but wait? Life and its trivial daily details goes on,
despite the fact that the earth has ceased to spin, the sun to shine, and night
and day to alternate. ... My family are so amazingly undemonstrative, but
I always know when my father wants to comfort me, because he calls me
'Kid', and therefore shows how I have slipped back to the age when he could
comfort me in more practical ways by hugging me, or shooing the nightmares
out of the room for me. Although I sometimes wish I was once more a child,
I know that is not true, for without having known and loved you (which*

I could only do as a mature person), I would not be complete – mentally, physically or spiritually.

Your Jenny

The following letter really does seem somewhat deranged:

11/06/42

Hillary took me to the Esplanade this evening, I forestalled any queries John, the waiter, would be likely to make by telling him what had happened. Our last meal there was wonderful. Every minute with you has been wonderful. Geoff died at once, and never knew what hit him. ... We also went to the British Lion *and walked through the churchyard. Each step I made was with you. Hillary may have been somewhere along, but you and I went down the four steps and over the paving stones. I have not yet had the courage to go down the Bayle Steps to the bus – for I know I should pause on the twenty-second step, and lift my face on the twenty-seventh with a laugh in my throat and expectancy shining like a star out of every bone of my body. For as long as I can fool myself I can keep going fine. ... Geoff was the only casualty on that 'grand' night, for which Harpie Lloyd [SO MGB flotilla] has received so many congratulations. He was actually on board Geoff's boat. I'll never mention this affair again, but wanted you to have all the details. ... Let me know you are alive soon, so these letters do not take on a nightmarish, hideous mocking quality. ... Do you remember the photo group, Geoff, you, Tony Law, Jimmie McCosh? Well its only Tony now.*

Jenny

12/06/42

It was a calendar month ago and just about this time I was talking to you. Tonight you went out and tomorrow you did not come back. I told them all it wasn't true when they tried to tell me, because I knew you were not on duty. So firmly was my mind convinced of that fact, that I had gone to sleep that night knowing that you wouldn't be going to sea, so I could sleep peacefully. ... I am once more in 'Solitary', everyone is at a dance tonight and I am left in charge. It is about time I was given some sort of responsibility, I have been in this job long enough and I know I am OK at it. ... Although my 'frivolous'" nature may daunt the old dears. ... Diana and I are going to Itchenor next Wednesday. My calendar begins on Wednesday. The sun stopped shining on Wednesday and I started counting days and then weeks. ... When you are sent home I will get my day off and go and spend the night at 26.

My love, my love, J

13/06/42

Today I did nothing at all, I did not even leave this house, I must soon pull my socks up or I shall be lost irreparably. ... I had a letter from each of our mothers today – Mummy's frantic. She feels a lot that she can't be a real help to me. She wants to know if there is a 'little Cornish' on the way. I had to smile! I'd love one, but know that without you it would not be fair. ... I don't want anything important to happen without you there too. It has been a wonderful ten months dearest – two separate minds, souls and bodies have met and become one. I am sure that has been said better. But it is unique because it had happened to us, and is sufficiently rare to be rather breathtaking. ... All this is so sudden it is still hard to believe. I was so happy and complete and then the bubble full of sunlight, love and friendship was burst. ... Your mother loves her enlargement of the photo and wants one of me to match for the other side of the mantelpiece. Look after yourself, and never forget how important, precious, and indeed essential you are to all of us.

Jenny

14/06/42

I am very disgusted with myself today, its awful to realise one can't amuse oneself or keep busy, but sink into a 'slough of despond' without the help of others. ... I should be out walking or something, but I just stay in my room and wish and wish. ... If I have thoughts about those I love to run around inside my head, I am kept happy. But how can I think of you when I don't know where you are or what may have happened. ... I can't think at all so

I behave like a selfish, helpless child. (Yes Sir, I will snap out of it). I shall go for a walk this evening, over the grassy hill, your hand swinging in mine – into the little wood, and we shall discover again the beds of violets, the clumps of primroses. ...

J

15/06/42

The wireless said the Germans were going to announce some prisoner's names in the next few days. I shall listen and hope.

Next day

Tomorrow evening early, Diana and I go to Itchenor. I am a little afraid of it. The little kitchen – the sofa (much too small for us), the funny little bathwater heater. ... The people we met there, are very concerned at the news. ... One almost wishes people would not be so nice, that it is better if the subject is just ignored, but that is not really true. Kindness helps a lot to make one feel a human being in an interested community – not just a star without a sky, or an unattached stone, like the ones in my 'other' nightmares. ...

Jenny

17/06/42 Itchenor

. ... This place is lovely now. ... He has laid carpets upstairs, and made the place look less bare – but for me, of course, it is quite empty. There are yellow roses all over the front of the house and around the bedroom window – they nod in through the window panes. How cold it was when we were here last. It is ideal now. I wish we could have had that week's leave – but then I smile at myself, because I realise we are going to have years and years on end. ... I miss you here worse than anywhere else, because I never saw any other human being in these rooms except you. Diana's presence comes as an ever constant surprise to me. ... I simply can't tell you how wild my joy is when I imagine your return. I wish I could lose myself more often in that dream and not the other nightmares. It's a very beautiful evening. The boats out on the

tidal mud are silhouetted against the sky. I wish you would come in suddenly through the little blue door, and the lamps would be lit, the curtains drawn, and then, sleepy, we would go upstairs and wait for the 'convoys to pass'. ...

Jenny

18/06/42

Back again – I couldn't think why you weren't at the station to meet me, to grin at me over your pipe stem. ... I wasn't very nice to Diana yesterday. We had a slight contretemps – but it was difficult to have her there in your place, and have her telling me what to do in 'my' house! She didn't really, and I didn't mean any of the things I said, and we have, of course, cleared it up. ... Your mother signs her letters, 'just like I signed his'. She is sweet to me and says she has a 'daughter' now. ... The doctor in Itchenor, was very insistent that I should not despair and not give up hope. ... I assured him I would never do that – he does not know what it would mean if I ever had to. ... If only you could hear what my heart is saying all day and all night, but there are no words.

Jenny

19 & 20/06/42

. ... The tin on top of my dresser gets heavier every pay day. Soon I shall open it and send the lot to the bank. I haven't seen anyone from W for over a week, but I believe they are all 'healthy' still. I keep up a habitual interest I suppose, and still worry. I guess it is difficult to stop something I have done for so long. Later: I see in The Times *that no more jerry builders are to be permitted after the war 'no more hideous buildings' – you should be glad to hear that! Also the Bill regarding family allowances has gone through, which seems a definite step in the right direction to me, although I am not qualified to judge. Boarding or private schools are going to be open to everyone not only 'people of means'. Although, what is meant exactly by 'boarding' and 'everyone' is hard to say. I have such pathetic letters from Mrs Elton. Apparently Geoff told her a lot about us both, she wants your picture to put with his as she says you were 'so fond of one another'. ... The strawberries and tomatoes are in,*

and I keep thinking what marvellous picnics you and I could be having. I am longing to go and order you lots of books and have them sent off to you. … I hope I did right in telling John the truth about you.

J

21/06/42

My darling, I had my first swim yesterday, and another today. It was wonderful. They have allowed us to go down the cliff under the house. It's very steep and a long way down but thoroughly worth it. … It will be fun swimming together when all this is over. You must come home and I will show you the pool under the cliffs at Lulworth – it's deep, and very cold, but a brilliant turquoise colour, and right inside the cliff one's laughter hits the roof of the cave and echoes all around as you swim. … How the time drags. It is only six weeks on Tuesday since you 'went out', but feels more like six years. … Why can't time go fast when it is full of sorrow and slowly when every minute is packed with joy!. … I know that essentially we are not parted and this will make no difference to our love, only strengthen it. … But one is seldom high minded enough to live on those thoughts alone. … All these things are difficult to put down on paper, but I know that since we are each with the other mentally, we are really not apart. I must go to bed.

I love you, Jenny

22/06/42

I have been out for a walk opposite for the first time since the 13th. Over the hill and then the stile, by Mrs Sinclair's (a wonderful women who used to give us eggs for tea!). *Then down the lane to the valley, and up the steep hill to the windmill. Do you remember the 'path the cow made?' How I said that was how 'all roads were made', and you told me gravely, (but faintly mocking me with your eyes) that you doubted whether the Romans had relied upon a cow for their roads! Do you remember too, the path to the windmill, how long it took to walk it, and the series of embarrassed cyclists and the policeman we left behind us! The grass is knee-high now, and the smell in the evening is heady. … bees buzzing in all the flowers. …*

J

As can been seen from Rick's letters to me whilst I was in Falmouth, he had a very good relationship with Nigel Pumphrey (his Commanding Officer in MTBs). Nigel had been at Dunkirk and Dieppe. He had also been in command when the MTBs attacked the *Scharnhorst* and *Gneisenau*, and was a Naval officer of some considerable renown. Shortly before Rick's battle on 13 May he left Dover to take command of a destroyer. His exploits were written up in the press. On 23 June I received the following letter from him:

Dear Jenny

It was perfectly horrible of me not to have written – not through laziness or through just not caring, but from the hellish blank feeling of wanting so fearfully to help. You see Jenny I was so very fond of Rick, and though I didn't know you half so well, of you too. Of course, it was miserably cowardly of me not to write, but perhaps you can understand the feeling of complete inadequacy that stopped me. Anyhow, thank goodness you wrote and snapped me out of it.

I haven't managed to get many of the details, so I have no idea what the chances may be of him being a prisoner. One can only hope. Oh Jenny it is a bloody war. I didn't know that you and Rick had decided finally to take the plunge, though I had hoped very much that you would. Oh Lord if things had gone differently, what a lot I would like to say about that, I admired and liked Rick more than almost anyone I ever knew – and that feeling was shared by everyone. Perhaps you would like this letter from Mark Arnold-Forster, not that you need to be told that we all felt alike.

30th May 1942 MTB 219

Dear V6 Sir

I expect you will have heard our heavy news, that Eric is missing with his crew. I can't really tell you all about it through the post, but it was one hell of a night anyway. It was a loss felt very much by the whole flotilla. I think we all had a lot of confidence in him as a leader and as a friend. Still you know what the situation is, and I suppose we can't get away with it always…219 is still being repaired but otherwise all goes well. …

I was most awfully glad to get your letter, and very proud that Rick liked me as much as I liked him. I do wish I could see you – letters are so hopeless. But you know Jenny don't you, that in the limited way that I can, I know what you are going through and even to a tiny extent share it. Goodnight my dear, God bless,

yours,
Nigel.

23/06/42

Darling Rick
I had the most wonderful letter from Nigel today – enclosing part of one from Mark to him. I'll save them for you, and with their help am longing to cure you of your low opinion of yourself! I never believed I'd receive such letters. He is a wonderful man altogether. He's been very 'busy', and was given a write up in the news. An Aberdeen paper called him one of the 'Fighting Pumphreys of Northumberland'. ... I have not seen anyone from W except a fleeting glimpse of Mark...I wish I could get to know Mark well...I like his face so much and should enjoy talking to him. However, I don't have much hope of that since you are not here to help, and Mark probably feels I would intrude on his personal quietude. ... The Warsaw Concerto *is playing in my ear, and it is a terrible thing, for it moves me right low down somewhere. ...*

Jenny

24/06/42

Rick – I suppose the fact that we saw each other, or at least spoke to each other every day has spoilt me, and so I understand my present feeling of despair and misery. ... Enough – but darling I am not going to make these letters merely 'bright epistles to a lonely POW', but more a small honest picture of my each days moods. As you said I believe we owe each other complete honesty, even if we make each other a little sad at times. My sadness for you is also my privilege. ... I can't even write straight, it is now 2300 and I have been up and about since 0315, I fear we may not get any sleep tonight. ... As you know I said I had never needed anyone before in my life, and a year ago I would have been a little truculent and defensive at the idea. Although I believed I was a separate entire individual, I now realise I have become part of a whole – a whole that we make. A paradox if you like! I need you when I am thoughtful, gay, tired, energetic, angry – almost I must have you to be a 'being' at all. ... This can't be a clear letter tonight, I do apologise...if only I could shut my brain off until I was sure of your safety. My imagination is not a welcome gift just now. ...

J

25/06/42

Sweetheart,

Diana and I went into D and met Granny [Paddy Granland] *and Mark in the movies. ... They were both very nice, Mark was particularly charming to me. I believe he has lost his shyness of me, possibly because, as I have lately discovered, he likes you so much and knows that you love me. I only discovered this evening how terribly cut up he is, he could hardly talk to me about it. ... These W people are so much a part of your environment that it always makes me a little sad, although at the same time being with them I am only nervous – (over excited!). It is now six weeks after 'the show' and I am more afraid of the worst being the truth than ever before.*

My love J

26/06/42

.... I can hear the noise I have come to dread more than any other. The boats are going out. If only I was able to do something to help. If only I could have been your Number One, your gunner, or a member of your crew, we wouldn't be apart now. If only the 'me' who is your friend and companion – your soul mate – could have been a boy, but none of those can I separate from the wife or the lover, and unless I am all, and a mother as well, I am not complete for you. ... I am afraid that the strain of waiting, waiting, is making me a bloody, bad tempered bitch. ... I am going home on the 2nd for forty-eight hours only. It is hardly worthwhile for so short a time, but any

moments I can snatch at the farm, the garden, the baby, Don and Joyce, are a relaxation from this place, which nowadays has me completely keyed up.

Jenny

27/06/42

My sweet Rick,
I am on watch at 0330 and will finish this then. The 'bouquets' I am getting about you are coming thick and fast. The latest is Dorian-Smith [Flag Officer Coastal Forces Dover?] 'Cornish was my most promising young officer'. ... Must go to sleep now, will finish later –

On watch: The morning is just coming up over the sea now. I wonder if you can see it too. But perhaps you have mountains or plains to watch the sun rise over. ... I learnt today that I had not got the story of Tony Lovell quite straight. ... There seems to be some talk of a float, the whole makes my throat constrict with terror now ... I can only wish that soon I shall know that these letters are not a mockery, but they are becoming increasingly difficult to believe in.

My all, Jenny

28/06/42

Once more in 'Solitary'. I went for a long walk today with 'Little Jenny'. I looked for all the places we had been to in the woods. They are so overgrown now I could hardly penetrate them. The paths are lost. Where the violets grew, it is now red with wild strawberries. I sat and picked them for a long time and had a conversation with the troll whose particular strawberry patch I was robbing...I am reading some short stories by William Saroyen. He was originally an American refugee I believe and became a citizen. It makes me proud to be an American when I read books like his, Steinbeck's or Fannie Hurst's for instance. They give a very clear view of America's unemployment and poverty problems and present them pitilessly, but also with a sort of tenderness – which I suppose may have come from their having suffered themselves. It is difficult nowadays with no-one to share my thoughts with, and these letters are so inadequate.

My love, Jenny

30/06/42

Darling heart, I couldn't write yesterday, I went to S [Sandwich] *to meet Rose. It was good seeing her – but I am finding it difficult to stir up much interest in anything outside of you. ... I had a letter from Abbi, (a boy who was at Gland with me) I believe I told you something of him. It seems he has landed the job I was trying for last year. If the news of you is bad I shall try and join him* [clandestine operations behind enemy lines]. *But how silly to tell you that, since I wouldn't be writing this if I didn't believe the news was going to be good...I have come out onto the cliff edge – it is late – 10.30 – but I can still see perfectly. It is hard to get used to this light. Clouds, rather like grey veils are flung across the setting sun...I am longing for the time when we can watch the skies from our boat – lie and see the limitless sky above us full of stars, the moon just coming up. When we can do just as we want anytime, anywhere. Not ever be restricted again by watches, duties, certain hours to go in or go out...I also had a letter from John Arbuthnott* [an old friend] *today, he said anyone who could 'inspire your love and admiration must indeed have been a great person'. ... Not true at all. I don't know why I am told by everyone that I have amazing 'courage' and that I am an example to all etc. If by courage they mean I have 'hope' then yes, and again yes – but I am too afraid to believe anything else. ... My senses are paradoxically deadened yet sharpened, i.e. I am capable of perceiving others feelings, pains, sorrows, but at the same time am emotionally at a standstill, waiting. ... Night is falling so I must go in and work.*

I am still and always will be your loving Jenny

1-2/07/42 0045

I collected a folder of yours full of correspondence from W. It was in a desk in the SO's office. W makes me feel quite terrible now, and yet I feel a fatal fascination for it and for the boats. ... You are so close to me every hour of the day – sometimes I feel your two hands, one each side of my face. They soothe away these confounded headaches, which seem to be becoming a chronic complaint. ... Soon for Gods sake! This is not so much a test of patience as of endurance...I long so to comfort you, and in so doing, bring that sense of peace and joy that only you can give me, to myself.

Your, J

03/07/42 The Farm

I wish you could meet Dom now, his table manners are a little distressing – he eats a dirty foot and a slice of bread and jam clasped tightly in the fist, off the same tray. His language consists of two or three words the most arresting being 'Bugga' – he has known how to say pretty or 'purtie' for a long time. On being chucked under the chin by some ''Pongos' the other day, when he leant out of the car window, he clearly enunciated 'purtie buggas', much to the delight of the whole squad. ... We have some bees too, now.

Jenny

05/07/42 ...

Darling, it is two months now. I have been so patient and kept on saying we would hear. ... I hope it won't be an elastic game, two then three then four etc. I do wonder if you can feel my thoughts around you all the time. ... When I was in London I met a girl I used to work with at the Embassy. She said, she couldn't recognise me and asked what 'I'd done'. I could have told her that I had fallen in love, lost the person I loved, and that I was living on a tightrope waiting to hear from or of him. ... I think now that the only things worth having hurt. ... What drivel that sounds, I can't concentrate there are so many people around. ... There are people talking all around me...I will go and see your mother soon, whether your gear has arrived or not. She has made me pairs of socks and God knows what, she sends me cakes and chocolates, in fact I am getting spoiled...I call her 'Mother C' now, she says you'd like it – I can't go on calling her Mrs Cornish, and I can't say mother because I have one of those. God Rick I am so terribly tired! Have been locating the Marlager [German prisoner of war camps for Naval personnel] *on the map and praying tonight.*

Jenny

09/07/42

As I lay waiting to be called at 11pm tonight, I found that in the semi-conscious state I was in, I could never the less think very clearly about you. The tendency sometimes is to remember you in the way other people see you – my fiancé, a Naval Officer, a brave young man. But tonight I heard your daily warm voice on the phone, met you at the bottom of the drive, had supper with you at the Royal Oak, *and I really knew <u>how</u> I missed you – how impossible it was that your boat should have been the one that didn't return. … Perhaps Rick and Jenny were people I dreamed about, and everything that happened to them a fancy of mine. Perhaps I shall awake soon, and find I am still Joan Gill, and quite alone. … I wish Nigel would write to me, I suppose it is too much ask though … I believe we will both come out of this nightmare and find one another. Only remember how I love you and believe.*

Jenny

11/07/42

Rick, I went and saw Doc T about myself, and he and I talked of you – but he is such a sentimental and emotional chap, I can't be altogether natural with him. However, I found out the truth about Tony Lovell. The HSLs [High Speed Launches] *found him and a German, possibly an officer, with the float from 220. It is awful to think they both might have been saved had we found them sooner – it was four days later. Two sailors of opposing sides though they may have been, they were two mother's sons to me. I met Tony Law today, he told me he was going home to Canada for his leave. But he will return. His pictures were all sent over to Canada by the Canadian Government and are on show in Ottawa* (Tony was a recognized marine artist of some repute). *They will go on tour. Do you remember the day you returned from R* [Ramsgate] *all covered in salt in your ancient suit and your sea boots, and I met you quite unexpectedly in D? I will never forget how lovely you looked with your arms full of sweaters and God knows what! I have not had a reply from John yet.*

Jenny

12/07/42

I have been reading Rilke this evening and comparing the original with the English translation and of course, noting how much it loses in translation. But there are some lovely things for us to read together, so many poems, and books too. ... When I am planning things like this, I am perfectly happy – but when I remember that it may all be futile the meaning of hopelessness is understood by me...I do hope we will hear soon, otherwise your warm clothes will not reach you in time for the cold weather. You will be in the northern part if you go to the Marlarger – that I have seen on the maps – the North West. The colours are rather lovely there in the landscapes I remember. Faintly purple in the summer evenings rather than blue, as though the red sun had suffused the blue. ... I think constantly of you and never plan the future unless you are by my side. If you were not alive, surely I could not plan so easily...I don't know where the natural ends and supernatural begins.

Jenny

13/07/42

It is the 13th of another month and still no news good or bad. Diana and I went to see the film How Green Was My Valley. *It wasn't as good as the book but it made me think how I would love a family of boys. All sitting around the table with you at the head, and with, God willing, enough food to feed everyone, good clothes to keep us warm and our own roof over our heads. You to teach them patience, a sense of balance and fairness, not to judge abruptly, if at all – and both of us to tell them where to find beauty and truth – and leave them to it to find their own. ... The day has come to an end again. ... If only this mad cruel folly would come to an end. Human nature in the individual and in the mob, are two separate things, and the one contradicts the other. Sometimes my dreams are so vivid I wake up weeping.*

Jenny

14/07/42

Today nine weeks ago I was talking to you, and saying I had washed my hair and was feeling sick and a lot of other silly things ... I am again in 'Solitary' – I don't mind it because you are here too, but that is not substantial enough for me at all times. ... Must try and get some sleep now, but I wish I could tell you how I feel tonight – just drowsily tell you – because you'd be right beside me.

Jenny

15/07/42

It's funny to have a free day and not use it all, or at least some of it – if only half an hour with you. ... Pagliacci is being sung in my ear by Caruso. Do you remember the evening when the soldier with the lovely voice walked over the hill singing and we listened to him? ... A wonderful thing happened. I had a grand letter from John. He really made me feel I had done the right thing in letting him know the true details. He has put my mind at rest anyway. He is very like you in his inherent goodness of heart and sympathetic perception of other's unhappiness. The ring you gave me has broken, the band of it. ... Thank God it did not break on the side you had written on. Little Jenny is looking at me reproachfully and begging me to go to bed. ... If only I had the initiative to do something real. It will come I know but I feel so feeble now and despise myself for not having terrific faith, faith enough to be unworried. ... I have grown up in the last two months, and am now, for the first time, sure about my beliefs, my strengths and failings. ... I have learnt not to assert myself so pugnaciously, but to let the other guy have a chance to say his bit.

Jenny

16/07/42

Darling the mist is swirling around the house in great waves, and I felt when I woke up this morning something terrific was going to happen. Little Jenny and I went for a walk over the cliffs and got very wet. I am really too restless to write you a letter and also I am getting impatient for a real address – not just your blue writing case to post my letters in. Your mother sent me another parcel today. Apparently your father keeps coming home, his pockets bulging with sweets and wafers for me and she says he's like 'a schoolboy with a present for his girlfriend'! I miss you so abominably it has become a part of me, like an extra limb, a really solid appendage which I am forced to take around with me along with my legs and arms. ... Joanne [our WRNS housekeeper for whom Rick and I had bought a farewell gift in Canterbury], *loves the decanter – and I love the memory of the day we bought it. I wish I could see the palms of your hands – I wish I could put my head on your shoulder again and feel all my sadness ebb away.*

17/07/42

Diana and I had Tony Law over for supper at the Esplanade. Tony told me that one of the wives of your crew had 'heard', but he hastened to say it was only a rumour, and also that news would not come till later. Oh God I am so scared. ... Diana has been most kind and I owe her an unpayable debt. She has withstood all the storms which I forced myself to control elsewhere, therefore they were even worse when they came, having been bottled up for so long. I can't even think straight I am so terrified and excited. I must stop. I am foolish with anticipation. ...

Jenny

18/07/42

I am on night watch again. ... I have not told your parents the rumours. This agony of waiting is made more intense by the knowledge that somebody has heard. I have learnt that the phrase 'I can't bear it' has no meaning at all. For unless you simply become the air, the wind or cease to exist you have to 'bear it'.

Jenny

19/07/42

I am becoming a little afraid that I am unable to think alone anymore, that my brain has ceased to be constructive by itself. I have nothing to talk about – articulate – only my perpetual hurt. … The evening smells so sweetly of hay. They have cut the field opposite. The rain has fallen for the last few days, only this evening did the sun come out again and bring out the scent of the wet sheaves. I know that the spur, the incentive I need to settle down to some sort of work again, is the news of your safety. I am glad, yet afraid, of the clarity of my memories of you. Glad because for a short time it takes me right into some particular moment – afraid because the reality of coming out of it is terrible. … So many meaningless hours are between us, and yet it is only yesterday you said goodbye to me after our day in Canterbury. What is so incomprehensible about this universal suffering – ours only a small part of the whole – though for us an entirety – is that it is man-made. The supernatural does not come into it. We are brother against brother, torturing each other – and here am I, never a patient person under any sort of tyranny, accepting our forced separation!. … There is nothing to say and yet there is a world of words – words I don't know – I haven't found my way to them yet. They belong to us, with the discovery of other lands and all else we will find – together. I never leave you. Remember that.

Jenny

The hay field opposite the house was cut, and afterwards I went for a short walk there. My thoughts were, as so often, on the war and the loss of young people. I wrote a rather immature poem of how I was feeling. In fact, I sent it later to my mother in America, in the hope that it might be published, and perhaps awaken some awareness of what the war was like in Europe. She sent me the refusal from one magazine, in which they explained that the mood of the poem was 'too negative', and at present, the authorities wanted positive, tub-thumping publications.

To Geoffrey and Legion 20/07/42

If these sheaves fresh greenly cut, were but the hay, wild flowers and the
summers yield,
Would I gaze fearfully about this field?
No! at my feet are all our crying dead,
The youth, ideals, the young despair of lovers,
Friends and brothers, all are lying here.
The sweetness in a smile, a rounded head are stiffly stark and grinning
murdered.
No more the warm blood pulses through our arm
along our lovers chair
Or fingers wander in our lovers hair. For they are buried.

21/07/42

Getting busy again. Cobb and his boys went out last night. Maybe you will
be seeing him. They did a wonderful job. God! I wish I was incapable of
fear. Although two of the people are gone that I loved – the one I loved most
of all – I am still afraid when I hear such news. I wish Tony would hurry
and go home, out of it for a while anyway. There are so many things to say
that are unsaid, and it seems must remain that way, for a while at any rate. I
wrote a poem the other night and am sending it to Time and Tide, *of course*
I will get it back.

Jenny

22/07/42

Its ten weeks now. Why we haven't heard I dare not ask. Sometimes I have
moments of utter terror when I look at the sea. I did tonight coming over
here to 'Solitary'. I wonder at myself – how I can go on day after day,
thinking of you as alive and well – I wonder at my audacity. I hate these
flashes of doubt, and the ghastly clear picture of alternatives. I push them
out of my mind. ... Doing nothing is making me fat! I have to talk like this
to stop myself saying the dreadful things that are pounding in my brain –

or the miserable pleas to fate or God which I perpetually and silently offer up. ... They are taking two weeks over mending my ring, but I told them how I missed it, so they are hurrying it up. They asked after you in Simmonds 'Where is he?' Ah where? I don't know how to answer them. I expect my face is a curious mixture of bewilderment, near to tears, and pugnacious belief in your essential safety. ... The stars are still shining through the Itchenor window panes, and I am still waiting and always shall.

Jenny

23/07/42

My darling there is a lovely moon shining on the sea tonight, but I cannot love the sea anymore. It is so pitiless and I am afraid for you when I look at it. My love and my need for your safety seem insignificant before it's vastness. ... The persistent fear of what the news will be if it should come from the Red Cross, sends me cold inside. This will be the strangest summer ever spent. Each glorious month going by uselessly, it might just as well be winter, for each day is but another twenty-four hours of waiting. ... Do you remember writing to me that the essence of our love was spiritual and unaffected by mundane, material things such as time and distance, that you could live on that for a time? I am glad that is true – if we had no spirit in common the situation would be quite impossible, and it would be hard to sustain our love apart.

My all Jenny

24/07/42

Went into D to do a little work for them today as they were shorthanded. I had supper afterward with Daphne Baker. I kept on seeing you in her sitting room, standing there talking to the 'Tiger' [the CO Dover Castle] at that party we went to, and kept remembering how I was racking my brains for an excuse to get you away! I remember thinking too that you were the only person (male) in the room worth looking at. But I may be a little prejudiced. We played Mozart's Symphony in G Minor on her gramophone after supper. It was on one of those evenings when, though the sun is shining in the sky, it is not shining on the trees, houses, or hillsides, but will suddenly pick out smoke from the train or one branch of a tree in the garden. Quite lovely. I think of you so constantly that in the company of others, I am either silent or just thinking of you. I must try and cure myself of that. I love you.

Jenny

27/07/42

I distempered the wash room downstairs yesterday, and nearly wept because it was no easy job – and instead of thanks I got a minor 'bottle' – and anyway I am on the verge of tears most of the time these days and have to be handled with care. … I wish I was treating your face for salt water exposure, and watching you play havoc with your wavy hair with a brush and comb. Hurry back and marry me.

Jenny

28/07/42

There is an enormous orange moon over the water tonight and I am sitting on the roof writing by the light of it. I feel sort of mad and exhalted. What a night this would be for the deck of the Lunenburg. They are going out, making the night throb and crossing the yellow path of the moon. I hope they all come back and wish they could bring you back with them. Barbara and I tried a bit of cliff scaling today. It was fun and we got right down and sat in the coarse cliff grass and were completely cut off. The night air is fresh and lovely. I can smell the thyme and grasses. … I feel my thoughts are much more vivid than ever my words could be tonight. I am with you and there I find my moon, my stars, my sun.

Jenny

That night I wrote and worked on the following poem:

Dover 1942

The air is fresh and cool like every other night,
Gently it lingers in my hair and blows across my eyes.
I can not see the stars, not yet the moon-path on the sea
My eyes, my ears, my every sense are listening to the throbbing drum of
engine noise,
The start of yet another night of gambling.
The dice are loaded and the adversary Death.

29/07/42

I had a bad fright this morning – I got a letter from your mother, and when I opened the envelope I saw it was only one side of a small page, and I was so afraid she was going to give me the worst possible news. I know now what it means to have one's heart 'stand still' – it literally seems to stop beating and ones breath hangs suspended and aghast. Thank God it was nothing. ... My family are moving back to London at the end of the school holidays. Daddy's 'Civilian Technical Corps' Headquarters* are going to be in town in the future. It is a pity for the sake of the baby, but Joyce will be happier I believe.

30/07/42

My darling Rick, the view coming over to 'Solitary' tonight was lovely. The opposite coast clear, with a slice of blue sky over it, and the sky from there until this coast overcast. It made it look like a lantern slide in a darkened room. I am beginning to get used to being alone – to walking about without you. It is not really being used to it, it is shutting out the realisation of the

---

* My father had organised a group of American technicians to come to Britain to help maintain the American engines used in the Coastal Forces and some RAF aircraft. The CTC wore RAF blue uniforms but were not under Military Law, which fact eventually led to some difficulties in discipline. After the war my father was one of the few Americans to be awarded the OBE for his contribution to the War Effort.

facts . I really don't know what I shall become like if this waiting goes on very much longer. A complete tortoise with all my senses drawn inside my shell! You must not worry about us all. We are bearing up fine and will be normal again as soon as we hear the good news. I am rather dreading going to see Mrs Elton tomorrow. I won't be able to write as I shall spend the night in Eastbourne with Esmé and the others in the night watch bed.

Jenny

31/07/42

Yesterday was very sad. I guess it was bound to be. Geoff's mother is a marvellous woman. She has kept her faith in her God and her religion. She loved Geoff more than life, but is able to say 'God must have had a reason for taking him'. I can't find God in all of this, and I am afraid now that you and he are perhaps together. ... This is the heaviest fear I have ever carried in my heart. ... Your Mother gets so worried about me if I don't write every three days, she gets in touch with Joyce to find out if I am alright. I feel she's really adopted me…Geoff did not die as soon as I had hoped, he was conscious and in pain at first. He said 'Are my crew safe?' and 'How's the battle going?' He then became unconscious and died after fifteen minutes. ... He had told his mother what he told me, that you were 'The finest person he had ever met of his age. ... '

Jenny

2/08/42

If someone had said to us when we were so upset about my going to Falmouth for two weeks, that a separation like this was in store for us – I should have simply disbelieved them and said that being without you, at this time particularly, would have been utterly impossible for me to stand – but I am still doing the same things day after day, and still have to start another day when I have finished one. ... Little Jenny has taken over a good three quarters of my chair, so the discomfort and the fact that I am on watch, may make this even more illegible than usual! I am dropping, so really won't go on. I wish I was going back to the 'High, light room with the moon casting shadows on the big bed' – the same room which used to have 'firelight in it in the winter'. Do you remember?

3/08/42

Went to D to find out about this delay with your kit. I know the reason for the hold up now. We won't get your things until your 'fate is known'. ...

Commander Leary was very abrupt with me, until he asked 'Who are you and for whom are you speaking?' I answered 'I am his fiancée'. I then went on to see Doc to ask him to get to the bottom of the rumour that one of your crew's wives had heard . I am working hard on that thing (W/T) which will make me a CPO [Chef Petty Officer]. As you know I never did much before, as I always rushed out to you as soon as I could. But now I have no excuse and must have something to concentrate on...Tony leaves tomorrow so I wished him luck if he gets married. I'll give him something from us both,

Jenny

4/08/42

Well, today it came. A signal about Davis, Jones and Holloway. Davis and Jones are POW's, I am glad for Mrs Davis's sake, she was in D when you went out, as I expect you know. Holloway was washed up and buried in Holland. But darling why haven't we heard of you? I am too afraid and sad to say much. I won't tell your people yet. It's not very good news and, perhaps irrationally, makes one's heart sink. That accounts for four of you. But something must be known of the rest. Please darling – or is it God I am asking for mercy? I am on watch again and must concentrate.

5/08/42

Maybe I shouldn't do this every night, but it is something to hold on to. I simply cannot bear to think that you will not be able to read these letters. ...
Mark and Bill Hay, now in command of Hillary's lot, are going for a rest –

they have, of course, put in for an immediate return. Mark was 'Mentioned in Dispatches' for the same night as you and Tony were. ... I can't ever find anyone else who will love me as you did, but perhaps I was not meant to be so lucky. Our life would have been wonderful. It will be. Nothing is really between us. ... This is quite apart from being in love, it seems to be a mental oneness which does not cease to exist even when we are apart and out of touch. Perhaps there is some place which we can make our 'half way house' and arrange to meet there.

Jenny

7/8/42

I arrived here at the Farm last night, dead tired as Daddy and I had a long journey in the guard's van yesterday. He looks terribly tired and has been working hard. As he will be going back to London at the end of the school holidays he wont be seeing as much of the Farm as before. ... The crowd in D is almost all new to me now, and there are a lot of our Allies, the 'big blondes' [the Norwegians]...you would so love it at the Farm now with both boys and Daddy at home – you could do so many odd jobs together. I can't help thinking of these things. ... I guess I am not as patient as I thought. But this particular news of Davis and Jones, does not help the waiting. ... The bees are doing fine. Joyce has painted the hive yellow and decorated it – and I can only hope.

J

After a few days in Dorset I arrived at the flat in London completely exhausted by a journey with thirty other people in the luggage van. The Salisbury races were the attraction which had induced all these people to 'travel unnecessarily'. It was amusing to see the English break down and talk to one another. The ex-barmaid to the well-to-do draper, the three bookies, (the fattest I had ever seen), squashing my poor Naval suitcase out of all recognition and chatting amicably to a Major and his very high and mighty girlfriend. I and a Chief Petty Officer, were jammed into the guards seat, dissertating on the merits and de-merits of married life, while we took it in turns to share our 'Love seat' with two youths who were factory workers

– and incidentally had the best manners I had ever met. When I arrived at
Waterloo, a rather small boy of fourteen or fifteen tried to act the efficient
porter and procure me a taxi. Maybe by reason of his small stature, or maybe
because, as he said, the other boys bigger and more grasping wouldn't 'wait
their bloody turn', I don't know, but the fact remains that at the end of a
quarter of an hour we had not managed to get a conveyance. So, although
it broke my heart, I told him I would have to take the Tube. Half way to
the Tube he pattered up behind me and told me 'he was going that way',
and would take my case. Grinning at him, I let him have it, as he seemed
pretty desperate for my tip. We shouted happily at one another all across the
station, but when we finally got to the Tube I had the greatest difficulty in
making him take the shilling I had ready. He was apparently doing it all for
love! I had to admit the whole incident helped my flagging spirits.

10/08/42

*It was so desolate coming back here in the train. I couldn't help remembering
how I used to love to sit and think I was coming back to you – but to
remember now that you would not be in Dover! I miss you so intolerably
I cannot help this continual repetition of practically my only thought. Bill
Hay was killed on Friday night just when he and Mark were due to go off
for a rest. It seems all the old crowd are either going down or are missing. ...
John said in a letter to your people that he thought I seemed a 'great girl'
and that he was glad he'd met me. He came out top of his class in everything
including navigation. The trouble with you Cornish boys is that you are too
damn good at – everything!. ... There is a world still to say, but it's only for
your eyes, i.e. not the Censor's. ...*

Jenny

10-11/08/42

*0215 I started this before midnight, but had to destroy it as it got crumpled
in the meleé we have just had. There is absolutely nothing to tell you, except
that I wish sometimes I could stop thinking about you – or at least find some
way of pouring out my incessant thoughts of you. I can't possibly tell anyone
but you what my thoughts are – because you are the only person to whom
they would mean anything. I am tired, and wish that these letters could say*

more of what is in my heart . Its your birthday today, and the only wish I can have for it is your safe return. I will be in 'Solitary' again and had intended going to bed punctually – circumstances permitting. However, it is now 2330 and Diana and I have been debating everything under the sun for the last two hours. For two people of such widely opposite opinions, it is amazing how well we get on together . I am so desperate for news, so longing for a reason for going on and on, I pray we may hear soon.

13/08/42

Rick Darling, I have just rung up poor Mark to ask him if Mrs Davis had answered his letter yet. When he came to the phone in my nervousness I spoke very badly, and when I asked him if he had heard from Mrs Davis today, I put the stress on 'day', and so poor Mark answered 'Oh God is he?' – thinking I had said the word 'dead' – the result was we were both so unnerved and shattered we could not talk properly and I feel a fool for not annunciating clearly. I have imagined telling him the news, good or bad, so often, that I feel a little weak now. I went out to calm down on the cliffs. It is dark earlier now, and there is that peculiar stillness, like the evening when you were kept so late and I was afraid. I felt I was in a truly isolated spot out there, and was almost awed by the stillness. Oh God Rick!

Jenny

15/08/42

Sweetheart, I came on watch intending to start this letter before midnight, but it was not to be. I have been very busy, it's now 0230. ... Granny [Paddy Granlund] *has left, and Mark is SO of your flotilla! He only got his second stripe about a month ago. It is wonderful for him. Your mother sent me a birthday present on your birthday. A blouse made from one of your shirts! It is a very nice blue stripe, your favourite no doubt! Don't worry, we will buy lots more for you together soon. I had tea with Nancy Bush today, poor little kid has certainly taken Tony's* [Lovell] *death hard. I must say it must have been pretty God-awful to have to write up all the reports on the action. ... Bill wrote me a nice letter today. He said I was 'brave and sensible' Wow!*

Jenny. I want you......

15/08/42 2300

I am reading William Shirer's book 'Berlin Diary' very avidly. I wish we had managed to get it before you left us, for I certainly can't send it to you now. [Shirer was an American journalist who remained in Berlin until the US entered the war, as did Fred Oeschner]. *You seem very close today and even almost comforting – maybe I am foolish, but it makes me so confident when it is like that – very feminine, premonitions and instincts. The boys are very busy these days and I am perpetually in a minor state of worry over them. But perhaps it is good that you are not here to worry over. If only that were enough, and if only one could be sure you were alive. … Darling there is an entirety to say in just three words.*

J

16/08/42

It was Diana's birthday today, so Diana, Barbara, Rosemary, Margaret and I all went to the Esplanade and had a good dinner. John (the waiter) has promised that there will still be some champagne left in a month's time to celebrate the good news with. So it must not be longer than that darling! We bumped into some MGB chaps and arranged for a party of ABCs to see the boats sometime and have a drink on board. I have always wanted to do that as they [the WRNS Abbotscliff] *don't have an uproariously gay time here. … I feel sometimes I am being punished for being so sure and accepting of the fact of your love. …*

J

17/08/42

Harvesting is starting opposite, and tomorrow we will get down to some serious stooking. I can't help thinking what fun it would be if you could come, and how nice you would look with your hair all bleached, and an open neck shirt on. How wonderful it would be to be doing some work which did not entail any nervous tension. … I want to pluck up enough courage to write to Nigel again and tell him to read this book of Shirer's. The trouble is it starts ones' mind off again on the old treadmill, and I am beginning to sicken at myself and my perpetual criticism – with no constructive ideas, as to what should be done, which, (however puny my voice), I ought to formulate. Because what is the good of removing one thing if you have no alternative? All my love-and my thoughts God knows.

Jenny
(later)

17/08/42

Just learnt you were avenged last night, tit-for-tat was played in full, and prisoners were taken. I am frantic to find out if I can't ask someone, or ask them myself if they know anything of your affair. Have rung Mark but he is 'out' I am very tense and excited. Must enquire further. Oh God protect you all! Have just phoned Daphne [Third Officer Baker], *and she promises to get questions asked tomorrow and phone me. Am hopeful, but also realise they may know nothing being 'Roberts'* [Raumboote, or minesweepers] *and not 'Edwards'* [E Boats] *They are also from further east, in fact just opposite. However, anything is worth trying.*

18/08/42

Daphne Baker is going to ask a few questions for me. I don't hold out much hope. Some more taken [POWs] *last night. But at the cost of Malcolm Ball – that beautiful boy. Granny has not been gone more than a week. The 'asparagus dining room* [an MTB on which we had an asparagus feast] *has been lost, but they were quite close in, and we have all those who were alive. God! Only Mark left and this goes on and on. Oh Rick it is such a terrible thing to lose all these young people. How futile it sounds in those words! I am so tired of this. Had a sweet letter from Geoff's mother. She prays for your safety and says that my love for you both would be completed it you are alive. ... Darling I am in the depths. It may be I would have died of nervousness now if you were still here. I certainly would suffer even worse agonies when I hear them going out. ... Harvested all afternoon – a dope, like opium.*

Jenny

The following poem does, I think, show a degree of maturer emotions than the previous one about Geoffrey:

Coastal Forces Dover Summer 42

I have not stood spray drenched and looked Him in the eyes,
Nor seen His profile sharp against the stars.
I have not scanned the sea's face long drawn hour on hour
Waiting for a moment by the year,
And sickeningly marvelled at my fear.
Indeed I never felt that surge
Of exultation, crested on the verge of lunacy,
Or grimly watched the floating moon betray us to our enemy,
Nor saw I, threads of blasting fire night-stitching my eternity.
I have not, with my hand-firm friends, laughed in my throat returning
Nor shaken Death's cold fingers off my shoulders in the morning.
But your eyes have been His mirror.
And your shoulders set defiantly bear the imprints of His hand,
They are for me to see there, and for me to understand.

On 19 August the Special Duty WRNS were ordered to Dover Castle to take part in a squad drill – something we were almost never required to do. It was the day of the landing in Dieppe by Canadian Forces and the Royal Marines. According to Anthony Cave-Brown's book *A Bodyguard of Lies* this was a deceptive manoeuvre designed to lead the Germans into believing it was the beginning of an invasion. Standing in the boiling sunshine, we could hear the gunfire and shelling coming from the French coast, while we went through our futile squad drill. Our little Third Officer fell over in a dead faint – I broke ranks and swept her up – carried her across the tarmac muttering 'This is all bloody silly'. Luckily the WRNS were not subject to court martial!

19/08/42

Darling the excitement has been pretty tense all day and the bustle constant. No news yet from Daphne Baker, she is having a baby soon and leaving the service. … Again in 'Solitary' and really feel so utterly depressed about the pace of the 6th, [6th flotilla] disappearances that I can hardly think. Its still so hard, so impossible to believe that we are not close and that you are not within reach, that I can't phone you or jump on a bus and be with you in ten minutes. Soon it will be winter again and how wish I could defy the elements and tramp down the drive in my duffle coat and sea boots to see you! I shall never forget how lovely you looked when we had finished our last lunch at the cottage in Itchenor, and you were in the little kitchen in uniform again, looking happier than ever before, drying a dish or something. I shall go and see your people, news or no news, kit or no kit. Your mother writes that she never stops thinking of 'her three, Eric, Jenny and John'. It is all a bit overpowering for me. I send my heart to your hands.

20/08/42

I went down to W today for the first time in ages. Saw Doc, and he told me young Nick was killed the same night as Malcolm Ball. Mark came and spoke to me, and he is going to ask 'I' [Intelligence] if I can ask some questions. … Doc suggested going to the hospital with me, but it is an awful risk for him. So, if possible I would rather do it officially. All this may seem gibberish, however it is difficult to be clearer. It is a beautiful night, a full moon and a breeze. I did some more harvesting today, but the wind was too strong for successful stooking. I keep laughing when I remember whose harvest I helped bring in 1939, and where [Bavaria]. Mark looked dead on his feet, they have certainly been busier than ever before of late. … My love tonight and all the other nights.

J

Today I took a party from Abbotsfliff on board one of the big Gs [MGBs] for a drink. They had arranged dinner aboard a converted trawler, and I cooked them a lot of Dover Sole. The others had never been on board anything before, and thoroughly enjoyed themselves. No news, from 'I' or, of Mark's enquiries yet. ... But I saw Mark again today...he has had a bad time with the Nicholsons [parents of a lost crew member]. *He is keeping up a 'yammer' at the authorities and will let me know if it gets anywhere. Angela Grandlund will be thanking her lucky starts – Paddy only left thirty hours before everything went sky high. ... I hope to God Paul does not come back here. I wouldn't wish anyone I knew here now. ... What I would give to hear your voice.*

Jenny

Next night

I didn't write last night, being weary and only getting in at 2230. I had spent some time with a young Number One in GBs. He is a year my junior and a Methodist Minister's son. Though fundamentally we are both open minded, he has the advantage over me of knowing and understanding how to reach God. It has of late been so 'hot' that I cannot attempt to describe it to you. It is now an accepted thing among them all in O that it is only a matter of time. I would be so grateful for a real belief when I offer up my prayer of 'Stop this please' every time I hear them go out. Darling I don't deserve to even have you to write to, if I am going to write you this sort of letter!

I need the 'bulwark of your spirit', which is something you once wrote to me in a letter to Falmouth. ...

Jenny

It is a very warm close night, but with a breeze up here. I have spent most of the time, before going on watch, sitting outside on the cliff, gazing at the moon and feeling a little numb and strangely 'afloat' – away from myself and my longing for your safe return – outside of myself and yet able to see myself. Partly due, no doubt, to being very sleepy. I had another swim off W beach this afternoon. I must try and not fall asleep on watch! Whenever I have to do something I don't enjoy, I tell myself, like a child, that if I do it I may hear good news. It was so beautiful tonight I could have wept at the futility of our days and years.

My hearts love Jenny

27/08/42

… Cobb's Number One is a POW. Taylor is his name. I do not know if any others are, as this was only a chance piece of information. The news has come through in five weeks. Why, oh why must we wait four months? Darling, I am terrified tonight, and yet must not let my fear ride me, or I shall be lost. It is like another world to me, the times we were together. To have you every day and always within reach – I am appreciating the help a person you love who knows you spiritually and mentally, can be. How wonderful a thing it was to have you here. Bill and your mother tell me John has 'got his Wings', but seems to be pretty sure of a 'safe' job. I wrote to Nigel the other night on watch, and only trust it was not such a terrible letter, as in the cold light of morning, I seem to remember it being! I am again in 'Solitary'. It is so hot that I do not know how I shall last the night here. … There could never be another person so good to me as you were, and for four months I have written to you everyday – belief in your being alive my only incentive for the daily trudge and round…I long for you in so many different ways for so many reasons.

Jenny

28/08/42

My God it has been hot! I am no good in this weather unless I am up to my neck in the sea, which is exactly where I have continued to be in all my free time. I had an evening swim at W today, and it was the loveliest I had had, the water cool and deep and green and no-one else was swimming. I do so wish I understood about Taylor's news coming through so quickly, and yours taking all these desolate months. ... The SB [Submarine Basin] where I was this evening for a quarter of an hour, to talk to them about Taylor, was lovely in the evening light. The sun was going down behind the castle, and the water reflected every cloud. Then, I wished as always when I see something beautiful, that I could know that you were alive, and that we should be seeing these things together some day. This is a long waiting, but I will never grow too weary.

Jenny

29/08/42

I went swimming at W at 0600, having taken Diana to the station to go on her leave. The house (W) was still, and all in it were sleeping. I crept out of Big Sam [the evacuation van] in my corduroy trousers and my uniform jacket. My footsteps sounded terribly loud on the shingle, and then I was in and oh it was wonderful! The high dome of the sky empty of aerial activity and deep quiet all around. I wished so very much that we could have been able to do that a few mornings, just for us to remember later. But I know that we will have countless memories of such things.

Jenny

31/08/42

I read in The Times *a warning little paragraph saying that is inadvisable to write more than twice a week on both sides of a page. ... I stood in the Market Square this evening waiting for a bus and kept remembering how crisp the air was in October and November. ... I told Mark that we would have been married, and also apologised for being a constant reminder of something he would probably rather forget. But he misunderstood me and was very moved and said 'Jenny we will never forget, we don't forget'. He's a great person.*

Jenny

1/09/42

It seems funny now not to write every day. But I am afraid I will have to keep back some I have already written, and show them to you as a sort of diary when you come home. ... Four months – and this time last year we were on our way back to Dover. The sight of your handwriting again will be the loveliest sight God could grant – and when I see you standing again relaxed, with your hands in your pockets watching something, as you used to watch your crew having a job done, then I shall I see the colours in the sky again and feel the joy in life around me...I seem to have dried up verbally and these letters are no longer easy to write – they are terrifying...I shall never forgive the two old ladies I overheard in the Esplanade saying 'They all marry too young these days – I suppose she will get a pension if he is killed'. Exactly thirty-eight hours before you were lost. Unbelievable fact.

Jenny

On 5 September Nigel Pumphrey answered my letter of 27 August, and added his voice to those people trying to persuade me to leave Dover. I wrote Rick as much of the letter as I could, from the security point of view:

5 September, extracts from N.P's letter:

... People aren't able to take more than a certain amount and you must surely have had your share – yes, I know the Coastal Forces boys don't get a change but they are actually <u>doing it</u> – and anyone who doesn't know the difference between doing and listening to it being done, is fit for an asylum. ... Yes the war is lunatic, crazy and sickening. But it is in the past that the real craziness lies. I think now more than ever that this war has to be gone on with – and at whatever cost. Not that I can see a very Brave New World at the other end – but because of the yet more sickening chaos that is the alternative. Sometimes I even do have visions of a New World that may not be too bad. I will tell you about it.

  I was at Dieppe (which must have been a nightmare on the beaches, but was a picnic for us destroyers, as compared to an ordinary MTB night) – and as I have since left HMS Brocklesby, *and am to build a new destroyer* *on the Clyde – I have been seized on by the Admiralty to do series of lectures to Tyneside ship workers on the war in general and Dieppe in particular, related to their work. Well, it is a hellish job – I haven't got the public speaking temperament, and there is a feeling, hideous and Judas like, that I am focusing on myself the glory of the Coastal Forces boys, and of the people who stormed the beaches. Sometimes it makes me feel quite <u>ill</u>. But it has a good side. I am seeing the working-man en-masse for the first time – I hadn't imagined my ignorance before. When I look at the rows of serious, hard, attractive faces, I realise at last, what superlative stuff we have got in this country we have the stuff, I am sure of it, to build up something fair and decent and enduring. But meanwhile the people who realised this such years before I did – people like your Rick – are being killed, and who knows how and in what form the directing power is to come.*

It is no use talking to you about Rick, Jenny. I don't know and can't know, what the chances are, and for unreasoned optimism I know you have no use. I am only glad you are brave enough to go on hoping and join you from the bottom of my heart.

Goodnight Jenny, God bless Nigel

5/09/42

... So I had let three days pass without writing to you. Partly because of my new decision to only write two letters a week, and partly because of a sense of desolation that I have been unable to shake off. I had hoped, so foolishly, that we should have news on the morning of the 2nd exactly four months in weeks from your being lost. Your Father had written to me that a man he knew had heard after four months. ... I had a wonderful letter from Nigel today. He is giving a series of lectures in the ship yards, while waiting for a new 'baby' and he is quite worked up about it – one because he feels a 'Judas' taking your Coastal Forces glories as his in public, and two that he has found the hope and strength of England in these men. ... Nigel is also, to my mind, one of the 'nation's strengths'. I am in 'Solitary'. ... I need you a lot, but knowing that you were there at all, would be enough for a while until you come..

Jenny

7/09/42

Sweetheart, I am tired nowadays. I guess I will be grateful for my leave which I am getting on the 14th. I heard from your family today. John has got his Wings, his commission, and most importantly, a job as a navigation instructor. Which although it will be away from home [he went to the US] *at least it keeps him out of a fighter plane. I am so glad for your mother ... I keep wondering how I could have wasted even a minute of our times together, and the fact that I was even a quarter of an hour late in meeting you seems incredible. ... After a spell of quiet I heard the familiar engines 'bumbling' tonight. I can only pray. ... There seems so many things we could have done now and didn't, and so many things that weren't possible then and are now, its cruel – but I know that if you are alive I am one of the lucky ones.*

Jenny

Later

The long white fingers of the mist are gradually closing in on me here in 'Solitary' tonight. I think it will be pretty thick before morning. It is a very eerie sight, fog at night, lying low on the ground in thick coils, before it spreads out into a general mist over everything. I am afraid it may be a busy night for Mark. I can but keep my fingers crossed. ... I am continuously brought up short by most vivid glimpses of you. I see you, and sometimes you and me together, perhaps only doing trivial things. I can remember the particular moment so poignantly that it hurts. My ink has run out, so I will stop for tonight.

Jenny

11/09/42

Darling, I am going to see the family at 26 on the last day of my leave, I do wish we could have news by then. Oh the eternal wishing, and God knows, eternal fear! There is so much I have to say to you which has been piling up in all these weeks and months and yet I cannot write it. Thoughts, which pass through my mind during the day and night. It is amazing how

close we are mentally, how I was in your mind and you in mine, so that in the end little talk was necessary. I am afraid of time – its merciless, never stopping, flow – and what it can do to both of us. And yet I feel that what we have is stronger than time, and will endure, unchanging, anything that the years may have in store for us. ... When I think of what you must be going through now, I feel small and ashamed at my grumblings. It occurred to me today, that the reason your people are so marvellously brave, and the reason I can take it all, is because you are such a brave person. Your strength and quietude seems to be in us. If I lost this feeling of your nearness I should know you were not alive, but that is all I have to go by, to believe in. and it is what keeps me hoping all the time. ... My letters to you are lousy now. I can't write them anymore. I am afraid – Forgive me.
Jenny

Weymouth [The Torpedo Base] 12/09/42

My Darling, I came to Weymouth on the first night of my leave, since Daddy was driving over and it seemed too good a chance to miss. It is strange seeing so many of the old faces again. I was so miserable in this huge hotel, when I sat alone at breakfast and watched them all. Dick Richards and Dreyer came down with their young wives and had breakfast before 'going out', and although I know perfectly well its no ideal life going from hotel to hotel, I would willingly have given my soul to be having breakfast with my husband. ... Mrs Davis wrote to me, she had heard from her husband, who 'harbours great admiration for his officer who handled the boat wonderfully'. All Davis knows, is that he, with Jones and Barrett (both wounded), were ordered to abandon ship by you and took to a raft. They were rescued after four and half hours by a German E. Boat. Barrett may still be in hospital or perhaps dead, and Jones cant be in the same camp as Davies, as he seems to believe he is the only 220 prisoner there. It does, perhaps give one hope, that, as you could give the order to abandon ship, you were not wounded? Joyce was very upset at my going to Weymouth now instead of later in the week, as she had prepared a 'royal feast' for last night. How I, and Daddy, hate depressing Joyce. Particularly these days. The whole bloody set up is getting her down so. ... I find the only defence I have against utterly succumbing to missing you, is lots of people around me, who natter at me and therefore keep my mind perpetually on the jump in order to answer them.

My visit to Weymouth and seeing Barry did me good, he has taken Gamble's orders seriously when he was told that I was to be his 'good deed' of the war! I feel mentally alive and stimulated for the first time since you've gone. It's been like a long fearful sub-consciousness. My heart is still numb, and will be, but I'm not dead mentally.

I have done very little except pick apples, dig a few potatoes and watch Dom, who is walking now, running around creating incredible chaos. I have also considerably over eaten. Joyce cooks immense meals and then apologises for having 'nothing in the house'. Mick and Jim are working as full time farm labourers. Up at six am and receiving sixpence an hour! They will have earned over two pounds each this holidays which I consider pretty good! I dread leaving on Sunday, although I am spending the night at 26. It is nearly five months now, but since Mrs Davis's letter I have given up speculating on what may have happened. Mercifully the full realisation of the truth is kept in the background of my mind by constant activity. But now and then it does come over me in a surge of unbelieving misery. Walt Disney has got a hold of the 'Gremlins', he is making a film about them and the proceeds are going to the RAF! Now, if Gremlins are not about the Coastal Forces, then I would like to know what are. I am annoyed! .... Edward Hallett Carr's new book apparently modifies his 'Twenty Years Crisis' and analyses the moral as well as the economical questions. It is called Conditions of Peace *and I would like to try and send it through to you. Perhaps you would receive it – I need you to bolster up my poor flagging intellect, and give courage to my heart. I need you to make me a just, saner judge, a calmer, truer speaker, and a slower, better thinker – to put worth into my thoughts, and words and joy into my blood again. ... I must go up to bed with little Dom snortling away opposite me – he has another cold. He calls me Jeya, the nearest he can get to Jenny. I had a good letter from John today. I'll send him all the odd scraps of news I get – nothing really – but one grasps at any straw.*

Ever Jenny

20/09/42

Sweetheart, I am again sitting up in OAL's bed [Rick's 'Old Aunt Lizzy'] *and re-living that happy night before Itchenor. Your people are very good to me, and your mother would spoil me un-mercifully if ever she got the chance! I would to God there was some news. They are so patient, but you can tell the strain is getting harder to bear. Bill particularly, seems all pegged out. I guess he takes it harder as he can't get comfort from small things, like me and my paltry cheer, the way your mother can. The nearer I get to you, to your days before you met me, through your family, from your exercise books, the book shelf, the snapshots I see, and the stories I hear, the more sure I get, if possible about us Eric – Rick. Your mother keeps on asking me 'Do you think' this or that, oh God what can I say? It seems to me in the light of events, foolish to surmise and yet it is so difficult to answer her that. You are far too close and real to me for anything terrible to be true. I cannot believe you are not alive. … I wish and wish and can imagine no greater joy than the first news of you. Your mother and I just look at each other and laugh when we mention that. Laugh in anticipating joy.*

J

23/09/42 on watch

Rick, it is very cold and winter seems so suddenly have come upon us. The same crisp air and the same autumn smells as last year. It was not so hard all summer, for we had not really known the summer together – except in dreams! But now, the cold makes me remember things, like the warmth inside your great-coat, the night we battled up to the **Royal Oak** *and you gave me a Whisky Mac' for the first time in my life. The way we used to meet wrapped up to the ears in your school scarves and how cold your hands used to get because you wouldn't wear gloves. … Mark tells me they* [the German prisoners] *know nothing. I am depressed. I find that a particularly silly phrase in the light of my perpetual mental state! With a lot of luck I might get a chance to visit my mother for a month, and have a rest, by doing a job on the side* [a few WRNS worked in Signals on board Atlantic liners being used as troop ships], *but I can't believe it yet or even it's possibility. … If only I could tell you of the ache and need of news.*

Jenny

26/09/42

When they called me at 2300 to come on watch, I was never so loath to come up here. I had been lying in the dark, and, for the first time since the 13th, I could picture you absolutely clearly. I lay remembering every line and expression of your face, and drifted off into a lovely haze of memory which it was hell to have broken off. There is terrific thunderstorm on, which as you can imagine does not make life any easier [interference]. *It is quite clear to me now, that, as you once told me long ago, although one may marry and perhaps love someone else, there is only one perfect relationship. One great one in one's life. Some never know of its existence, some meet it too late, and some have it and lose it (God forbid). … This is so foolish I hardly dare say it, but I feel this impression of your nearness (not spiritually but actually) these last three days must be due to more than the September weather and the wishful longing of my heart. Either you are writing, or your letter or news is near, or you are! All of them are too good to be true, but are, all the same very powerful sensations. Must concentrate – and not on you.*

J

27/09/42

I have the strangest and yet wonderful ability to see you clearly again, which I have not had since you were lost. A cloud came between me and your face. I have noticed this before, with my mother. It is absolute torture trying to remember a loved face and not being able to. There must be some explanation for it. Also, I find I am once more able to think, and have constructive thoughts of my own again. I had not realised, before this awful mental lethargy fell on me in May, just how dependent I was on you. Apart from anything else I could not have a single thought without you as its driving force. I am sleepy, and in 'Solitary', I love you darling and wish I had you here to make you believe it.

Jenny

1/10/42

Another month begun, and five months without you, or news of you, ended. Your mother wrote me a very brave letter today. She is beginning to feel like me, that you may turn up any day. No news, just you. I rather dreaded her feeling that, as I know how slim the chances are. It is October, and this time last year we were really well away! I believe we had even staged our scene on the front, when I had a minor brain storm and you resorted to shaking me and telling me to shut up!. ... Jim George is going home on leave and taking Mummy's Christmas present with him, as no parcels are allowed to the States now. I wish I knew you had sufficient clothes and food. ... What a day it is going to be! Your mother says she feels the tension of waiting will snap like a thread and she will break down – that is, of course, the danger of her wonderful control – the ultimate and terrific joyful relief. God keep you and let you know every minute of the day and night how I love you.

J

4/10/42

Later

...I have just finished a book about Jamaica. Tantalising in that I want to go there soon, and see for ourselves – with the boat. I must live an awful lot in my dreams these days, and as you once said to me, that is sufficient for a time. ... I would give all earth and heaven to be able to find comfort with you. To know that my dreams are not meaningless and futile.

Jenny

5/10/42

The first and foremost purpose for my writing is always to try and communicate to you how much I love you. It is of course impossible to describe the way I feel. I expect you are feeling the same, and so can appreciate that. Jim George, [a Canadian in C.F.] has told me some extraordinary things about 'that' night, which even the W boys don't know. Suffice it to say the Chief

*of Staff said he would write a report that would get you the VC, and took
24 hours to do so. You have only to produce yourself to get a 'gong' [medal],
but nothing can be done whilst you are still 'Missing' – what a word and
how it haunts me. Rick, I always told you that you were brave, braver if
you were afraid. J*

7/10/42

*Yesterday, I went beyond Ashford – quite a trip-to have dinner with
the Chester Beattys, friends of Daddy's* [an American- Irish copper
millionaire who donated Egyptian papyrus' to the British Museum
among other things, and was later Knighted]. *It was terribly kind of
them to ask me. I had a grand meal savoured with an extremely stimulating
conversation. I could not stop wishing all the time that you were there. Often
I would stop talking and leave a space where you voice should have been. It
was so very easy to imagine how you and 'Chet' would have discussed the
present problems. I needed to sit there and listen to you both and longed to do
so. On the train journey back I longed for you too. To have you with me on
such occasions, and to be able to talk over the evening with you afterwards,
is my idea of heaven these days. ... Your mother said in a recent letter, that
the important thing, once we knew your address, was to put your mind at rest
as far as we were concerned. It made me feel a little guilty that my letters
are a long moan.*

*My heart's love
Jenny*

13/10/42

*Only it is Tuesday and not Wednesday 13th. Today I have been aboard for
the first time since I was aboard your boat. Brian McGinty who has Mark's
old boat, showed our 3rd Officer Walker all around on a 'Cooks tour', which
I had promised I would arrange for her ages ago. This evening I was asked
to attend a farewell party given by a pal of Jim George's. I went, and the
remains of the old flotilla chaperoned me. Dick Saunders, McGinty and
Mark invited me to dinner at the 'Crypt' and were generally so good and*

kind to me that I was hard put to it not to weep. ... I am afraid now-and have not even been able to write these letters of late. ... So small and frail a thing is my faith at times. But my love is strong. What good are words.

Jenny

18/10/42

... I feel I haven't written for at least a year to you. I am so very afraid. Had a parcel from 26 yesterday and a sweet letter from your mother. She thinks we will 'hear this month. God! I don't think anything anymore, but know I cannot begin to live without some sort of surmising – some hope. I had a rather grim boarding school reunion in town and didn't get back until yesterday. ... I hate putting my feelings on public view now. They become diminished some how. ...

I am anxious about all these reprisals on prisoners which are going on and try not to think anything too awful...I go about thinking of our life together, I am terrified that I have had my only life with you, and lost it. Jim George went to the 'Big House' [The Admiralty] *when we were in London and made more enquiries into it all. I hope this brings some results. What I would give to awake from this nightmare and meet you at 2 o'clock in the Market Square.*

My love J

20/10/42

So sharp is my actual conjuring up of you wherever I go, that is has become hard to bear. Today I saw you and Geoff in F, walking along side by side. Your long, rather stooped, yet graceful walk, your old suit, Geoff with his stick. ... There was a long article on CF today in the papers, and they are slowly realising your worth – they called Nigel (who got a bar to his DSO), 'Won't go home Pumphrey'. It is a pity that the public have to have things juveniled-up for them. God! I miss you. ... It's funny after all your doubts about me and your parents I have become so fond of them quite without you. Or perhaps it is true that I have, since you have gone, grown if possible even closer to you and that this is indeed the 'firing' of my love. I have a good book called Faith in Living *by Lewis Mumford. You may have read his* Culture in Cities *– but I can't have it sent to you I am afraid. I send my heart for you to hold in your hands.*

J

23/10/42

I went up to town yesterday and saw Rose. She has suddenly got herself engaged and is to be married right away. He is a Major in the RA. I hope they will be happy, but Rose knows what she is about and wouldn't marry unless she was as sure as she could be. I have never forgotten how you told me one could never be sure of marriage – but I know that I am as sure as it is humanly possible to be. I would give my eyes to be your wife now. ... I spoke to the First Lieutenant W all the way back down to D in the train. He is a much nicer and deeper man than I had imagined. He also has belief in your returning, and it makes me feel happier for at least a couple of hours to talk to people who knew you. Daddy, Joyce and I went to see a film acted in and directed by Noel Coward. It is the story of HMS Kelly *and is called* In Which We Serve. *It is one of the most magnificent films I have ever seen! Coward has put his finger on what I can only describe as the Navy atmosphere. Even the Navy is enthusiastic about it, which is a pretty good recommendation. I was really upset, but also incredibly uplifted. I can't concentrate, there is slight bedlam going on here. I can only think of each and every day we met and how I was surrounded by your love, and so safe, and wish I had married you – but I don't suppose it would be any different now if I had. I love you Rick, that is all that is important and as you once said 'What is true but that I love you'. If only I could give your mother something concrete to hang on to. I pray for a little of your courage.*

Jenny

27/10/42

Rick, yesterday was Monday and my free day. Today is Tuesday and my afternoon watch, and tomorrow morning I will go up to the Watch Room and go on watch, and it will be exactly six months to the day and the same watch! It is an uncanny feeling to realise you spoke to me then, and tonight is the fearful night. ... I wish I could write to you as often as I want and not have to ration myself. The trouble is that tonight, as last night, and all day I want to write to you the way I did when you were here. But how can I? A love letter could not tell you anymore how much I love you than these stilted letters do. I had a terrible dream the night before last. You were somehow miraculously back, and you came to a dance where I was acting as a hostess to a lot of Tommies. You would not look at me and wouldn't believe I loved you. You drove away with Commander Eakin, and I ran after you begging you to stop and listen to me. I flung myself at the back of the car you were driving but you wouldn't stop and I fell on the ground. You looked back and just left me there, and I prayed to die. I awoke in floods of tears saying 'oh terrible, terrible'! [This dream seems to be a throwback to my early childhood, when I was so unhappy in my first boarding school and I ran after my parents car when they left, begging them not to leave me there] *...I am so afraid Rick, this cannot be true! I feel like a bewildered animal and could literally swing my head from side to side seeking a way out of my pain. Doc was in tears the other day when we spoke of you – he is so soft he embarrasses me, yet I know he is a fine fellow.*

My love Jenny

28/10/42 0200

Darling, tomorrow Rose gets married. It is difficult to realise that in this period of six months of my inactive waiting, when I was almost unaware of the changing seasons, she should have met, fallen in love with and married her Desmond. It makes one see that time only has meaning in its relation to individual people. I am to be her Maid of Honour. God knows what that entails, except holding her bouquet at the proper moment, spending a lot of money on flowers to wear, and having quite a time avoiding people's cameras in my shabby old black coat. I am on night watch, so I shall look like the wrath of God anyway! I have little patience now with this sanctifying of the marriage act, but go because I am so very fond of Rose ... I have spent the last three hours reading some of your letters. It hurts me to remember that there were only two of them after Itchenor and one a very sad one. I keep it to remind me of the fact that something I did aroused such miseries of jealousy and heart searching on your part. In fact, when I imagine that these, my letters, may not be sent or read, I indulge in a perfect orgy of repentance for not having made every moment of our time together idyllic. The last phone call haunts me too. I hope you took me 'to sea with you' that night as usual, despite it. Because otherwise, I may not be with you now. I was almost afraid this morning that if the IC [Intelligence Centre] *phone had rung at about 12.30 I would fall over in a dead faint or something. As it was a telegram from Rose stopped my heart.*

29/10/42

My dearest love, back again from Rose's wedding and in 'Solitary'. I am a little tired after night watch, not sleeping, and the strain of being a so called 'Maid of Honour' at such an affair in the Brompton Oratory! I don't know what it is like when Catholics get married, but Rose is C of E and the service took eight minutes exactly. It was gabbled at them, and they were married! Why should it now be sanctified in the public eye that Rose and Desmond can live together because of eight minutes of unintelligible gabble having been said over them? I remember how you once said in a letter, that you and I were married when we told each other we loved each other – just as simple as that. And that can be even without living with each other. We may be apart – even further apart than I can cross in my life (God forbid), and yet I know that we belong, and that there will never be such hope of perfection for me if you do not return and live your life with me. ... It is an awful strain to have people perpetually asking me when I am going to get married. I miss you so, but hope and pray you don't miss all of us too unbearably. I want you to know that the knowledge of your safety will make it all quite different, and I promise not to moan anymore.

J

1/11/42

... Another month has begun. It will soon be Christmas and I remember what fun it was to buy your present. I shall get you something this year too, and all

the time we are apart and save them up for you! I go to Eastbourne the day after tomorrow and stay the night with Geoff's mother. It wont be easy. I cant tell you how much I admire her faith and courage, and I suppose, envy it. Mick and Jim have their birthdays soon and Micky will be fifteen. The war only has to go on for another three years for us to see them in uniform. I have been for a walk along the road we took years – minutes- ago. It is rather lovely now, all the autumn colours are at their best. One-day darling I want to show you the American fall. It is the most gorgeous sight. I want to show you the long red-roofed barns and the white clap-board farmhouses, with maple trees and lawns right down to the red dirt road.

Jenny

In November 1942 the Cornishes were informed by the British Red Cross that the Admiralty had informed them that 'Lieutenant EAE Cornish was missing presumed dead'. I, and Rick's parents and brother, continued to believe in the possibility that he had survived for a very long time to come.

6/11/42

A letter from your mother today. The Admiralty have sent an official 'Missing presumed dead' notification, and the King and Queen have sent 'regrets'. Of course, I wish they could have been spared that. Although it changes nothing, it is bound to make them feel there is less hope. I am afraid. My faith in your being alive is being expressed, in the only way I have, by this letter. Somehow my love I cannot believe you are not alive. I cannot see any future without you. I am going to '26' next Sunday. I expect your things will be there by then, and perhaps I will be a small comfort and help to your mother. Typically of her, she withheld the news for five days and then sent it in the middle of a letter in a parcel of food. She really is wonderfully brave. If there is any mercy, God will certainly send you back to her.

Jenny

12/11/42

For six days I have walked around in this nightmare of condolence letters your parents have received from various organisations. I have wondered how I can help them this weekend. I have felt such sick fear, alternatively with a determined hope. ... I find it impossible to imagine myself not always beside you – your brain my support in doubt, your hands my healing in weakness, your presence my very life's breath. ... Daddy wrote and said, so typically 'I can't help feeling that there is still a chance that the nice friendly lad who dug with me in the farm garden is alive somewhere'. I feel as though I am carrying a heavy weight around with me – it has grown heavier as each month has passed. Only you or news of you can lift it. I came pretty close to being killed last night, but in the flash of the explosion I saw your face, and knew that if I could be spared then you must be alive.

J

[While waiting at the bus stop in Folkestone Harbour a shell had landed in the street. The glass from the plate glass window behind me stood up in my hair like some kind of fantastic tiara.]

13/11/42 7am

Darling this has been stewing ever since I came back from Mrs Elton's on the 2nd, but I don't seem to have had a chance to write about it until this last hour of the night watch. It was inevitably a very heart-breaking visit. She keeps on insisting that she and I must both pray for your safe return. Did you know that Geoff joined the Coastal Forces, fully aware that the slightest wound would kill him unless he was with a doctor and could get instant help? The blood clot in his leg had never dispersed since his phlebitis. But they didn't notice it when he had his medical so he got in. ... With any luck I shall get Christmas leave this year. Do you remember Christmas night last year, how you and Nigel put the world to rights over my poor head in W? I remember how you all looked in your white sweaters ready to go out. I can hardly believe all those things happened to me now. ... I am afraid that if I said anything about what I have felt these last few days, you would get an even poorer letter.

I love you J

14/11/42 0600 hours

… Doc has appointed himself my flaming sword or something – your champion – the other day on his way out to Abbotscliff he admitted he needed a wife and asked me who I could suggest out here. … Why am I talking about other people when it is you I never stop thinking about? The latest news worries me in that I have had wild dreams of you being on your way home – but the latest new 'developments' would check any such activities – or at least hamper them. Apart from that it seems as though, down a long vista we can really see hopes of peace. I go to your people tomorrow for forty-eight hours. I hope and pray I can be of some use to your mother and father. She wrote me such a sweet letter, and said my 'brave letter' made her feel a coward for having given in. God! Since Daddy has sent me the letters he has received from the Red Cross, with references to our 'Great loss' I don't wonder she was bowled over. I am not brave – I am perhaps stupid, or stubborn, for, despite my cold fear, I will not believe that you are not alive. It is sometimes an unbelievable thing to remember how you would stand on the dockside looking down, hands in your pockets, pipe in your mouth, and how your head would lift when I came near and you would smile at me. …

15/11/42

Here I am at '26' for my forty-eight hours, and your family are as good as ever to me. Bill has lost his original shyness of me and we can talk very easily now. He is amazingly fair and balanced, as you are. I believe I really do give your mother hope and strength, and if that is true it is all I ask – apart from your return. … It seems to me there is simply no life without you, that is why I am sure you are alive. You would have some way of telling us if it were otherwise. … I want above all thing to be your wife, and hope we don't have to wait too long, because I want us to be young when we have to amuse the 'Empire Builders'!

J

17/11/42

Have just written my part of a joint Air-graph to John. The more I learn about 'Eric' the more in love I fall. They have spoilt me beyond belief, even to a pound note with my morning bread and butter, which no amount of protesting could alter or deter! Bill and I went on a long walk and he told me he had gone to see a clairvoyant who promised they would try and 'reach Rick', so as to put his mind at rest as to whether he was alive or not. I was rather dismayed at the news, and told him that I believed most of these people – who are very active at present – were charlatans.

22/11/42

Darling, I am in 'Solitary', it is hard to have to wait a few days in between writing to you. I wish that all my thoughts, day and night, could go down on paper for you to read. I met Tony Law and Mark yesterday. Tony has just got back – a married man now. He looks very happy and his face has lost its nervous tenseness. It is always a shock to see these familiar faces, there are so very few now. I am beset with you tonight. Such vivid memories, the sound of your voice, the way you stood, the eager lines of your face when you were interested in what you were discussing with someone. ... It is easier to live day by day in my own surety of your safety – hard to drop into the true facts and still be sure.

J

Later, 0230 hours

Today after night watch I go up to town to celebrate Thanksgiving Day with Daddy. ... You said in one of your letters to me last year, that you thought perhaps you could bring me 'patience'. I do not know if I am interpreting the word correctly when I say that in these last seven months I have had that, and in a way from you. Almost as if you stood over me, were actually, physically urging me to have patience. I feel it is you who makes me have fortitude. I do not understand when people say I am 'wonderful and how do I keep on'? What else is, or was, there to do? Bill wrote me a sweet letter today. I am happy because I believe he knows where he is with me now and trusts me, even entrusts me with you. ... Mrs Elton has asked me to go to Geoff's grave with her. She is a broken woman, I wish you could come with me.

J

2&5/12/42

To go into D makes me into a creature not fit to be lived with – and yet I cannot bear the thought of leaving. Mrs Elton tells me I should. She also very kindly said I should perhaps not go to Seddlescombe to see Geoff's grave, but remember him alive. When I imagine what may have happened to you, I am like a child having a nightmare – but the calming parent must be somewhere in me too or I should become a little insane. How selfish my letters are! I don't see how I can avoid that. All I am conscious of is that I love you and I am afraid for you – I suppose that is selfishness.

Chapter 6

Heavy News and a Move

5 December

Mrs Davis has written me and told me that her husband said in his letter that he saw 'The First Lieutenant [Tony Lovell], CO, Coxswain and Trained Man killed' before he left the boat. But if that is true who gave the order to abandon ship? And how did Tony get onto a float and be without a scratch when he was found?. ... Oh Rick what am I to tell your dear mother?. ... I shall not write any more of these until I have hope again, I am terrified.

Jenny

10/12/42

I don't know what to say. Doc says Davis is probably a little deranged. Your people rang up that same day, and asked me to come as your kit had arrived at last. Well – I got back here this a.m., and darling it has been terrible to see your uniforms and things. No letters are returned, no negatives or photographs of Itchenor, which I need so badly for enlargements and prints – and Rick, we found your Kapok suit! Why hadn't you got it on? Oh God I must find out from Mark what you were wearing, and if you had a life jacket apart from the suit. ... Oh the sight and smell of your clothes, the great-coat that we used to wrap around the both of us. You must be alive. I cannot, dare not, and will not, imagine anything else. This is more terrible than anything I could have imagined – to see the words 'EAE Cornish deceased' was not possible – is not true.

My all, always J

16/12/42

Oh my love, it seems so hard, there is so much doubt and fear to contend with. As our love seemed to grow daily when we saw one another every day, so it still does. An all engulfing, aching thing it is now. I went to W today to deliver some things. Just as I was going to leave, the door opened and Paul Berthon walked in, with Mark and Chris Dreyer. I had a horrible moment – I felt myself go pale and gasped and stammered, and then I thought I was going to burst into tears so I couldn't say a word. I took a terrific pull at myself and hope I managed to pass it off. One has no idea how one will react to that sort of shock until it comes. The last time I saw Paul was when he was here with you. ... I went over to R [Ramsgate] yesterday. You were quite right, there is absolutely nowhere to stay. I spent the night with the WRNS. I had a short talk with Lieutenant Commander Wilson, and he, when I told him I believed you to be alive – said quietly and thoughtfully, that he would not be at all surprised. ... This dread!

My heart to you, J

20/12/42

I spent the 17th and night at '26'. They were very cheerful after my news of your second safety suit, and your father, though quiet, was as good as ever to me. Of course your mother spoils me! The farm is as welcoming as ever, but you are here too. ... When I go home to your family now, I always think of your doubts and worries as to how I would take them, and your seeing them through what you imagined, were my eyes when we were there together. I know no sweeter person than your mother, whose entire life consists of Bill, Eric and John and always has. Your father is an idealist and a very fair man. They both see amazingly straight still – no element of hate or 'tit for tat' do they have in their make-up. ... When you come back I want you to come and see Mrs Elton. Geoff apparently never stopped talking about you to her. I need to have peace with you soon, you are the only person I wish to spend my future with, and only with you can I attain that peace, and have joy in all things trivial or grave.

My love J

That I should live every day ever deeper in you and yet not be able to write each day sounds perhaps strange. Even though I was at home, there has never been a sadder Christmas. I no longer speculate – I simply, dumbly hope. Daddy has said I must find an outlet and an absorbing interest in something, but there is no interest for me in life apart from our future together. … I had a foul journey back to D, sat alone in a first class compartment, until I got the horrors. I realise that these days I dare not be alone. I dare not think for long because of the state I get in when I do. I wept like a baby on Christmas Eve. Your people rang up the next day. I can't be of much more help to them now. The almost cocksure hope and surety I used to have at times, has gone completely. There is only this agony left. But Rick, the only thing that it has (perhaps cruelly) made quite sure of is my love for you. We – (you were there before me), have reached the ultimate of unselfish love.
I have nothing more to say J

It was on this train journey that I had the following experience – I had decided to add to my travel voucher and pay extra for a First Class ticket. I was feeling very down. It was late evening as I took a seat in the First Class carriage. I did not put on the dim reading light, but sat in the blue-lit gloom of the carriage with the blinds down. The door of the compartment opened and I was aware that someone looked in. After this had happened twice, I thought I was, perhaps, stopping someone from finding a seat. I switched on the reading light overhead and said 'Are you looking for a seat?' I saw gold buttons, a white shirt and gold stripes on the sleeves. A voice answered 'No, no that's OK' and the door closed again.

Two minutes later a young man opened the door once more and said 'You look a bit low, come next door to our compartment, I have a box of *Fanny Farmer* chocolates.' He withdrew and I felt I was behaving in a foolish manner. Also, I have to admit, I kept repeating to myself *Fanny Farmer* chocolates – where would he get them? [They are an American brand]. I did go to the next compartment where there were three young Fleet Air Arm Officers sitting together. One had 'Australia' on his shoulder and another had 'New Zealand'. My host had nothing. After we had exchanged pleasantries for a while and said where we were stationed, this young man, who was very tall, dark, and with large dark eyes, kept looking sideways at me. Finally he said 'You look so like a portrait of my Great Aunt Mary'. I said I hoped it was a portrait of her when she was young! – But then – on looking at him and noticing his hands and his signet ring, I said 'You're a FitzGerald!' Indeed he was, and not only that, but his father and my grandfather were second cousins.

For several months after this, he sent me long telegrams about the *Götterdämmerung* (probably referring to Scapa Flow where he was based). Several months later on 28 May 1943 he was killed. At this point I began to think I was bad luck and I should not get to know any more young men. My granddaughter Celestine Lyons, has found his name on the Memorial for World War II victims who were pupils at Downside School where she is studying. I now have a photograph of him. Shortly after his death I wrote to his mother in Ireland and she very kindly answered my letter. Many years after the war, when my mother was living in County Cork, she met his mother – Lamorna Purcell FitzGerald, and her family. Her daughter had married an Italian Naval Officer before the war. The stress of knowing the danger both these young men faced on opposing sides must have been very hard.

29/12/42 Back in Dover

. ... You know Mark was, and is, fonder of you than maybe you realised. He is a great person ... he calms me and gives me amazing peace, with his quiet and rather ironic way of watching God's will being done. He's changed in the last dreadful months. He's learnt poise in the hard school. ...

After Rick's boat was lost and Mark took over as SO of the flotilla, I gave them a small silver plaque to put on the wall of MTB 219's ward room inscribed with the Breton Fisherman's Prayer: '*Protégé les mon seigneur. Leurs bateaux sont si petits et votre mer et si grand*'. After his next action he told me that it worked a treat.

This year can mean so much to us all one way or another. It is bound to mean everything or nothing to your people – and to me. I was rung up by Mark and asked to come with the 6th Flotilla to a dance on the 31st. So I went and for the first time since May I seemed to 'see' the world. I did not much enjoy what I saw but Mark is the best possible person for me to do such a thing with. He is very fine, and I feel nearer to you when I am with him than any one else. He has the DSC now – and about time too. Few people could have come through this summer as he has, and so well.

When Mark died prematurely in 1981 his obituaries were moving and insightful for those of us who had known him. One tribute from a former CF associate said:

There were quite a few heroes in MTBs and MGBs which operated in our Narrow Waters – the Channel – there is probably no one who served in these boats for any length of time who would argue that Mark Arnold-Forster was probably the bravest and best of the whole lot...[he] came to HMS Hornet in 1940 when I was training; a small, wiry, slightly hunched, scruffy Sub Lieutenant. It is perhaps not widely known that Dover was a rather special place during the war. In clear weather you could see occupied France from the roof of the MTB pen. Potential action was less than an hour away...and one was always at short notice for going to sea. ... The war was exceedingly close and ever present. These factors produced a special sort of strain on everyone there. ... The German forces opposite tried to bring ships through the Channel. These convoys were normally of a single ship with many escorts – M Class , Trawlers and R. boats [Mine Sweepers], frequently more than 20 escorts. This made them formidably difficult and dangerous to attack at close range.

.... I was in Dover in 1942 for some 6 months and lost 3 boats, and 3 CO's from the 5th and 6th flotillas in 10 days. Mark took part in these battles with quiet self efficiency and the utmost bravery...doing what was needed quietly and effectively and without fuss. He was a tower of strength and a wonderful example – and he kept it up for four years.

Rick had often told me that it wasn't so much that Mark was brave – but that he seemingly did not know fear.

Mark did not mention that he spoke German while he was in Dover as he wanted to stay in MTBs and feared he would be brought ashore to work as an interpreter or translator.

After the war Mark became a journalist and wrote the script for *The World at War* which became an excellent TV series and is still frequently repeated on television. Charles Wheeler who worked with Mark after the war as a correspondent described him as: 'self effacing, modest and a loner when pursuing a story.... His name was forgotten, but not by those who knew him.... He was the kind of person I would like to have been. That's why I describe him as my mentor'.

10/01/42

Dear Rick
You are indeed an obsession now. How I long for it to be a happy one! There is a beautiful picture of you which I got out of your camera, sitting in the window of your cabin in W. ... We never leave one another. We have been so much together since you left. I wonder if it is as painful for you. I think that perhaps activity of some sort does help a bit. My heart wherever you may be.
I feel this kind of letter writing doesn't get us anywhere and I am beginning to find it difficult to find enough of the drive needed to do so.
Goodnight Jenny

In January 42 Christopher Dreyer, another Royal Navy friend had written to me:

My dear Jenny, I have been meaning to write to you ever since leaving Dover without saying goodbye. I rang you up before I left, but you had gone to London, and so I have to write instead, which is easier in some ways, but still very difficult. So I shall go blundering on, when in the course of conversation, you could tell me, quite nicely, to shut up and look after my own affairs. Jenny, what I am trying to tell you, so long windedly, is to leave Dover. It has been the scene of good share of unhappiness for you, and the atmosphere there is bad for one, except in small, infrequent doses. By the time you reach the introspective and self-pitying stage, you have gone far enough and it is time to go. I feel personally that your present trade is too related to mine, which has caused much of your unhappiness. Why not try something else, where your qualifications can be as useful. Now I have blundered sufficiently. Don't bother to answer this ill-mannered and probably ill-timed letter. But please give it some thought.

God bless you my dear, may you be happy soon.

Yours ever

Christopher Dreyer

Many years later, retired and living in Devon, we met, and became very friendly with Richard and Romola Dreyer. On meeting them, I had asked Richard if he was related to a Christopher Dreyer and he replied that Christopher Dreyer was his first cousin. At Richard's funeral I met Christopher again for the first time since the war, and we had a long talk about the Coastal Forces.

1/2/43

Darling, darling Rick I can't write these anymore. And yet I have to believe you are alive or I could not go on. I awoke this morning to an envelope from your mother, and since she always writes to me in her parcel I thought it must be news of you – and I said to myself that I did not want life without you beside me. I can't marry anyone else, in all fairness, one does not marry another knowing such a thing to be true. I go to '26' on Saturday for forty-eight hours. I only hope we can give each other hope and cheer. John wrote me he would not give up hope, even after this show was over. I agree with him. We have known you. You are alive. ... I want to be your wife, friend, companion and the supplement of you.

Jenny

On 6 February, a Commander Day wrote to me from the Admiralty in answer to a letter I had sent to him regarding Jim George's account of the chief of Staff Dover writing recommending Rick for the Victoria Cross. He says, among other things:

According to later information he lived up to the high expectations we all had of him in overcoming the severe difficulties of the weather at the time so that he made close contact with the enemy and sank one of them. Piecing the various pieces of information together there seems little doubt that having made his attack his boat was rammed and sunk by the enemy ... several survivors were picked up from the action but not, it must now be accepted, Eric Cornish. As you rightly say there is no posthumous award other than the V.C. Or a Mention In Dispatches and the latter award was made. ...

Later that year, I also received letters from one of the surviving members of Rick's crew from POW camp. He told me how Rick had been 'hit in the head' and had gone below decks to scupper the boat, by staving in the bulkhead with the axe fixed to the wall that he had so often shown me.

The obstinate faith in Rick's survival by both our families is the reason for the apparent, unreasonable continuation of my letters.

7/02/43

Here in your home I can't answer sometimes when your mother speaks to me. ... I keep trying to picture how you will be when you return, when you'll come, what the circumstances will be – but I can't imagine it, so it makes me afraid. All I know is that I will be barely conscious anyway! It's so foolish to even attempt to put such a thing on the paper. Oh for your arms around me, and your presence.

Jenny

Quote: 'Nothing ever happens to me darling!' While I was with Rick's parents, Bill opened my eyes somewhat and filled me in with what exactly had occurred at Dunkirk, and with some of his other exploits before I met him. I knew that he had been at Dunkirk, but I imagined he was there with the MTBs acting as a sort of shuttle between the ships and shore. In fact he often acquiesced when I suggested this. I never questioned him about these things. They are sometimes best not over-remembered. It appears he was still in training at KA [King Alfred Officers Training School] when he was sent down to Ramsgate and asked if he would take a little 'pleasure boat over to France'. He was given two ratings and left to follow the destroyers. In fact, he had been given a Cross Channel paddle-steamer. He had orders to pick up as many troops as possible. They arrived at about dusk and worked all through the night. They first took a party of Belgians to the nearest destroyer and the Skipper said 'Our chaps first if you can'. They worked for two and half days evacuating the soldiers. The Tommies morale greatly impressed Rick, although he said the worst and most difficult part of the operation, was trying to impress upon the soldiers (most of whom could not swim) that wading out to the waiting boats was less dangerous than being *sträfed* by the Luftwaffe on the beaches. With rifles held above their heads they would walk out, often until the water reached above their mouths, their faces masks of fear. The paddles of the boat fouled on the seabed, and Rick had to dive over the side several times to free them. He was eventually hauled on board exhausted. The CO of a nearby destroyer ordered them alongside. He went aboard and collapsed. The next he knew it was 7am in Dover and he was in the CO's bunk. He had apparently passed out after a strong dose of rum!

Another time in Dover, when he was Liaison Officer to the Norwegians, he was out one night with his MTB. They went over a mine and broke in half. A destroyer picked up their SOS and rescued them after an hour and a half in the water. Later they were caught going up the river mouth in Portsmouth and were dive-bombed. The bombing became a 'little accurate' so they rowed ashore and waited until evening before returning to port. Probably his greatest exploit is still to be told. This young man I love was fast developing into a hero before my eyes. He told me that when he finally came home to '26' after Dunkirk, he and his mother had the following short exchange:

'You?'

'Yes'

'Sit down and I'll bring you a cup of tea – you're back then?'

'Thanks. Yes'

Before I went on watch on the night of 16 February 1943, I wrote some of my thoughts down on paper – not to be sent to Rick in a POW camp but to get them off my chest:

The sea was up to the base of the cliffs, and on the grassy point where I stood I was suspended between sea and sky – nothing intermediate, no hiatus of earth, just all immensity, and fearful in its awesomeness. The insignificance of my own sorrow struck me again, as it had two evenings before, when the evening star was gazing in unblinking tolerance at the ageless joys and sorrows of the earth and her microscopic creatures. Yet, in my newly awakened awareness, I had the temerity to beg that I should not be without the solace and the inspiration which my love for Rick had achieved. That he, who aspired to have a balanced mind and heart so that he 'could understand and help his fellow men better', was in his quiet, wide-eyed way, great, seemed only to make the rejection of belief in his death more essential. In the clear eye of my mind I could see him, his face turned up to the grey five o'clock skies, his hands gently propelling him through the water – long fingered hands, white with cold – bony wristed. His life-saving suit puffed and buoyant around his face open to his pain. The fear of leaving life in his eyes, the insistence in his brain that he make the effort to live, to gain the shore – to return. I know too that he and I will wait, 'through many deaths he will come knowing that I wait'. He will come as in the following Russian poem, which appeared in the press about this time. It became a sort of mantra for me. The amazing courage of the Russian people in their ordeal was a frequent subject of many newspaper articles.

Translated from the Russian:

Wait for me. I will come.
Wait for me.
Forget the sadness and the pain,
The weeping and the dreary rain.
Wait for me.
Don't heed the voice that says
"The light has gone from out your days
He has gone, you only wait in vain".
Wait for me.
I will come through many deaths
Knowing that you wait.

Those who do not wait
Cannot understand
That the hours that you wait
Are like the reaching of a hand
Across a deathless time
Wait...I will come.

7/03/43

My dearest love, I had hoped that I would find some of your clear minded strength in me. That I should have learnt enough from you, even in a year, to be able to live without you for a year – but it isn't so, I'm afraid. I am as nothing without you and life is like a passing show at which I stare unseeingly. I realise my complete pre-occupation with you is a form of extreme selfishness but I cannot stop it. I regret so much that I did not realise how happy we were together. How vivid would each moment be, could you but return. I think I would be conscious of our amazing completion until I died. I speak to you all day and yet I cannot tell you how I really need you. You are my second half, without which neither my mind nor body can function properly. I am so small to be afraid and to give up my hope. If you can, and wherever you may be, help me to be worthy of you, dear Rick.

14 and 23 March 43

I find I have little control over my emotions these days, a fact I deplore, because I cannot bear the idea of foisting my unhappiness on other people. Hearing Renee Cunningham's voice over the IC [Intelligence Centre] *phone hit me somewhere, I feel so utterly sorry for her.* [She was a recent Coastal Forces widow]. *Empathy and understanding for other people, is perhaps an asset for them, but it doesn't help oneself. Too much can only add to, not lessen ones sadness. ... Loving you Rick, I am becoming less of the poor part of Jenny, and some of the great part of Rick. I can only thank God that I can still hope, for without that I could not answer for myself. I am continuously aware that words are inadequate, and despair of ever being able to tell you what this year has been like. If I try to be brave I feel it may*

be helping you somewhere. … If only <u>I knew</u>. It's worse since spring came. …
Itchenor seems yesterday and yet a century of agony ago. …

<u>Rondel, Francois Villon:</u>
(Le Souvenir de Vous me Tue)

… Your memory is death to me
My only good the sight of you.
I swear by all that I hold true
That joy without you cannot be.
When I your face no longer view
I die of sadness yea – pardie!
Your memory is death to me. …

On 3 April I went into *Wasp* to collect Rick's typewriter. However, there was a rather acrimonious discussion about it when I arrived, as the dentist had apparently given it to his Petty Officer.

4/04/43

I suppose I am being very foolish letting such a small thing make me weep, but darling, nobody has ever been unkind or even brusque with me in W before. I also know that no-one, including the dentist, would have spoken to me that way if you had still been in W. I never go into the place without seeing you at every turn – pushing the door of the Officer's Mess open, slapping your gloves on the QM's desk, and then coming to where I am waiting. I wonder how much longer I shall be able to wait <u>hopefully</u>. I never realised how alone I felt before you went away. Perhaps the real answer to that is that no one else's company gives me such completeness. Certainly nobody has ever given me such a secure and protected feeling. Nobody could hurt me if you were standing there beside me – this spring is too lovely and too desolate to explain rationally.

J

April Dover 43

As I sat waiting at the Naval Dockyard slips for firewood, I watched the sea racing past the outer harbour walls, white horses on a grey sea. It was running pretty fast. The seagulls were wheeling without moving their wings, hanging and slipping over the swinging mast heads of the MLs [Motor Launches] alongside. The sky was crossed and re-crossed by their masts and pennants. The White Ensign and the Norwegian Cross together flying taut in a fair sized gale. The sailors were struggling along the Mole dragging heavy sacks. Their hats held on by chin straps, bell-bottomed trousers flapping around their legs. All the paraphernalia of a strewn dockside lay about, the small slate grey vessels were picked out here and there with red and black and their yellow gas detecting spots. The sea and sailors are my life now. Sadness mingled in a song of love and admiration for all sailors, every ship, everywhere, this morning.

15/04/43

Here in D it's hard to stand and wait. Today you are so much with me. Walking beside me all over these streets and squares. In Barclays Bank I even feel you open the door for me, and am amazed that others cannot see you too. So clear – walking close, your hand taking mine. ... Sometimes I walk with, stand and feel you so strongly, it is too vivid to bear. I have to stop still, my heart seems to fill my throat and ears. ... I long for your gentle eyes to calm my heart Rick.

J

30/04/43

My darling the mist lay heavy and a dense grey about this house, it shrouded the sea from here. All seemed lost in its muffling neutrality and impenetrability. I felt it was my life at present, that was enclosed in sad, wet, deep fog – no light or even hope of light in sky or sea. I thought hopelessly of our love, of your happy, deep and utterly sincere eyes, of how my life could only be with you, and surmised for the thousandth time, if you would be able to escape and return to us. Your mother and father's joy! But I was sickeningly without the flash and triumph of my ever springing hope. ... I lifted my head and the mist had cleared, I saw the light evening sky and the sea – albeit cruel and grey. I could look at solitary wheeling gulls and demand again 'Where is he – give him back to me – to us'. ... Even a desperate knowledge is better than an everlasting fog of uncertainty to blunder through, asking the same interminable questions and praying the same desperate prayers. If only I could hold your hands again, or even know it was too late! Come back.

J

16/05/43

A year ago yesterday was the terrible Wednesday, Rick – but twelve months don't seem to have made any difference as far as my feelings are concerned. I feel as sad, as sure you will return, as desperate and afraid, and God I love you so!. ... The violets carpet the Hougham Woods again, the primroses and bluebells. I remember you so well in the sun. The way the sky looked then – the running clouds, the willow copses, the way you sat and smoked your pipe in your shirtsleeves. I kissed you last night in a rather terrible dream, but the kiss was like a drink of water after thirst has been a torture for a long time, and I groaned aloud. ... I can say no more tonight. I would wish to dream of you, except that I always dream that you come back and no longer love me.
Jenny

23/05/43 0245

My darling, I think I ran the full gamut of emotion tonight – except that I cannot, nowadays, reach the heights or even the upper slopes of joy – but I certainly plumb the depths. My depression culminated in a storm of desperation – possibly self-pity, but I was afraid of the empty stretch of nothing ahead. No tree even in the landscape. I was desperate for some work to do to give life a purpose – if you are gone, inevitably a vicarious purpose, but how can I even contemplate a job – probably the one I thought of before I fell in love with you, i.e. the one risking danger and/or disappearance for some time, if I do not know at all whether you are alive or dead? I can never take liberties with my life, for it is yours. And I cannot be in any way cognisant of your whereabouts, or if indeed you will ever need me again. It is not a good situation. Also, I see myself not only as myself, suffering, for though we may have had something fairly rare and unique between us – so many women and families are suffering the same way. So many more will do so. I can only see this lost generation sinking deeper into its sadness, and futile waste, as the war years go on. This all built up to a weep – which did me good I suppose, also I was able to tell someone about it. … I cannot go on without you. … So please, even more for your mother and father, and the world's sake, return.

J

27/05/43

Venus is hanging enlarged and shining in the sky, which has not yet quite changed tonight. There is wonderful scent in the air of herbs and grasses – a smell I have never been able to pin down, which seems to be the very smell of summer itself. The wind is soft, and tonight I would like to climb right down the cliff face until we reached the point over the sea, with the loud waves in our ears – and then I would lie with my head in your lap, with the sky immense and limitless above us. The feel of the coarse cliff grass under my hands, and the sky – the sky – I am intoxicated by the sky! A mystery I may look at and never feel the frustration of wishing to understand or go deeper than the clouds, the varying colours, the depths, the stars, moon, and the ecstatic lift it gives my heart to lie and gaze thus. If only I could have you here, or at least know that one day we shall have these long languorous nights and evenings together. Evening is our hour, the blue green fading into the night, the gentle breathing of the earth.

J

In the late August of 1943 I was finally persuaded to accept a change of station. I made sure I could take Little Jenny with me, for she had become my most sympathetic and constant companion. I was sent to Cromer in Norfolk. We were in a country house about two miles outside Cromer. Our HQs were in Felixstowe, and necessitated quite a train journey if we had to report there for our pay or other reasons. Norwich was the closest important town, and a bus ride away. The area was full of the US Army Air Corps, and raiding German bombers and 'Doodle Bugs' were overhead night and day. The atmosphere was entirely different from Dover. We were distanced from the Coastal Forces operations and could only occasionally go to Felixstowe to meet some of the young men serving in MTBs, MGBs and MLs. The only good thing about the change was that I was closer to Burham-on-Crouch and could visit the Cornish's there on rare forty-eight hour leaves.

On one of my shopping days in Cromer, I met an elderly woman and got into conversation with her. She asked me to come to tea with her one day and to bring a couple of my friends. I went with two of my new associates, Helen Davidson and Dorrit Klatzow. During the meal our kind hostess said 'I see you are all wearing rings on your engagement – wedding fingers, you must tell me all about your husbands'. Poor woman! Dorrit's husband had died of radiation exposure as a result of working on the early atomic bomb, Helen was also a young widow whose husband had been killed in the Fleet Air Arm, and I could only tell her that my fiancé was missing. Her face lost all of its colour, and she was quite obviously shocked. I suppose she may well have been one of the thousands of women who lost their loves in the First World War.

By this time I was a Chief Petty Officer, and had a blue long-service stripe on my sleeve. Once, when I had to go into Felixstowe to collect my pay, and was coming out of the bank, I found myself face to face with an older, regular RN CPO. He looked in disgust at my cuff buttons and my good service stripe and spat on the pavement. I had never seen an Englishman spit before, and I was very upset. A similar, but more light-hearted, occurrence was when I and another Petty Officer went into Norwich for the day. In the town centre two ratings were walking towards us, and one of them turned to the other and said 'Cor, look at those two great big bloody POs'. When we exclaimed loudly in dismay, they turned around and said 'Its alright ducks we don't mean it'.

I still wrote infrequently to Rick in a sort of obstinate assertion of my belief in his survival. These letters are quite simply, as I said at the time, an expression of agony.

10/11/43

Last night, once again, a terrible vivid dream of you. I found you at last, you turned around and your deep blue eyes lit your face and your mouth grew soft, and then you raised your hands and with an infinitely tender gesture touched both sides of my face in a sort of wonderment. ... Every breath I draw is drawn in you too and each breath you draw, I feel in my own being. ... You are alive, alive and slowly we must surely meet. Without you my heart and soul are shriven. ... Come back to us. So often I write to you, but cannot put pen to paper.

2/12/43

I do not know if it is weakness on my part which allows me to write this. A thing I have not allowed myself to do since you have been missing. I want, have wanted so often to write you a love letter. ... But how can I permit myself to write such things that may go to a POW camp. They would only make your imprisonment more unbearable. But I will show you this example of what I shall never be able to put on paper adequately. Once again it is December. The air is cold and crisp, soon the deep winter will really be here, the blizzards and snow. Oh! How you and I could stand on a winter's night and hold each other and forget the cold and wind and snow! But now I want to know that each door that opens can only be you. When I go to meet someone it can only be you. I want to lie and watch the morning sun shining on your face – to wake you or leave you asleep without fear of time. But what of this terror? How can I, we, combat it? I can't go anywhere now without seeing you, the pain and longing suffocates me – perhaps that is fear. I can see your eyes so clearly, your hair, lips and the set of your shoulders as you stand. The way you walk, quite surprisingly gracefully. The light in your quiet face when we meet. The way you gently kiss me. The snow on the shoulders of your great coat when I returned from Falmouth. How I ran to you under the dim station lights. The way your hand lay in my lap in the bus after our last day in Canterbury together, palm upwards, light coloured and strong, the nails square and pink. The fingers gently cupped and relaxed, curving inwards. I looked at them and knew no other hands could give me such joy along my cheek, gently turning my face upwards. . . . The square finger tips and quiet flowing from palm to wrist. Oh Rick, sweet-eyed and gentle mouthed. Above all else I long to see your face again and slowly, without hurry, feeling each second of expectation watch you come to me and gently turn your head to kiss me. The sweetness of your breathing almost an intoxication. My darling you are my completion and I yours.

God! Come back and never leave me.

J

11/12/43 at '26'

My beloved Rick, this is once more in your home and I am doing a little cooking. Your mother is in bed and not very well. Your records are once more being played. The music means a lot to your father, for he can picture your face and posture as it was when he last saw you listening to it – and to me, for I know our hands are the few which have handled the records. The cadences and crescendos, the deep sad tones that move me, have moved you, you have felt the same surge of gaiety and release at the same passages – so I am listening with both our ears. So vividly, sweetheart is your face before me. Cruelly so, since two days ago Tony [Rolt] *wrote me that Mickey Wynn* [who was in the same POW camp as Tony, having been the only MTB on the 'Dam-buster' Raid and subsequently taken prisoner] *had heard you were hit in the face. You do not know my heart how I lie awake and see it all – but perhaps you do know. For nights now I have been quietly trying with deep concentration, to open myself to your total submersion in me. I have felt the strength of you pouring into me at times, and my heart has thudded heavily and has been enclosed by yours. This feeling of unity and oneness is hard to explain. That some people have experienced it before us does not make it any easier to put down clearly. How much would I give for the sight of you, the closeness of your breathing, your near physical presence, your mind and gentle reasoning to help me – your sweet whimsical expression while you consider my half-formed but definite ideas – pipe in mouth, your lips gently curling at the corners, and your eyes smiling sideways at me. I can see your hands, the very lines on your palms, the way your ears grow close to your head, and the way your shoulders are held, relaxed, yet strong, when you stand hands in pockets and discuss, and*

gaze at, your boat. The way you wave your hand and simply say 'Colour',
when we pass a newly turned ploughed field or a hedge fresh in new spring
green. … My own dear love Rick

J

5/1/44 0300 Night watch

We've gone over to a New Year sweetheart, and with it has come a new
friendship for me – but also a recognition of the knowledge that I love and
will always love, you. I have had a panicky feeling the last few days – have
been unable to reconstruct your face as vividly as before, but it comes back if
I don't try, and don't frighten myself by not achieving a really vivid picture.
I am so weary of waiting. I love you Rick. Where are you?

J

2/2/44

I dreamed of you again last night. It has been several weeks – and I do so
long at the end of each stretch between dreams, to see you again as before.
You were infinitely clear to me, each tone of your face, the colour of your
eyes in your different moods – each of your movements. This time I dreamt
you and I both knew that I was dreaming, and we were so happy together –
you were teasing me. Mark Arnold-Forster sat and watched us, and I turned
to him and said 'Look at Rick, when he is this clear to me in dreams, do you
wonder I do not give up hope' and he said 'It is wonderful'. It was – but I
long for the reality.

24/02/44

My darling I have been trying lately to straighten out my thoughts and
emotions…and know now that what I have always felt in moments of
intense longing for you – even after two years – is true. I still love you as
always. The sadness I felt before is not as intense – so nullifying – not such
actual agony to endure. … The sadness I perpetually have now is that I am
conscious ever more that I can no longer bring you up so vividly in front of

me at will – at any moment I choose – though I still have flashes of the same clear sight, and can see you and feel you so close to me, that it is an awful, painful, sorrowing joy…I can only feel maternal and protective love for the people such as Ned, my new friend, who say they love me now. I no longer know whether I have actual faith in your being alive. I still say I have – even to myself – but time is a ruthless destroyer of hope. I know I only want a life with you and will therefore continue to live in hope, be it weary and long – until I know you to be dead. … Dead to the world. But you will always be with me until I too am dead. Sweet Rick how am I to be a good, – a real-person without you there to show me?

4/04/44 Felixstowe

I have been once more reading your lovely letters. I read them each time with reawakened pleasure. A sweet suffusing joy at how vividly they bring you in front of my eyes – a dreadful dragging pain that I cannot answer them now – talk to you – know you are somewhere accessible. The sharpness of my longing does not seem to have abated through the years. I had a wonderfully hopeful letter from John. He and I still have this 'unreasonable hope and trust' in your living. I still picture and always will picture my future as part of you. You and the future are inseparable in my mind. Often I do not think beyond tomorrow, if I feel afraid for you. But when I do think of 'after the war' then it is of you and me I think, the warm private dreams we have dreamt together crowd in on me demanding realisation. You once said of them '…No – they are not nonsense, they are too strong – we must be strong too, that is all. That I believe – and I believe unceasingly all you say is true – as true as that I am your love and you my life – come what may.

J

27/07/44

Night watch
My love for you Rick is now a sick desperation or a dull hopeless ache. The knowledge that you are quite irreplaceable has taken nearly two and half years to prove to me that I can love no other, yearn for no other fulfilment

except with you. But even more, (for physical passion is arousable up to a certain point), that mentally and spiritually you are the only completion I can ever have. Thinking and acting can only be of a real meaning with you as my companion, my heart's journey-man, and more. You are the person I want to live and end my days with. I am twenty-four and half years old now, and have matured considerably since you loved me. John is back in England, we have met and discovered to our mutual pleasure, that we are quite unembarrassed and feel close to one another, in both loving you. Your absence rather than your presence makes us close and at ease with one another, I cannot yet, and never will until proof is given me, stop hoping and believing in your return. ...

Jenny

19/09/44 The Base, Felixstowe

Granlund has just come up here, and with his familiar face reopened all the old memories of Dover. Just now I saw someone walking slowly toward the boats, slim and yet strong looking, broad shouldered with a head of thick dark hair and a certain mannerism of hanging his head deep in thought – which you had. But you also used to hold your head very high and stare at the sky.

Jenny

22/09/44

Boulogne liberated. We shall know something perhaps soon. John and your parents are going to Burnham tomorrow. I am going down on Tuesday. John's voice reminds me so much of yours on the telephone. Darling I want only to be your wife, your friend and life's companion. I remember so well how we would look at one another – particularly I am thinking of the hall in the Esplanade when as I came downstairs again, you would stand against the far wall, your blue eyes shadowed and so full of pupil they looked black, and you would look at me with all our love in your face. ... Rick you are life to me.

Jenny

When the war and the battle of the English Channel were thankfully coming to a close, I was posted to London. I shared a flat with Rosemary Gilliat, who had already left the WRNS. I was sent to work on the top floor of the bomb damaged Peter Robinsons department store on Oxford Circus. The office was receiving all captured documents taken in Germany as the Allies advanced. The staff were a mixed crew of Army, Navy and Air Force from both the British and US Forces. The Jedburghs' were also bringing us plane loads of captured material. The Jedburghs were a clandestine organisation which included members of the British SOE, American OSS, Free French, Dutch and Belgian armies who had been dropped by parachute into Germany, France, Holland and Belgium to organise sabotage and guerrilla warfare, and to lead local resistance. The name is probably taken from the town of Jedburgh in the Scottish border country. Their training bases were moved from Scotland to Peterborough.

In the meantime, my father in London had been approached by Fred Oechsner, an American journalist who had been in Berlin until the US declared war on Germany. He told my father that the Americans were looking for 'US citizens who could speak German'. My father replied 'I only know one, and the British Navy has her'. A short while later I was 'on the carpet', and accused of telling the Americans what I had been doing in Special Duties – specifically 'listening to German submarines'. Thank God they had got _that_ wrong at any rate, and, combined with my father's good connections, I was let off with a reprimand rather than a spell on the Isle of Man in an internment camp. Actually, the OSS (for it was they) had never met, or interviewed me at all. They had put two and two together and made six. They had gone to the British Navy and said 'You have an American citizen in the WRNS listening to German submarines' I told them to keep well away from me from then on – and certainly until the end of the war in Europe.

In the Peter Robinsons office I was put to work trying to ascertain whether the so called '_Werwolfe_' were having any success in Germany's struggle to defend itself. Most of the _Werwolfe_ were very young boys who were sacrificed, quite cynically, in an effort to delay the fall of the German Army. They defended such things as bridges and highways for a short time, but I could glean nothing of any meaningful defence. One of the other jobs the

Navy gave me was to study captured police documents, mostly gruesome civilian crimes, having little or nothing to do with the war. I was also sent, alone, down to a publishing house in the East End of London to compile a comprehensive volume of all existing German uniforms – Military, National Socialist and Civilian. It was a period of almost stagnant depression, sadness and ennui.

At the end of my job in London the Navy offered me a post as interpreter between the British and German Navies in either Hamburg or Bremerhaven. But I felt that I had had my fill of the war, its results and its bitterness, so when the OSS approached me again, and asked if I would be willing to go to Germany with them, I accepted.

Like many people of my generation, my life, my memories and beliefs have been, and still are, greatly influenced by my experiences in the Second World War. Now an old woman in my nineties I am often racked with sadness and remorse about my histrionic dithering in 1941 and 1942. It is perhaps a slightly mitigating fact that I was just 22 years old when my fiancé, Rick was lost, and that I had always had doubts and reservations about marriage because, I suppose, of my parents divorce. But the terrible fact remains that he was never able to be completely sure of my love and our future together. My letters to him, written over two–four years, show how I grew up emotionally and very painfully, as each day followed the last in hope and longing. Losing Rick has been a very real and recurring sadness in my life.

Chapter 7

Post War Germany

In May 1945 I met some of the people I would be working with in Germany, among them Julia Cuniberti (Bimba), who became a dear and life long friend. After a few days in London, in and out of the very classy OSS Brook Street address, we picked up our khaki uniforms – to my horror – and were told to meet early next morning for our transport to the airfield from where we were to fly to Germany. As I climbed into the back of the open truck, a despised forage cap in my hand, a WAC Officer in full rig said to me 'You know, you have no right to wear that gold stripe on your cap unless you have been in the Army for some time!'

I said 'Oh yes? And how long have you been in the Army?' she replied two years, and I then said 'Well, I have been in the British Navy for nearly five years and have the right to wear any damn cap or stripe you can dish out'. Poor Emma Paxman (for that was her name) left me strictly alone from then on.

On the flight I sat in the plexi-glass nose of the Liberator bomber and watched the French and German countryside far below me in a disbelieving post war vision. We landed in Wiesbaden and were taken to our future Headquarters in the Henkel Trocken Sekt Factory in Bieberich. We were billeted in requisitioned apartment houses with every comfort. Bimba and I shared a flat and were both assigned to the 'Registry' in a large central reception area. The floor above surrounded the area with a balcony of gilded railings. One day, as I worked at my, admittedly rather boring, job sorting mail and various orders for the huge staff assembled in Wiesbaden, I felt someone staring at me. I looked up to see a young Army Officer with very blue eyes peering at me through the railings of the balcony. In the Mess Hall later, the same man continued to stare causing me a certain amount of confusion, and, I have to say, annoyance.

Bimba and I had been subjected to knockings and scratchings on our door in the evenings from various officers of the US Seventh Army Corps. On one occasion I opened the door angrily and an officer said 'Gee honey, please let us in, we haven't seen an American girl in over a year now'. I replied heatedly that I knew many a man and woman in the British Isles who hadn't seen their husbands, wives or sweethearts for at least four years, 'So go away and grow up!'.

On leaving the Mess Hall, I was approached by the blue-eyed young OSS Officer. He was wearing US uniform but with a few odd additions – a white silk scarf at his neck and a swagger-stick under his arm. 'What's your name?' he asked, and I replied rather coolly 'Gill, and what's the scarf for?' He explained he was a member of the 'Caterpillar Club', and that its members were those who had bailed out of their aircraft, and then had some of the parachute silk made into a scarf and embroidered with the date of their escape. His name was Jean Nater. A few days later I received a letter, and a beautiful flat basket of freshly picked strawberries on a bed of green leaves. The letter below was written by a friend, André Pecquet, in Jean's name – talk about Cyrano de Bergerac!:

To our friend in town. How are you? This morning with Jean, we were working – yes really working – hard – picking up strawberries under a very hot sun – indeed – of a sudden Jean said 'Lets us pick some for our friend in town' – the soul of a poet I no longer possess – perhaps too many small and big things, some would say events – happened here and there – but reverting to my story, well our work had a different meaning – as a matter of fact, it had a meaning – last time I saw you, so very sad you looked. Before the War I spent some days in England – an old lady would tell me – I do not imply that you are old! 'When I feel sad, I allow myself to remember a day full of laughter' – and I am certain you had – will have – such days.
Our best regards
André and Jean

Both young men were stationed near Mainz in a mill on the Main River. Jean was the officer in charge of a group of very disparate people, mostly born Germans – professors of Philosophy and Mathematics, adventurers and ex-agents – who had been dropped behind enemy lines during the war. There was also one very charming and out-of-water, US Marine Officer called Carl Muecke who became one of Jean's closest friends.

André Peccquet was an American Army Officer born in France, and he and Jean spoke mostly French together. He had been dropped into 'Maquis' territory, and he told how he and his companions had been overrun. He had managed to conceal himself in the undergrowth for several days, within hearing distance of the Germans. Apparently he survived by staying absolutely still and licking the dew from the leaves. Both he and Jean had later been recruited to fly in Mosquito aircraft on the OSS's 'Joan and Eleanor' operations, also known as Carpet Bagger missions.

Towards the end of the war the OSS had begun to fly these missions, which were named after Alan Dulles's daughter and sister. They flew over occupied Europe and Germany. The operators were multi-lingual officers, whose task was to trace, identify and communicate (by VHF radio) with agents on the ground. Jean's account of some of these missions and the Mosquitoes that flew them are recorded in a book by Martin Bowman *The Men who flew the Mosquito*.

Jean had written:

When I first met the 'Mossie' it was an impressive machine. Small, slim and sleek. Our models, mostly phote-recce veterans, had been stripped of all arms and armour, and the bomb bays had been stripped of bomb racks. Navigational equipment was left intact and there was tail-warning radar to tell the pilot if there was anything on his tail. To fit in the 'Joan and Eleanor' operator, his radio receiver and wire recorder, our squadron riggers had adapted a small hatch on the starboard side of the fuselage, just aft of the wing. They had fitted a makeshift seat close to the bottom of the fuselage; this was hinged and held together with elastic parachute cords so that you could pull it down to sit on. Great in theory, but when you shifted your backside, the seat tended to collapse. Imagine yourself all togged up in an electric flying suit, a pile lined flying suit, wearing felt flying boots, a chest pack-chute and an emergency oxygen flask strapped to your leg – you are hunched over in a crouch in front of a radio and antennae which had to be rotated and a wire recorder which was apt to shed a spool!

(One of Jean's trainers was particularly dissatisfied with the wire recorder and said that: "the spools could work loose, and then you had wire all over the place"!) *It was not very comfortable. The thing that bothered me most was the long-range, bomb bay fuel tank. It was just forward of me and my gear, looking much like the rear end of an elephant backed up against a low fence. Because the 'Joan-Eleanor' operational flight usually lasted between 5 to 6 hours, the ground crew would top up the tank to its full capacity. As we climbed up fast, over the Channel, the fuel would expand and be sucked into my compartment, where it would bubble in the bottom of the glass camera port just under my feet. Being on oxygen, you couldn't smell the stuff. The mere sight of it forced you to make an important decision: Tell the pilot and have him abort the mission; or tell him and add that you will stay for the ride. As we gained altitude and reached our operational height of about 35,000ft, the temperature inside the fuselage was about −20ºC, and the danger of an internal explosion was greatly diminished.*

One of Jean's operational flights also reported in the book, was of the night of 24–25 April, 1945 and he writes:

Although the war in Europe was visibly coming to an end, it was still almost dogma among Allied commanders that the German Army, particularly the Waffen SS, would mass in southern Bavaria and the Austrian Alps for a Wagnerian final battle. If we could get agents into the Alpine Redoubt we would be well placed to defeat Germany's final stand. Our flight target this time was south of the Munich area. After a light supper (belly gas is to be avoided at high altitude in unpressurised aircraft), we were kitted up and taken out to Mosquito PR.XVI NS707, waiting on the runway. The pilot was First Lieutenant James G. Kuntz, whom I knew, and the navigator was Flying Officer Bob Green, recently assigned to the squadron, and on his first mission.

I was helped to squeeze into my compartment. The hatch was closed and I locked it from the inside. I quickly tested the 'Joan and Eleanor' equipment. I had been issued for the first time with silk gloves to wear under my heavy, heated flying gloves, and these made it much easier to manipulate the 'Joan-Eleanor' gear. As usual the 'Mossie' got off fast. We flew south over the

Channel and once over France began steadily climbing to our operational altitude. Cold, noisy, but steady. I turned on my tiny lamp, (no gas bubbling in the camera port thank God) and tested the equipment again. The intercom was on and I could hear the pilot checking our position. Kuntz said 'We're at altitude, but still some way to go'. Time went by. Suddenly I heard a French accented voice asking us to identify ourselves 'Or we will open fire'. Kuntz cut in: 'That's French AA [anti-aircraft] – I won't answer them, they'll open fire, but the bursts will be way, way below us'. Then he announced 'We can see the bursts below us'.

It was dark and I was cold. Kuntz suddenly announced 'Tail radar has gone on! I'll do a sharp 360'. A '360'? I soon learned what it meant. We turned sharply and I was pushed down into my bench. It collapsed. Still we went around. We levelled out just as quickly. Kunz said 'Jesus! Something's flown past us! It had a tail light! Maybe it was one of the new Messerchmitts we've heard about'. Was it true, or was Kuntz just keeping me awake?

At about 22.00 hours Kuntz said 'Time's right – we are on target, do your stuff Jean. I'll fly a large figure eight' So it began. I turned on the 'Joan-Eleanor'. There was static in my headphones. I began turning the antenna. It was functioning. I began calling the agent's code name, repeating it twice and then identifying myself with the name I had been given. I repeated this procedure several times in German. If the agent was at the rendezvous at this time, remembered his code name, his transmitter was working, and there were no German military within fifteen yards, he must hear me and respond. Silence. Nothing. I tried again and again. Green checked our position. We were where we were supposed to be. Kuntz changed the flight pattern, around and around and back and forth we went for fifteen to twenty minutes. Nothing. Kuntz suggested we return to base. I made one more call. No answer. I agreed with Kuntz. I was sweating and cold.

My altimeter stayed at thirty-five thousand feet for a long time, before moving down. Kuntz told me we were deep into France, so he had come down lower. I must have fallen asleep. The bouncing and whipping of the aircraft woke me. The altimeter had us at five thousand feet. I asked Kuntz where we were and he replied in a tone of great relief that we would be crossing the Channel soon and then he would go down lower. I watched the altimeter come down and level out at a thousand feet. Despite the bouncing and shaking I felt much better. The altimeter started down again to five hundred feet. In my mind's eye I saw the water below us and the cliffs of Dover before us. The altimeter went to below a hundred feet and then lifted. 'We are over the coast' said Green. We climbed to three thousand feet. Smoother, much smoother.

About 10 minutes after crossing the coast, one of the engines began to miss and the aircraft shuddered. Kuntz ordered Green to switch on the reserve fuel tank. I assume he complied, but the engine did not pick up. Instead it started to shake itself loose. Kuntz began calling for an emergency landing. Two stations answered him and gave him a fix, so the navigator could work out a course. Kuntz told them we were at 'Angels 3'. Then he saw the port engine begin to burn. He ordered us to bail out. He called 'Green's out! Jean, Jean, when are you going?' I told him, 'I'm going!'.

In theory, the Joan-Eleanor operator was to 'Kick out the hatch under his feet', and go out head first, but going out into the roaring darkness head first was something I could not do. I went out feet first and got stuck with my legs banging outside on the fuselage. My 'chute had stuck on the hatch frame. I tried to disengage it with my hands, as I did so I smelled smoke. I was terrified that my searching fingers would spill the 'chute inside the aircraft. 'Relax' I thought. Then I was outside on my back, the aircraft going away from me with the port engine burning. I pulled the ripcord. A long strong tug on my shoulders and body and a God-given quiet. My 'chute had opened!

Actually, Jean told me that he had decided he was lost, but that when he gave up and stopped struggling his muscles relaxed and he shot through the hatch. After swinging once he landed in an ATS (Army Territorial Service) camp. Seeing a crack of light in a door he collected his 'chute and knocked. He was let in by the CO of the camp and his wife. They asked him if he would like something to drink and when he enthusiastically said 'Yes please' the CO's wife brought him a cup of tea. A short while later the police arrived on a bicycle. He was subsequently picked up by an RAF lorry. The next day he and Kuntz joined in the search for Green whose body was found in a wooded area. Kuntz said that Green had told him his 'chute harness was too tight' to fasten, and so he had probably fallen straight through. One interesting thing about this operation was the fact that in a news report at the time only two crew members were mentioned. Jean's presence in the tail of the Mosquito was not reported. Presumably because security was still tight.

When the 'Joan and Eleanor' operations ceased, Jean was told he was to go to the Pacific to train in one-man submarines. These were to be used against the Japanese Navy and the operations were quite probably little more than suicide missions. However, his excellent knowledge of German was finally recognised and in May 1945 he was sent to Germany.

When I met him he had been in Mainz for about a month or so. On one occasion when he and Pequet came into HQ in Wiesbaden, Jean suggested we go to the Red Cross Club and have coffee together. For the first time we really had a chance to talk, and discovered how alike, in some respects, our backgrounds were. We were both 'displaced Americans'. Jean's father was a Swiss-born first generation American. During Jean's early childhood he had worked in the US with Fisk Tyre Company and later General Tyre and Rubber, travelling extensively in Europe and the Middle East. His frequent absences, when he was travelling, by train, boat or automobile visiting his distributors in the Middle East, the Balkans and Greece, were very long. At the time of the Great Depression (1929), he moved the family to France. He left Jean's mother, Jean and his younger sister Priscilla in Paris when they first arrived in Europe. The fact that Jean was not in school at this time greatly shocked his Swiss paternal grandfather, who undertook to give him some basic tutoring. He was put to work standing at an old fashioned draughtsman's desk, doing reading, writing and arithmetic. His grandfather had studied lace design in St Gallen Switzerland and he was an excellent draughtsman. (We still have two of his pictures which he gave to his parents in 1881). Often when Jean's mother accompanied her husband on his trips, Jean was left in the old man's care. One of his mathematics lessons was in the form of frequent visits to Longchamps race track. They travelled by Metro and Jean remembered the suffocating feeling of being crushed between several portly men, his nose on a level with their lowest waistcoat button. At this time he suffered from frequent chest colds, and when he coughed in the Metro his grandfather would order him '*Crache!*' (spit). But Jean refused, mutely pointing to the signs '*Defense de Cracher*' which were very visible in the carriage. On arrival his task was to work out the *Paris Mutuel* figures before each race, a thing he dreaded. However all was forgotten when his reward was a large, crisp, ham filled *baguette-au-jambon* at lunch time!

On one occasion, when he was quite seriously ill with a chest infection, his grandfather called the doctor. After examining him, this man lighted some newspaper, and putting it inside a large glass stemless cup, approached the bed telling Jean to lift his pyjama top. He was to be 'cupped – to draw the noxious germs out of his system'. Jean, a 9-year-old American boy, leapt out of bed and fled the room in terror, thus ending his grandfather's and the doctor's efforts.

Jean told me of his youth in Austria, in Greece and the Middle East. He spoke particularly of Vienna and Beirut, two capitals, for which he still had a very great affection. I found his tales of foreign lands, of the customs, sights and foods in glamorous places, extremely beguiling.

Then and later we talked of our beliefs, our philosophy of life, of what we felt about the war, and of how we had many good and dear friends in Germany and Austria. I told him of my love for, and loss of Rick, and he was grave, understanding and sympathetic. He told me of his failed marriage to an English girl, who had been born and brought up in Cairo. Shortly after they married she had been unfaithful to him. In his bewilderment he had applied for any and all, if possible dangerous, postings.

In 1939 he had begun his University career at the American University of Beirut. When the family had to flee the Lebanon and go to Cairo in 1941, he had tried to join the British Forces. One day, walking down the street in Cairo he ran into one of his old Professors at AUB, named Steve Penrose, (later the President of Amherst College in the USA). Penrose had joined the OSS after having to leave the Lebanon at the beginning of the war. He recruited Jean into the OSS, and he was later put in command of a Greek *caique*, or fishing vessel, delivering arms and mail to the Greek Partisans in the Aegean. Operating out of Alexandria, he and his crew of Greek fisherman and sailors, moved around the islands. Sometimes putting into Turkish ports where they would pick up water and supplies and in order, he told me, to let the restless and, one gathers, 'randy' crew some time ashore – eating, drinking and 'going with the girls'.

Jean's descriptions of his adventures at this time were interesting and fascinating. When he first went to sea with this Greek crew, he was allotted a so called cabin below decks. He found the cramped quarters in the bows, the stink of diesel fumes and lack of fresh air not to his liking, and so slept on deck. He wore a mixture of British Navy and US army uniforms. An American hat, and British Naval sweater, sea boots and bell bottom trousers. If his crew wanted some fish for their dinner, they would lob a hand grenade into the sea and scoop up the resulting stunned and dead fish. The problem with this method is that they frequently lost a finger or two. If an octopus was caught the cook would hang it at the masthead until it was dark and quite dried out. He would then cut it into chunks and throw these on top of the hot stove in the galley. Apparently they were delicious.

When they had to go ashore for water or supplies they would often hoist a Turkish flag and go into Turkish waters. On one such occasion, when they were tied up alongside the mole. Jean was approached by the local Turkish Governor who told him he had an American flyer in custody, and that he felt sure the young man wanted to escape and return to his unit. He allowed that at night there would be very little security; in fact he would see to it that there would be none on the dockside. He said he would turn a blind eye to the subsequent 'disappearance' of the US flyer. Jean went to interview the young man in jail. To his acute embarrassment he had to inform the Turk that the prisoner had said he was in no way interested in escaping, and that the last thing he wanted to do was to return to his base. He would wait out the war where he was, or in Ankara.

On another occasion when they were in the small bay of a Greek island, an aircraft suddenly appeared overhead and dove down on them. The entire crew, without hesitation, jumped overboard. Jean was left alone desperately waving his US army hat and hoping the pilot would see that he was not an enemy craft. He had spotted that the diving plane was in fact an RAF Hurricane. On another occasion in very rough seas, he and his *caique* were entering a Greek harbour, when they were loud-hailed by a British MTB. 'Oo are you?' enquired the skipper with a strong French accent. Jean replied he was *caique* number so-and-so out of Alexandria with a US Commander and Greek crew. On shore he was warmly welcomed by the British Coastal Forces, and duly wined and dined in their tiny wardroom. The wardroom hatch was always left open for air, and there were a certain amount of anxious glances as a lookout was kept for 'You know, the odd hand holding a grenade'. I suppose it was on one of his returns to base in Alexandria, that he was told he was to go to London for special training. This, turned out to be for the 'Joan and Eleanor' operations.

Towards the end of his time in the Mediterranean, he had been issued with a Leica camera and, since he spoke a fair amount of Greek, told he was to photograph the disinterment of Greeks who had died, or who had been executed, during the Greek civil wars between the resistance factions. The idea was to prove that atrocities had been committed by one side or the other. Very often Jean would be called over to photograph a corpse with an arm or leg severed, or some other disfigurement, and although it was fairly obvious to him that these had been caused – by mistake or on purpose – by a spade, he was assured that it was proof of torture and 'crimes against humanity'. The smell of these fields of death and decomposition did not leave him for a very long time. It saddened him, as he was fond of Greece and the Greeks. He had made many Greek friends when he was studying at Athens College when the family were living in Athens in 1934–36.

Once Jean and I started to see each other regularly, we had several very interesting, experiences. We went on part duty, part recreational drives together. We often picnicked in the Taunus Mountains where I had spotted a tower that I thought looked as if it had been an RDF (Radio Direction Finding) post. We suggested to our superiors that we should go and explore it. My wartime experience with the British Navy, and both our German speaking abilities – in case we met anyone up there – would make this possible. We duly set out one day to the tower and did find a great many documents relating to the RDF operation, which had been carried out from there. We also found some boxes marked ammunition, and decided we should take these to the US Army post we had passed on our way up the mountain side. The track was extremely rough and bumpy and we could hear the boxes bouncing around in the back of the Jeep. When we arrived at the post the young Lieutenant, to whom we handed over our cargo, blanched. The boxes were full of grenades, and according to him could have been activated by our very bumpy ride!

On another evening, on one of our drives out into the countryside, this time along the Rhine from Bieberich, we were driving back when we spotted a group of children walking along the road carrying sacks. It was well after midnight. The cherry trees all along the roadside were heavy with fruit at this time of year, and we guessed that they were carrying sacks of cherries. We stopped the Jeep and asked where they were going. The older children replied 'Bieberich', so we told them to climb in. When we were helping them, we realised that the sacks were very heavy and discovered that they were, in fact, full of potatoes. I took the smallest child of maybe 5 or 6 years into the front seat and sat him on my lap. There was in indefinable smell of infection coming from his head, I gently moved the hair away from his ear and could see he had a bad, and certainly long standing, ear infection. They told us they were living with their mother in a stable in Bieberich. When we arrived there we accompanied the children into the severely bomb-damaged building, and found their mother entertaining a man. They were drinking wine and seemed quite unconcerned that the children were not home so late at night. I told the mother that she must take her youngest son to the hospital the next day as he had a bad ear infection. We also told her that she and her male companion should fetch potatoes themselves from distant farms, and not send her young children out on the roads at night. They must have been walking at least 10 km, to and from the farms along the Rhine.

On another occasion in Bieberich when I was talking to the GI guards outside the women's quarters, a 2x4 US army truck, driven very fast, crashed into a horse drawn cart at the gate and did not stop. The vehicle was smashed and the occupants were thrown out onto the road. The horse was down and obviously injured in its foreleg. I went first to the old woman who was moaning and crying loudly in the middle of the road – but she seemed relatively unhurt. The young man however, was badly injured and unconscious. I told the GIs to call an ambulance at once, and kneeling down, held the young man's head. A little later he opened his eyes and said in accented German '*Bin Ich in Himmel?*' (Am I in heaven?). Later, when he was in hospital, I took him some cigarettes and PX (Post Exchange) treats, and he told me his father was dead, that he and his mother were refugees from Estonia, and that he had recently graduated from Law School. On later visits I took him books and writing materials. Alas, the result was that when he recovered he came and waited to see me outside the main gates of the

Henckel Trocken Factory. He thanked me for taking his horse to the vet, and looking after it, and declared his devotion.

Post-war occupied Germany was not the ideal place, or setting, for conducting a courtship. Jean and I were already affected – perhaps traumatised – by a lot of what we had experienced. We were also very aware of our empathy and even sympathy for what the Germans and Germany were going through. We both spoke the language very well, and had an understanding of the psyche of our many German and Austrian friends and acquaintances. Although the Germans I knew at this time, and earlier, were anti-Nazi and mostly Jewish, I have never witnessed such abject homesickness for their countries as I encountered among these German friends and former classmates in exile in England and America.

The bombed cities were still full of rubble, and decomposing bodies were still buried beneath it. In the cemeteries some had often been so summarily buried in shallow graves, that the heavy rain storms would expose the tips of their boots among other things. In the forested hill-sides of the Taunus there were large German Army *Lazaretten* (hospitals), full of war wounded – mostly amputees. As we drove past in our Jeep the men would call from their windows and shout at us. Artificial limbs were still largely unavailable for the majority of them.

I have always loved horses and riding. One day when Jean and I were leaving Wiesbaden in his Jeep, I saw a very short GI riding a rather large *Zweibruecker* horse. These horses are middle weight 'warm bloods', and are bred in the Rhineland specifically for equestrian sports such as dressage, show jumping and eventing. I asked Jean to stop the Jeep, ran over to the horse and rider and asked 'Where *did* you get that horse?' I said how much I admired the animal and the soldier very generously told me that, as he had very little free time, I could ride it any time I wanted. The horse was kept in a riding stables in Wiesbaden owned and run by a certain Herr Weiss. The following week I went to the stables and saw the horse in his stall. His companion was a half-grown kitten which would jump into the manger and bat at the horse's nose. When the horse felt he had enough of this teasing, he would pick the kitten up, usually by the tail, and drop it on the floor in the straw. This game was repeated at intervals, and it seemed to me they were both enjoying it.

I told Herr Weiss that I would be riding the horse, and started going down to Wiesbaden from the champagne factory in Bieberich every afternoon after work. I first rode the horse in the tan–bark, and soon realised that he was very young and had hardly ever been ridden. He was enormously good natured however, and we got on very well. Later, I started going out for longer rides in the Taunus countryside. As I rode through the town to get to the fields and woods, the people in the street would look at us and admire the horse and say '*Prima! Prima!*' From then on I named the horse Prima, which means something like 'first class' or 'great'. The assistant stable hand was a youth called Gert, he was an excellent rider and when I couldn't ride myself I would ask Gert to exercise Prima for me. He introduced me to several Wiesbaden youngsters, there were about six of them – the daughter of the local *Gast Haus* – (actually the oldest one in that part of Germany), the son of the local pharmacist, and several others. They were all riders, and although fraternisation was officially frowned upon, I formed a club called the *Reiter Gruppe*. We would meet after riding, I would bring cookies and chocolate from the PX, Marianne would bring wine from her father's *Gast Haus*, and the pharmacist's son would bring *Wein Geist* (spirits of wine, or alcohol). This is sometimes used to adulterate or strengthen the wine. It was the first time I had heard of such a thing, and certainly the first time I had tried it.

Often Jean would come to watch me and I would look up and see him sitting at the ringside. He would bring me something to eat, as I would usually miss the meals in the Mess Hall in order to ride. It was not possible to go out for a meal anywhere in Germany in those days, because officially no fraternisation was permitted. One evening Jean was also invited to join our *Reiter Gruppe*. The young decided to trick him into getting drunk and really *gepanshcht* (adulterated) his wine with the Wein Geist. He kept his head however and it was a merry evening.

Gert and I would sometimes drive out in a horse and cart to the neighbouring farms to get hay, and, if we were lucky, oats for the horses. Herr Weiss owned a very fine *Zweibruecker* horse himself. Before the war he had been obliged to become a member of the *Reiter SA*. If you were in a position such as his and did not sign up to the SA, you were hounded out of your profession. He had adopted Gert, a war orphan, and had given him a home and a job. A few years after the war, Gert used the skills he learned from Herr Weiss and had a successful career in charge of the stables of the King of Greece. But at this time Weiss was extremely worried, that because of the so called 'de-Nazification' going on in Germany at the time, he would lose his stables and his livelihood.

As the US Army group in Wiesbaden prepared to return to the US, I went to see Joe Finazzo, the GI who owned Prima, and asked him if he would sell me the horse. He said he would think about it and told me to come and see him in his Master Sergeant's office. On several evenings while we were talking about Prima, lower ranking GIs would be coming in and out carrying full duffle bags which they would deposit in a corner of the room. I said to Joe 'I hope you are not dealing in the black market?' Joe laughed and said not to worry my head about such things. He told me he would like to take me back to St Louis and build a house for me 'on the hill'. He also said he would never allow me to see the 'gambling joint' which he intended to open, but would keep me in innocent luxury 'on the hill'. Many years later, when Jean and I lived in St Louis I came to understand what he meant. The all Italian area of St Louis is known as 'The Hill'. The shops, street names and businesses are all American Italian and even the fire hydrants are painted in Italian colours. I told Joe, who was all of 5ft 5", that I was flattered, but there was no way I was going to join him in St Louis. He finally agreed to sell me Prima for $300. I had about $100 saved, but had no idea where I would get the rest of the money. I was not even sure that I should do such an extravagant thing as buy a horse. However, one night I was with the GIs in their club, and watched, appalled, as they played 'craps' on an army blanket spread out on the floor. Hundreds of dollars were won, and lost, by the jubilant GIs who would scoop up handfuls of army 'Scrip'. This was currency printed and issued by the US army to be used in occupied Germany – it was exchanged for US dollars when the troops were repatriated. These notes were stuffed into their shirt pockets before continuing the game. I decided then and there that I would somehow borrow the extra $200 needed to buy the horse. I asked Bimba to lend me $100, to which she very kindly agreed, and then, despite my mother's warning that one should never accept anything from a 'beau', except flowers and chocolates – I borrowed another $100 from Jean – I could buy the horse!

At this time, even though the war was over, Jean was still able to claim additional pay for 'flying time'. He went on several flights with the US army pilots serving in Wiesbaden with the OSS. I had told him of my dream of seeing Prague and the Karlsbruecke again, and so, when he heard that he could accompany the crew of a C47 going to Prague on an official visit, he talked to the crew – all of whom were friends of ours – and they agreed to smuggle me on board as well. I borrowed one of the co-pilot's hats, stuffed my longish hair into it, wore officer's army trousers, a battle jacket and dark glasses. I already had a pair of flying boots. I sat in the co-pilot's seat wearing gloves and hoped I would not be spotted by any of the important senior officers who were flying to Prague on business. A couple of them did come up to the cockpit to talk to the pilot, but I turned my head towards the window and pretended to be listening carefully to my headphones.

Jean and I, and the aircraft's crew, were left on the airfield while the VIPs went into town. The Russian soldiers and personnel, who were still in Czechoslovakia, surrounded us and made their, by now well known, request for '*Uhr? Uhr?*' (watch, watch). They rolled up their sleeves to show us wrist watches almost up to their elbows. However, I am afraid we were a disappointment to them. The Czech air field staff invited us into the terminal building and treated us to beer and *schlivovitz* (plum brandy) and we all swore life long friendship. Not being fond of beer, I innocently allowed myself to be plied with *schlivovitz*. Later, obviously feeling no pain, I climbed onto the aircraft's wing and had my photograph taken. Our return trip was without incident apart from one difficult moment when someone said to Jean 'Aren't you wearing Jenny's rings?' I had asked him to keep them for me in case my hands were noticed wearing them and my disguise discovered.

We continued to see a lot of each other that summer, and I came to slowly realise that I could perhaps love someone again. Jean wrote me letters whenever he was away from Wiesbaden. In March 1946 he wrote:

21/03/46

Tonight in Wiesbaden you are with friends – young people who are among the chosen few to meet the real Jenny, and I am happy for them, for after these years of struggle and betrayal, they are nurtured by your gentleness. 'Gentleness' means all the qualities of kindness, truth and, in your case, an uncanny understanding of and belief in, humanity. ... I too am one of them, and something more. That something more is growing. A light is coming into my darkness. ... Berlin is now a miserable town. I have seen very little but that was enough! Whole sections look like Frankfurt [A town that had been flattened in the bombing raids]. *The broad avenues have a horrible naked look, flanked with burnt out buildings and stumps of trees. All the famous buildings ruined – the Diplomatic Quarter is razed to the ground and the canals are impassable. In some streets the Russians have left burnt out tanks grinning like skulls, mocking all that is around them. They have painted these monstrous machines gold and raised them on pedestals as monuments. Surely a salute to militarism. The weather is foul too, rain all day. ... Every time I see a Russian my stomach slowly contracts with uneasiness – victim of my own propaganda!*

Je t'embrasse Jean

Although we realised that we had an awful lot in common and were very happy together, it was a complicated relationship for many reasons. Shortly after we met, the mill had been returned to its owner and Jean was sent to Marburg. I wrote to him there:

I'm glad for your sake you've left the mill. It was no sort of life for you, or any active young man, and probably may have caused you to dash off with me on our escapades and adventures, and feel that you urgently needed something I had to offer. I don't say I know this – I say it's possible – and for that reason, for both of us, this is a testing time and it's good we are not able to see one another so frequently. But I miss you a lot ... the point is – can I stop the dramatics, and you grow up a little, in order to see if we can also be serious and responsible together. I didn't mean to write such a serious note this time. ...

He replied:

Your note is so full of you that I feel you are by my side as I read it. You are probably right when you say that this short separation will do both of us good

*and give me time to think clearly. … I will try to be 'grave and responsible'
as you say in all my dealings with people, but the best I can do is calm down
in some respects. … For the first time in my life I appreciate the pleasure and
goodness of friends. … Somehow there has always been something missing
until I met you.*

J

A short time after this Jean was ordered to report for duty in Wiesbaden. He
began 'running' agents on his own. One day a young ex-German army non-
commissioned officer arrived in Weisbaden with a lorry-load of film which
he had driven, at considerable risk, through the Russian occupied zone of
Germany. The films turned out to be of the so called 'Katyn Massacre'.

By 1945 most people in the know had heard of this atrocity which took
place in the forest of Katyn in Poland. The German Wehrmacht claimed
they had discovered a very large mass grave in the forest when they were
advancing in 1940. Reportedly, some local people told them that the bodies
were of Polish officers, and some leading intellectuals, who had been executed
by the retreating Soviet Army. By 1943 the Soviets were counter claiming
that the crime had been committed by the Germans.

The films which were brought to Wiesbaden by Johan Hirschlander (not
real name) were delivered to Jean, and he and I were ordered to examine them.
We sat up under the eaves of the Henkel Trocken Factory in the summer heat,
to go through the large number of photographs. It quickly became clear that
the perpetrators of the executions were in Soviet uniform. We reported our
first findings to our superiors. The next day we were told not to continue with
our research, as the films were 'not of any interest' to the Agency. The films
were taken away and we heard no more about them. For years afterwards,
whenever the subject came up, Jean and I would wonder what had become
of the evidence we had seen. It was still being argued which country was
guilty of this crime. We assumed that the films were in the CIA archives
in Washington DC. However, in 2011 I was very distressed to learn, from
the Internet, that not only were the counter accusations continuing between
Russia and Germany as to which country bore the guilt of the massacre but
that both the British and US governments had been aware of the truth in
the 1940s. At that time it was felt to be more important to keep the Soviets

as allies, engaging the Germans in the crippling war going on in the Soviet Union, than to uncover the truth about Katyn. Such discoveries never fail to make me despair of mankind, of wars, of their many deceptions, and such terrible truths as are described in Anthony Cave Brown's book entitled *A Bodyguard of Lies* - a direct quote from one of Churchill's speeches: 'Truth is so precious that she must be protected by a bodyguard of lies'.

Although the personal relationship between us was developing into a more serious affair, Jean's (it seemed to me) rather ambivalent attitude towards me, and my very definite doubts and continued state of mourning over the loss of Rick, gave rise to the following letter:

Wiesbanden 45

.... It's strange. I am so afraid of being hurt by love again – I see now that you need to know <u>who</u> it is you love – when and if you decide to love at all. Joan [his wife] is associated with love in your mind, and I am perhaps an extraordinary dream-like occurrence in your life. But I can't take that Jean – I need help, utter peace, love and companionship. I must know where I stand because I am so confused a being at present. I don't love you in the way I loved Rick, but I do love you dearly, and right now I need you. ... Tell me soon what you really think about the future – and go and see Joan too – for your sake as well as mine. God bless, I give you a kiss on both of your eyes.

J

In the following weeks Jean did go and see his wife to ask for a divorce. He went on leave to London and arranged that they should meet there. To his relief she too wanted a divorce, as she had met another man she wished to marry. I also went to London and stayed with my family. I was in central London one day planning to meet my old WRNS friends Rosemary Gilliat and Charlotte Lefroy for lunch before going down to see Rick's parents in Bexley Heath. As I was walking, head down as usual, on South Audley Street, someone greeted me and I looked up to see Jean coming towards me. He joined me and my friends and treated us to lunch. Later he took me to the station to catch my train and gave me a bunch of violets to give to Mother C.

That year the OSS closed the offices in Bieberich. We were moved from Wiesbaden to Karlsruhe. The Henkel Trocken Factory was handed back to the Henkel-Ribbentrop family. I left Prima in the care of Herr Weiss and Gert until such time as I knew what the future held. The new headquarters in Karlsruhe were in a large modern apartment block which became known as 'the tenement'. The Mess Hall and club were in a villa higher up in the town. As can be seen by his letters at this time, Jean was suffering from doubts and depression concerning his failed marriage:

Dearest Jenny

This is one of the very few letters I have written to you – we have always been so close that I have been able to tell you vive voix of the small things that I hold true. Having bungled one responsibility, I am gaily ready to take on another one – namely you – without being able to prove to myself that I am even capable of supporting myself! This is very foolish of me, and I know that I must take a firm grip of myself and pull myself together by sheer will power. ... I must learn to concentrate and not drift hither and thither. What is wrong? Surely it is not conceit that hides my mistakes and thoughts from me, for I see them writhing before me and I am ashamed ... I want so badly to make a success of my work, for myself and for you. Perhaps they are right, I am not fit to do this job – yet I know I could and make a good job of it too. What is missing? Please don't think I am the victim of my family. For since I know my faults doesn't it follow that I should be able to rectify them?

Jean's superiors would often come into my office in the mornings, and ask me if I had any idea where he was, as they wanted to talk to him. At this time it was touch-and-go as to whether they would be keeping him on in the Agency. They were yet to discover his true talents and potential and were using him in an administrative position. I would reply that I had seen him somewhere around that morning, but did not know where he was now. I would then dash over to his living quarters, galvanise him, tell him I had pretended that I knew he was up and about and doing some job or other, and urge him to get to work on the double and show his interest in, and eagerness to remain in, the Agency in the future. He was eventually put to work with Emma Paxman, drawing up a concise and extremely informative list of agents and agent potential, which duly impressed the powers that be.

By the time we were moved to Karlsruhe Jean and I had come to realise that we were falling in love with each other. But that I, for one, had not committed myself, can be seen by the expression of love and loss I wrote of in several unfinished poems at this time, such as the one below:

Germany 45

Rick

Ah! I would dream I saw your tender eyes and face,
Hold your long hands, and sleeping, enter your embrace.
My loves sad dreams and waking searching for your arms
Are growing like far hills half seen through mist and rain.
I dream now only of the pain
And wake to know that you are gone.

Seventy years later I found Rick's name on the vast Naval Memorial in Portsmouth: 'Lieutenant Cornish, Eric Alfred Edward RNVR, 13/05/42, aged 27 Mentioned in Dispatches. Additional information, BSC London. Son of Alfred Edgar and Lily Jane Cornish.'

Chapter 8

Jean

Despite my somewhat obsessive mourning for Rick, Jean's sweetness and understanding aroused my love in return, and we decided we were truly committed to one another and would get married on our return to the United States.

I left Karlsruhe before Jean to return to Washington, where I had been offered a job, still with the OSS. I told Herr Weiss I would be returning to Germany, left him some money for the horse and hoped for the best.

I was sent to a US army camp in Le Havre before shipping out, where the living conditions left a lot to be desired. Before leaving Germany, I had bought a miniature dachshund to give to my mother. When I arrived in the camp, I shared a room with four other American girls from different war jobs in Europe. Each one of us had a dog. We were warned that we would not be allowed to take the dogs on board the troop ship when we sailed, but we all decided to try and smuggle the animals on somehow. After a very long and frustrating stay in the camp we were finally able to go aboard. I draped Liesel (as I called the little dog) over my arm and put my overcoat on top of her. I and all the other girls managed to get our dogs on to the troop ship.

On board there were hundreds and hundreds of hungry-eyed GIs and only five girls. Before we left the harbour the Captain announced over the loudspeaker that if he found any dogs on board he would have them thrown into the sea on leaving port. A few miles out of Le Havre, while the French coastline was still visible, it seemed as if every GIs duffle bag opened and disgorged a dog of some description or other. None of them were thrown overboard.

In order to escape the soldiers' fascinated stares and attention, we were allowed to spend our days in a gun emplacement on deck. Our cabin was extremely cramped, three sets of double-decker bunks for five girls and five dogs – three of which, including mine, were very sea sick. It did not make for a comfortable voyage. It was quite rough a lot of the time and our lunch was usually a pack of peanut-butter crackers and an orange. More or less guaranteed to make you throw up in a rough sea. I was befriended by the First Officer of the ship and he gave me leftover treats from the crew's meals, often steak, which we and our dogs would all share in our gun emplacement.

On arrival in New York the ship was delayed for about two hours whilst a troupe of ageing entertainers danced and sang on the dockside. The GIs (particularly the New York and New Jersey men) became really mutinous. Many of them could actually see the districts in which they lived, and they had little patience with the rather pathetic efforts of the singers and dancers on shore.

Eventually we were allowed to land and I walked off with Liesel. I had to go through a dockyard full of rusting bits of marine equipment like a depressing stage set. The little dog ran ahead of me, and after a while I saw, behind a link wire fence, my mother and Milo, who was still faithfully working for my grandparents. We drove to New York enroute to Connecticut, with just one stop, to allow me to buy a large, vulgar, orchid corsage for my mother.

Jean's several letters to me from Germany at this time are evocative and informative.

In one of them he says:

13th June 1946

Darling Jenny
... It is raining here in Berlin too, wet and cold! The flight up was very bumpy and I suppose the trip down tomorrow will be worse. Everything is just miserable, and I feel as I were wrapped in black silk velvet and stuffed in a damp refrigerator. If you were only here how different things would be. Heidelberg holds little charm any more, all I want to do is get to the States as soon as possible to see you and hear the wonderful sound of your voice. Sandal, [his nickname for me] I am miserable without you. All I do is think in circles. When are you going to write, I am so impatient to get even a postcard from you. Nothing to do but read and re-read those little notes you sent me. I received a letter from my father yesterday in answer to my cable for help. The answer was not very pleasant. He refused to do anything in

connection with the divorce and wound up quoting, 'Marry in haste relent at leisure'. I shouldn't have expected anything more – my reply was that I wanted neither help nor advice … and yet, further on, he said he would do anything to help me in any other matters. He had spoken to some people about me and believed that I might be able to take over his old job in the Middle East. This suggestion appeals to me – however matters can only be settled when I get to the States. He has not answered my tirade on Egyptian labour – probably he just shook his head and doubted my abilities at business – thinking I have not changed my rather 'adolescent ideas'. But Jenny we'll show them won't we?

And a week later:

Pecquet came to see me in Heidelberg the day before yesterday. He is looking less haggard but is still as bitter as ever. The brush off he got from the Organisation, who still doubt his account of his time with the Maquis, is still on his mind and he swears he will settle the score. … The outfit is due for a considerable shake up in the near future I hear – this 'au secret'. *Only native-born Americans will be employed and they must be married to native Americans. A lot of heads will fall by the way-side and a lot of people will quit in righteous indignation. Although the dismissals are to be cushioned as much as possible, many are going to be hurt. Of course, some naturalised citizens will be kept. However these must 'be extraordinary cases and must be kept to a minimum'. If this policy is carried out, I imagine our work will become very incoherent and the whole outfit will be back where it started. No discussion has yet taken place and to my knowledge no one has been victimised. … Sandal, je suis a toi pour tous jours.*

J

Jean arrived back in the States about two weeks later and we arranged to meet my mother in the bar of the Barclay Hotel. She was dressed, as only she knew how, in an immaculate black suit and a hat, the upturned brim of which was covered in large white daisies. She looked amazing and Jean was duly impressed. We told her that we were going to get married, that Jean had to go to Reno to get his divorce – the lawyer who would be representing him was a connection of my father's, and that I was pregnant. She took it all seemingly in her stride, and we arranged that later that week we would all go to meet Jean's parents who happened to be in the States. They were to return later to Alexandria in Egypt, where Jean's father would once more be with the General Tyre and Rubber Company.

We went out to Orange, New Jersey, where Jean's parents had rented a flat. His mother was painting her nails and did not bother to stand up or greet us properly. When my mother, trying to lighten the atmosphere, said how happy she was that Jean and I were to be married, Minna (Jean's mother) replied, 'I think it is a pity'. It was not a successful visit. Jean's father had been 'too busy' that day, and I did not meet him until some years after we were married. Jean's parents did not come to our wedding, send us any message on the day, or any subsequent wedding present. His mother apparently told him that he should return to her and be 'her boy again'.

When Jean left for Reno to get his divorce, I went down to Washington DC and returned to work in the Reports Department of the SSU, as the OSS had been renamed. We needed the money. While I was working it was belatedly discovered that I had been hired at a very low salary in London with the rank of CAF 7, which was comparable to that of a Janitor in the Government buildings in Washington. The head of Reports offered me a very considerable pay rise, and higher rank if I would come and work with him. When I told him I was going to get married, he said that it didn't matter and I could still work for him. I tried to explain that I would want to go wherever Jean was stationed, and that I really wanted to be a wife, and probably a mother. I also said I was not particularly interested in a 'career'. I was met with looks of disbelief.

Jean's letters from Reno, where he had found a job as a ranch hand, were descriptive and sometimes very funny. He wrote to me on the long train journey from New York and said:

I have suddenly felt this great urge to write to you, talk to you and in this way be close to you...without your conscious mind and your thoughts the whole world would become senseless. ... At times I feel a nameless terror – a hopelessness about 'old mankind', and I want to run away with you and build a life of our own in some far distant land. Not isolated and living only for ourselves, but in a community where some of our ideas, and some goodness, would bring help and love to others less fortunate than ourselves. I feel that I must study and learn, striving for the truth, and, in a small way, pass on the learning to our children and others. ... The night before last I had an argument with all sorts of people at 'Soap Box corner' on Columbus Circle. I was drawn into the arguments by idiotic anti-British statements, based solely on emotion and the American habit of automatically bristling at 'Imperialism' – especially British. These so called orators did not have the knowledge, or the facts, of those who speak at Hyde Park Corner – or the politeness. One champion of the 'American Fighting Spirit' took great offence at my pro-British arguments. He swore that there was something fishy in my remarks and that he was going to find out what or who was behind me. The situation could have been very embarrassing. I shall write at length from Reno, the train is very unsteady.

And on 9 August 1946

Dearest heart, well at last I am here and everything is rolling and under control. The train ride across the Continent was like all long train journeys, interesting at times. The scenery was truly magnificent, but I think the most awe-inspiring thing is the immensity of this country. In Europe one would have crossed country after country and come into contact with new people, costumes and food every day. Here everybody is still American, only the scenery changes – plains, rich fields, snow capped mountains and desert. ... Would you marry a ranch hand? This morning I went and bought myself some farmers clothes and a big straw hat and hired myself out to the 'S bar S Ranch' in Wadsworth Nevada, about forty miles east of Reno in the desert. As a ranch hand I am a good nuclear physicist! Tomorrow will be a great trial – I will either be in hospital with a broken neck or in bed with a broken back. Chores at 6.30. Feedin' five hundred chickens, waterin' the horses and chasin' after the stock. Then a ride to the dam to see how the irrigation is working. After this we all fall out to the chuck–wagon for 'chow' (breakfast to you). What pitfalls await the innocent? I do not know. I can only hope and pray. We got to the ranch at six this evening and I met the other hands at the bunk house. Gary is an ex GI with one leg, and Woody reads nothing but wild west stories! We get three dollars a day and all meals. Imagine getting paid for chasing cows. Cows? There is one s.o.b of a bull here. He is an ornery critter – which is frequent in bulls. ... I hope my rather erratic note from Cheyenne did not frighten you. It was close to my feelings on many things. ... The quiet and peace of the desert is so wonderful! This country is very much like parts of the Lebanon and Palestine – the bright moon, deep shadows and soft desert air. A great vault of dark blue and infinite emptiness. Worries seem to disappear and man is so insignificant.

J

As Jean began to acclimatise to Nevada he wrote me several letters about his ranch-hand adventures.

August 12

... The first part of this letter probably does not have the humorous swing of my usual letters. Please try and read between the lines. I am being distracted by this character Gary, who is outdoing himself telling me Western stories sotto voce ... he is doing his best to make me into a rancher, and is a very, very patient teacher – even controlling his temper when I hitched the team to the wagon and crossed the harness and reins. The result was chaotic, instead of turning to the right when the right rein was pulled, the team came together with a crash and tried to shoulder each other off the road. Poor horses! They were ready to break down and sob. ... Today we spent most of our time repairing leaks in the irrigation ditches, and hauling rocks two miles up the river to build a dam to raise the water level for irrigation. Tomorrow we cart more rocks. So you see darling I am kept very busy. ... The nights are especially beautiful Sandal, yet it means little to me alone. ... Little things to be admired with you mean more than all the treasures of the world seen alone.

On 13 August I answered him ...

Darling I had your two letters from Cheyenne and Wadsworth when I got home last night to Aunt Woodies. Please never again say to me 'I hope I did not scare you with my letter written on the train' – or anything of the sort – you should know me well enough by now to tell that I want exactly those parts of your mind and spirit that are shown in such letters. ... We see so eye-to-eye on such things, and again and again I wish that it were possible to slip away from situations that are so averse to the way of living that I consider good. ... The little man who put you up at the Army and Navy club came to see me and asked me what he should take to Germany as 'hand outs'. Thinking of course that he meant for the German population, since they are the people over there that need such things, I answered bully beef, oatmeal, chocolate, sugar, tinned butter, cigarettes, etc. and his face was a picture 'Is it that rough?' I then discovered that he meant to alleviate the poor and meagrely pleasurable life that the organisation's female personnel lead! So I said: 'God I don't know'. 'Nylons, lipstick, nail varnish?' says he. So I gave up and said: 'Hell yes, gardenias, minks, those poor girls don't see these necessities year in and year out!' Never mind maybe Registry and Communications will appreciate him. ... I had a terrible spell of weeping last night – it isn't that I am not happy about us – I am, and I am so grateful I should be offered a second chance, but I remember Rick's loveliness, his family – it was his birthday on the eleventh, and I feel again that awful aching desolation of 1942 in Dover, when first Rick and then Geoff went, and night after night another boy would die. One became afraid to ring the Mess and ask for anyone by name. Only two men out of Rick's flotilla survived that ghastly summer. I wept for the individual as well as the national suffering of the war in England and the consciousness of what they were fighting for. I wept for the years of crowded, smoky trains, black booted soldiers and airman, and slippered bell-bottomed sailors. I wept for the bombs and the shells and the little people living in such chaos with only their own integrity holding them together. ... So poignant is a people at war, Jean.

All my love Jenny

Jean wrote again on 14 August

Darling please forgive this short note. I am very tired this evening and my bottom is worn down to the bone. Riding in this country is ever so much more difficult than those lovely excursions into the Taunus. Here they ride for business, not for pleasure, and all the training, and 'posting' and correct seat, aren't worth a tinkers dam! Even the horses don't understand style 'Hold your legs rigid and just loll with the rest of the body'. Swell, but I can't do it, and these Western saddles would be fine substitutes for some fiendish oriental castrating device. Five hours this afternoon, chasing horses and cattle through the river flats and over the desert. I damn nearly wept with pain! Last night was different. Jenny, how you would have loved it. Gary and I went for a long ride after supper – rode out into the desert to see the moon come up. A burnished silver disc, turning the cotton-woods into living water. And a cool breeze. Jenny such wonders make my mind cry out for words to describe them to you. God but I wish I could write and tell you of the mysteries hidden in the soft purple hills, the delightful sensation of cool air coming through one's shirt and chilling the sweat on your body. ... Can't we forget, lost in a dream of our own, the tragedies of life! Or must we always push and fight for such things as these? We should not be in want, and yet we are beggars asking for scraps of peace, of love, of kindness. Answer – I must hear your voice. Goodnight J

On 29 August I wrote about the wedding plans and then:

As to the other question – the state of the world. I hope that by now you are getting an occasional newssheet to read, because, although they are as bad as bad can be, they are indicative of the way this country is thinking these days. The feeling is both violently anti-'Red' and violently anti-British. The Palestinian question is the subject of long drawn out, sentimental and libelous news reels in the movies. The conditions on the Jewish refugee ships described as rivalling concentration camps, (quite forgetting that in most cases the 'Romanian Red Cross' or some such organisation, has chartered the damn crates). The port of Haifa is described as eagerly awaiting these Jewish immigrants and of building homes for them. People from Polish and Balkan slums and villages, are perhaps not so eagerly awaited, nor will they be easily housed or provided for by the meagre economy of the Jews in Palestine. ... And my dear NO ONE mentions the little problem of the Arabs. So what? The British clear out and in two hours will we have the streets filled with bodies of both Arab and Jew? No, the American public is certainly not finding the answers. Hell! What a mess. And before we start looking for the mote in England's eye, lets get out of China, where we have not even the excuse of a Mandate. What in hell the answer is to those poor buggers in boat loads off Palestine, or to the Chinese question, is something I can only ask God. We spit in the eye of Russia at every turn. Not only politically and diplomatically but by the very insolence of journalistic phraseology 'Red' this and 'Red' that, and never the 'Soviet Ambassador' or the 'Soviet Government' or the 'USSR' always the 'Reds'. I don't think that war is that imminent darling, but I think that this country is full of God damned fools that would fight Russia, and would then perhaps happily turn around and fight Great Britain, incongruous and unbelievable as that would seem to you and me, or any other thinking human being. The Yugoslavian mess is, however, undeniably the work of the Soviet State – and the attempt to get Upper Mongolia and Albania into the UN, is also undeniably a political move to insure Russia more votes from her sponsored satellites. What everyone seems to forget, is that we, and England, and every other great power that has ever been, have also managed to gain foreign prestige by trickery in politics. As to whether I think that this Organisation [OSS] is the best thing that you and I can do to help – there I would like a long talk with you. This Office, and all offices here are not conducive to making me believe that we are, unfortunately, anything but children as yet in this field of work. The British are so far ahead and we are too spread out over too many piffling little subjects – not enough of them real intelligence targets. If they manage to collect their good elements together and become the thing that America certainly has a crying and urgent need for, then I am all for there being such an organisation, and I should be proud to be part of it. But the way you and I feel about other offers, and the idea that you would like to see come to life also seems to me a good plan. The Middle East and the Balkans are the hottest spots in the world today. What price then the sort of assistance you could offer? High I would say. ... Quite frankly, whatever we decide will be right as far as I am concerned. We are so lucky to see eye-to-eye, (and heart-to-heart – I couldn't resist reminding you of that however inappropriately). ... Jenny

Jean replied on 2 September

Some of your remarks on the Jewish Palestine question are not, shall we say, up to the Jenny standard. The Jews in Palestine I believe are quite ready to greet the refugees with open arms. The Jewish population in Palestine will be able to give shelter to at least the majority of the homeless. Remember that the Jews are a very clannish race and through their suffering are capable of great compassion for their less fortunate brethren. And this compassion is backed up by the millions of dollars supplied by Jews in America for just such purposes. The economy of the Jew in Palestine is backed up with money from Jews throughout the world. It would not be profitable immediately to settle Jews in Palestine in vast numbers, but in time with peace it might be done. However, I do not believe that the solution for the Jewish people lies in Palestine – such a solution will only foster more nationalism in a world already choking with a surfeit of nationalism. No! The solution lies with every individual in the civilised world. We must forget that the Jews are cursed with the cross of suspicion that they have been carrying through the ages. We must forget that there is such a thing as a Jew – if he is a man, welcome him to your home. How often have we spurned the Jews – how often have we added shame and indignities to what the Jew is carrying! Jenny the answer lies within each and every one of us. They have suffered and we must help them. Let the so called democracies help the Jew to forget his chauvinism. … If only I could talk to you when I feel the words well up in my heart. Man's universal desires and needs are fundamental and we avoid the issue when we dress him in false sentiments. Food, work, love and happiness are all he needs. Forever J

On 12 September he wrote to me about a supper he had been invited to by his lawyer's secretary at her mother's house. After clearing up the garden for her, he was regaled with an excellent meal. He told them both of life in Germany:

I described a soldier's life in Germany and all the pleasures a pack of cigarettes and a candy bar could purchase! I am afraid I laid it on a bit thick. I told of the brandy ration in Germany, and now the shocked mother is going to write to her Congressman! Then today, the secretary, Mrs Merton, in fear of the Labour Unions, said the army should be turned loose on strikers. I, never failing partisan, roared the battle cry 'to the barricades', – and now am a Communist and probably wont ever be asked to supper again!

How is the strike affecting New York? Reports have it out here that the city is virtually paralysed and that the situation is very serious. Few of the people in this State realise what an industrial stoppage could mean to America – they have little or no feeling for labour, and although they can sympathise with the wage earner in these days of rapidly rising costs, they do not believe that labour is justified in striking. Most people here are actually afraid of any 'radical' thought or action. I have spoken with some people, and they look upon me as a radical, because I say that I believe a worker is entitled to much more than just a bare living wage. Labour unions are abhorrent to some of these people and their ignorance is astounding. A woman college graduate, seriously asked me why there were labour unions! She finally admitted that collective bargaining was necessary in order to allow people to get ahead!

Our letters crossed. I had written to him from Aunt Laura's house where I had experienced several days of recurring unhappiness.

September 10th

Please forgive me for letting five days pass without writing. I have, actually, no excuse, but I thought it better not to write to you in my present mood. … I didn't write because I was in two minds whether or not to post the two letters I had already written – calling the whole thing off. Please don't panic it is nothing to do with you – just that I have been so desperately sad and so sure – still am – that these moods of sadness – lets face it – because of Eric and possibly the whole war – will recur most of my life Jean darling. Can you take it? Can you forgive me? It isn't that I don't love you, it is just that I know that one side of me, which you will never miss, will never get over being sad. Will write again later.

Jean's immediate reaction was to send a cable telling me 'never to write like that again. Even your sadness is part of the Jenny I love. I am with you no matter what'.

He followed up with a long letter.

13 September

I never thought two pieces of paper could have quite the effect on me that your letter from Stratford has had. ... This letter is so difficult my love. My heart is full and yet words don't come to me. I can't fight this with logic. Here human emotion defies all logic, and probably for the first time in my life I am speechless. Yet I know the answer lies with us – in our love – it is the only thing that will free you from the ghosts of the past. ... Jenny I can't hold you and tell you that you are everything to me – that my love, our love, is as strong as your first love. If Eric brings you moods of sadness and holds a part of you in bondage – a part of you that I may never know – I shall fight it with my very soul. ... Remember <u>our</u> plans, our talks of the fights that lie ahead, <u>our</u> new world. ... I too can be sad, and as I have said want to cry out in protest against all the futility and horror of war. I feel pity for all sadness and for life, a pity that wants to fight to help those crushed by such futility. You and I can help in our way, and, in helping, our lives together will grow and be fulfilled. This I know in spite of all uncertainties. Have I failed you Jenny? Please turn to me in your sadness... Or are you afraid I won't understand? I do understand. And I can take it. I haven't had much time to seek out that side of you which will 'just never get over being sad'. Let me try to find it – let me try. ... This letter of yours frightened me terribly, and yet it is the final link in the chain welding us together. I realise that if you had any lasting doubts about us, you would certainly not spare me or yourself. That is just the way you are. ... The day is finally drawing to a close and I am very tired. ...

J

On the sixteenth I wrote asking him to forgive me for writing in the way I had while we were apart – and said that I had never promised or said anything to him that was not true. I told him of the wedding plans and said that my father – Don – was as '*gay about it all as a drunken cat*', and that he and my brothers Mick and Jim had tidied up the 'sacred spot' in the garden, and I had chosen the mill stone for the pastor to stand on. I closed '*your letter deserves a very wonderful answer, but my words too seem to have dried up, you have both my hands, and they will stay with you, don't disbelieve, just come soon*'.

Finally the power of attorney arrived from his wife Joan, and Jean returned east. He stayed in New Jersey with my Uncle Hal and my father, who had come from England to give me away. During the weeks whilst Jean was in Reno, my mother had been busily making my wedding dress. Material was difficult to come by, but we managed to find some Chinese damask silk, my aunt Margaret borrowed a beautiful antique lace veil. I spent the last week at my grandparents and later my Aunt Laura's house in Connecticut. Uncle Hal's Scottish housekeeper had made a three tiered wedding cake, and decorated it most beautifully with little pink billed, blue eyed doves and curlicues. We were married in Aunt Laura's garden, with the performing minister standing on a great millstone. We left for our honeymoon in a haze of happiness, driving a brand new Buick that my father and uncle Hal had hired for us as a wedding present.

As a treat before the end of our honeymoon, we spent one night in a hotel in Lennox. For dinner we had champagne to drink and chose a huge claw-snapping lobster for our first real celebration.

We returned to Uncle Hal's where my father was still staying before returning to England, and had a peaceful week together. We went down to Washington and checked into the so-called 'Officers Hotel' opposite the Union Station. As I hung my clothes in a walk-in cupboard I was faced with an inch-and-a-half long albino cockroach – the room was infested with them. I later learned that in US cities, as in the Middle East, one has to learn to live and let live as far as cockroaches are concerned. Jean admitted that he admired them, as tenacious, indestructible survivors of the dinosaur age. We found a room to rent in Georgetown, Washington. There were four married veterans renting rooms in the house. The landlord told us all he would do anything to help the 'returning heroes'. Our room was furnished with a small collapsible table against the wall to eat our meals off, and a double bed whose springs were so broken that we had to push our footlockers under the bed to stop it too from collapsing. Three of the young wives had already had miscarriages, and shortly after we moved in I began to loose blood. The gynaecologist in New York recommended by my father suggested I go and have bed rest at my grandmother's in Connecticut.

After ten difficult days in Connecticut, I asked the doctor if I could return to Washington and Jean. I told him of the difficulties of the place where I lived and he said he thought it would be alright. I was very glad to be back, but the next day I was losing water – and here I have to admit I had no idea of the significance of this. When I met Jean for luncheon and told him what was happening he said 'your water has broken, I will phone the gynaecologist'. He told us to come to the hospital right away.

I was frightened, but also excited and full of very second hand knowledge about child birth. I held on to the head of the bed in classic fashion each time I had a contraction and tried to keep calm. When the nurses came in, I told them about my contractions, and they smiled dismissively. I later heard them talking and laughing outside my room – '*she thinks she is having a baby!*' I was, after all, only six and half months pregnant. I swore I would die before I called them again. Later a young intern came in and I told him I really thought I *was* having a baby. He took one look and ordered me to be taken to the delivery room.

I was completely anaesthetised, and only remember coming-to and seeing the red, almost "string-bean"-like baby beside me in an oxygen tent. Apparently the doctors went out to Jean waiting in the hall and asked him '*what has your wife been doing?*', '*she keeps telling us to lie down here comes another one!*' Jean replied dryly, '*she has been in a war*'. They told him that the baby was too premature to survive and that he should tell me she was dead. He came in and sat beside me and said 'Jenny we have a daughter'. My father wrote me a letter from England which I have treasured ever since.

Jenny, dear I do wish you were not so far away. Jean's cable has just arrived and although it was reassuring about you, it is hell not to know more about my little granddaughter. ... It is hard to hope for the best, when we aren't sure what would be the best ... if it should prove impossible to save the baby's life, please do not feel too unhappy about it. To send my love to you and all that goes with it is all I can do.

Love Daddy

But Annabel – for it was she – never looked back. She had no 'blue spells' and no other noticeable complications at this stage. Jean would take the daily bottle of expressed mother's milk into the hospital – which to my great pride even had cream on top. He was known as the "milk man". The nurses were very kind to him and they loved their 'baby doll' as they called Annabel.

At this point Jean was ordered to return to Germany to take up his new job. Annabel spent five weeks in a hospital incubator before she was allowed to come home to me. She had to be kept at a steady temperature, could not be washed with water, and her feed of mother's milk was to be augmented with a soya drink.

I was left alone in the small flat we had rented in downtown Washington. It was in a four story office building opposite *Ruby Foos* Chinese restaurant, the lights of which flashed red, yellow, blue, green all night into our front window. In the basement there was a hairdressers and the central heating boiler was also down there. As the day went by the salon would get hot with the dryers and clientèle warming up the room. The hairdresser would switch off the central heating and would usually forget to switch it back on at night.

On the ground floor there was a tailor's shop. I frequently had the bad luck of losing the head of the mop when shaking it out of the back window. I would have to go downstairs to the tailor's and explain I needed to recover the mop head from the space behind the building. Time and again the tailor would be standing behind his bolts of cloth, looking out of his front window, vigorously pleasuring himself! After a couple of these disastrous encounters I gave up on the mop altogether.

On the second floor was the office of the Union AF of L and CIO (The American Federation of Labor and Congress of Industrial Organisations). But nobody was in the building at night except myself and Annabel. The door to the flat did not lock properly, and I had to jam a chair under the door handle and against the bottom step of the stairs. In the mornings the entrance of the building would be full of empty cans and broken bottles. The winter of 1946 was one of the coldest on record; the garbage men could not make their collections and the restaurant bins were overflowing. The snow was deep on the streets, and sidewalks were slippery and dangerous. I telephoned the hairdresser every evening and asked her to please not forget to turn on the heating before she left. The roof began to leak and I had saucepans to catch the drips all around the crib. Two electric fires were trained on this as Annabel needed to be kept really warm.

Finally, when Annabel was old and strong enough to travel, I asked for, and received, my travel papers from headquarters. There were tickets for the ship SS *John Erikson* out of New York. I travelled up and checked into a hotel near to the docks. I had to make up a formula to augment my breast milk. I rang for the bell boy and a young Mexican came. I gave him a small saucepan, two bottle and nipples and said 'please boil these and bring them back in the saucepan and do not touch them'. He told me not to worry, that he had six brothers and sisters and he knew all about bottles. He later returned with the tray, a snow white cloth spread out on it, and every bottle, nipple and top laid out in a row! So much for not touching anything. I washed the whole lot again and trusted in God. I suppose we are all paranoid with first babies, particularly premature ones. The next day, they telephoned me from Washington and told me that the *John Erikson* had burned at the dock. We would be sailing on an ex-troop ship - a 'Kaiser' ship as they were called. Gigi was to sail with us, and within twenty-four hours we were on our way. The baby, my mother and I, an English woman, her daughter and Nanny were all in one cabin, the ship's so called Sick Bay – all of 15ft by 25ft with five bunks and a crib for Annabel strapped to my bunk. The Sick Bay was right next to the door into the crew's quarters, and often in the evenings the crew members would stand leering in the doorway. Meals were taken in the Mess at long trestle tables sitting on backless benches. The stewards would pinch our bottoms as they put food on the table.

We landed in Southampton and took the train up to London where my father and Joyce had arranged for Gigi to go as a PG (paying guest) with a professor and his wife. She subsequently moved from one house to the next over the following years, ending up in Ireland which she felt was her home from home. Wherever Jean and I were posted she would come and stay for prolonged periods. Bensheim in Germany, Vienna and the Salzkammergut in Austria, Virginia, Zurich, Paris, Baghdad and Washington DC.

After a few days in my parents London flat, we left by train for Germany. We arrived in Paris at the Gare d l'Est. Taxi's were as rare as hens' teeth. However, after a longish wait, one arrived and was immediately surrounded by a crowd of eager customers. The driver said he had finished his days work, but after a few words from Jean, and a look at the baby in my arms, he declared, '*Mais alors, pour les bébés je vais au bout du monde!*'. He put our pram on top of his cab, and took us to the Eduard VII Hotel.

The hotel was shabby, and as comfortlessly post-war in atmosphere as everywhere and everything in those difficult days. They found a crib somewhere. I thanked them profusely, while looking in horror at the pale pink, extremely dirty crib in question, I washed the whole thing in soap and water. The sheets were clean and there was a big turn down so I wasn't afraid of the blanket. Paranoia somewhat calmed, I fed and put Annabel down for the night, and Jean and I went around the corner for dinner. A very nice willing chamber maid agreed to look in on the baby and let us know if all was not well. I do not remember how we got to Bensheim in the Neckar Valley where Jean had requisitioned a house.

After about six months in our rather imposing 'Dianahaus' so called because of the bronze statue in the garden, we moved into a more practical villa for our family home. I had to go to the Post Exchange in Darmstadt for food and other household supplies. It had been heavily bombed, the streets were little more than roughly cleared to make a free passage for vehicles and carts. The rubble was still piled high and the stench of death from the unmissed and unfound bodies in the ruined buildings was everywere.

We had brought Prima from Weisbaden, but it became clear to us that he was not being cared for properly in the stables of Battenberg castle, above Bensheim. We were told by Jean's house man Heinrich of an Arab brood-mare farm outside Bensheim, owned by a widow who lived there with her two children. We went to see if we could stable Prima with her. We introduced ourselves and asked Frau Heuck, the owner, if she would be willing to let our gelding run with her mares; we told her we would try and find fodder for her horses and would at least be able to transport hay and feed for them. She agreed to take Prima and afterwards we saw her frequently, becoming good friends. We often had supper with her and her family. She was a proud and reserved woman and would accept nothing from us of things in short supply such as sugar or coffee. Our meals with her consisted of mashed potatoes and applesauce, plus, it must be said a very good bottle of wine from her cellar. Her husband, I believe part Jewish, had died in a concentration camp. She was left some very valuable works of art and artefacts, among them paintings by Gaugin and Van Gogh, some of which she had bartered for fodder for the horses. She also had two wonderful figures on her mantelpiece, one a mediaeval carving of St Florian the patron saint of firemen, and the other a large tan and cream pottery T'ang horse – which I often admired.

Later that year Jean was informed that we were being transferred to Vienna. Since no vehicles, farm animals or riding horses could be taken out of the country, I realised I would have to give Prima up and asked Frau Heuck to find him a good home. She told me of a young cavalry officer who had lost a foot in the war. He had married a local farmer's daughter, and could use a good horse for getting around the property. He came to Frau Heucks and I liked the look of him and the way he rode, so I told him he could have the horse. He said that his father was from Pforzheim, where the main artisan industry is the making of jewellery, primarily with silver and semi-precious stones. He said he would pay for the horse with some of these. I told him I did not want anything like that, but would be grateful if he could supply Frau Heuck with potatoes and apples from his father-in-law's farm for her staff. He was to collect Prima in the next couple of days.

When the day came for him to collect the horse, I was very upset. Frau Heuck said nothing but certainly noticed my distress. We had a last dinner with her and when we were leaving she said to me: '*I put a package for you in your VW*'. The following morning I brought the package into the house and unwrapped it. It was the T'ang horse. I was really rather startled and worried by the generosity of this gift. I took it to an antique dealer in Wiesbaden, and asked whether, in his opinion, it was a genuine piece of T'ang pottery. After carefully examining it he told me that as far as he could tell it was indeed a T'ang horse. I immediately returned to Frau Heuck and said that I could not possibly accept this gift. She asked me why I felt I could not and I replied because it was a real T'ang horse. She said she was aware of that, had bought it as such, and in any case she had *given* it to me. For some years after this amazingly gracious present, whenever we had to move quarters, I would have Annabel or some other baby under one arm and the T'ang horse under the other. Before coming to live in England in 1977, I sold the T'ang horse, and the proceeds were the down payment on our first house.

We drove to Vienna in a wonderful touring Mercedes which had belonged to the German army. We draped anything we could not fit into the boot, including such things as diaper buckets, on the outside of the car. En route I discovered that Annabel had cut her first tooth, although she showed no signs of distress during the whole long trip. We arrived in Vienna and moved into a flat in Grinzing. It was here that our very happy, varied and interesting marriage and life together, for the next sixty-four years, really began to take shape.

Acknowledgements

My thanks to my grandson Lee Andreae, who was there for me at the start of this operation. Also to David and Minty Philips who arranged for my interview with BBC Radio 4; to Oliver Warman for his help and advice; Mike Maccoy for professionalism in teaching me how to begin to use the computer; to Olivia Lyons for her generous legal help; Miranda and Max McKay James for guidance on how to market and promote the book and to Claire Bujniewicz for her unfailing patience and professional help with the computer and its diabolical unfamiliarity. Without Claire this book would never have seen the light of day and my gratitude can never be fully expressed. I also thank the editors at Pen and Sword for their encouragement and interest so early on in the creation of the book. I thank all my loving and supportive children and grandchildren, and finally, very late in the endeavour, I profoundly thank my niece Montserrat de Muller-Nater, who literally 'saved the day' when I broke my hip.